To
the memory of
RODNEY POTTER ROBINSON
I affectionately dedicate this book

Sources For The History
Of Greek Athletics
In English Translation

*With Introductions, Notes, Bibliography,
and Indices*

By

RACHEL SARGENT ROBINSON, Ph.D.

ARES PUBLISHERS
CHICAGO MCMLXXXI

a revised edition of
The Story of Greek Athletics
Copyright 1927 by Rachel Louisa Sargent
Renewed 1955 by Rachel Sargent Robinson

Reprint of the 1955 Private Edition:
ARES PUBLISHERS INC.
7020 North Western Avenue
Chicago, Illinois 60645
Printed in the United States of America
International Standard Book Number
0-89005-297-2

PREFACE

This book is a revision, or to express it more accurately, a tardy completion of a pamphlet which I compiled in 1926 and published privately from 1927 to 1933 under the title of "The Story of Greek Athletics." The immediate purpose of this publication remains the same as that of the earlier one: to bring together, in English translation, for use by students at the University of Illinois, the principal ancient sources for the history of Greek athletics. However, it is now my hope that a wider circle of readers will also be interested in this exposition, since many new details have been added to the original book.

Thirty years ago, when the late Professor Oldfather introduced his new course in Greek athletics at the University of Illinois, he found it difficult to assign outside reading to his students, because English translations of the less-frequently read classical writers were either not suitable or not available at all. As a favor to him, since he had recently spent so many hours guiding me in my doctoral studies, I was glad to undertake a translation of Philostratus' essay "On Gymnastics" and of Galen's "Exercise with the Small Ball." These he added to the collection of translations which he had assembled. Almost immediately I caught a glimpse of the need for a better-organized and more comprehensive collection of the athletics source material. With the help of Professor Oldfather's

advice on matters of bibliography and choice of selections, I completed the first brochure. Brief explanatory comments were written
for each selection, though they were, for the most part, merely re-
worded excerpts from modern writers on Greek athletics. There
were few notes, no bibliography, and no indices. The collection,
incomplete as it was, has experienced a surprisingly long life; even
after its formal withdrawal from publication, parts of it have remained in almost continuous use to the present day.

For many years after the first appearance of my "Story of Greek
Athletics," I continued to hope that the book, in its final form,
would be a publication in which three friends would participate.
But the fates willed it otherwise. Professor C. A. Forbes, at my
invitation, did actually finish a careful critical reading of my own
translations in the original book. Professor Oldfather always
hoped to find time to write the history of Greek athletics which I
had visualized as Part I of the new book, and to prepare a collection of illustrations from his own photographs. But important
prior obligations for the decade 1930-40 -- obligations which overtaxed even his seemingly boundless capacity for research -- left
him no free moment. All plans for any sort of collaboration were
abandoned in the decade of 1940-50. In 1945 Professor Oldfather
met with a tragic death; in my own household sad events for nine
years precluded a continuance of my studies.

It has been a source of great satisfaction to me, on returning to
my long-planned book on Greek athletics, to find that a need for it
still exists and that my Alma Mater still stands ready to proffer
me an assisting hand. In the present edition three new chapters
have been written for periods barely mentioned before: The
Legendary Origins of Games at Olympia; The Rise of Organized

Athletics; The Hellenistic Age. The funeral games which occupied
so much of the text before have, after Homer, been limited to discussions in the notes. Many new translations have been added and
representative evidence from inscriptions and papyri has now been
included. The rather full notes seek not only to explain certain aspects of the translations but also to provide essential information
for those who would investigate more deeply the many unresolved
problems of athletic history. For each of the nine periods into
which the dozen and more centuries have been divided, I have now
written a short historical sketch in which the current trends in
athletics are emphasized. The information in these is drawn
directly from a fresh examination of the sources and in a few instances I have reluctantly been led to conclusions which vary from
those expressed by previous writers.

Acknowledgments due persons and institutions for their assistance in the preparation of this book are of course many, and there
is danger of some regrettable omission over such a span of years.
The select bibliography lists the modern writers whom I have
found useful for background material on the various aspects of
ancient athletics. Among these the books of Professors Krause,
Jüthner, and Gardiner have been most frequently in my hands. To
the late Professor Oldfather and to Professor Forbes, I am deeply
indebted for the assistance indicated above and for many other helpful consultations. To Western Reserve University, where I was
Associate Professor of Classics from 1929 to 1931, I am grateful
for secretarial assistance which enabled me to finish a first revision of the original book. To the Harvard University Press, I
express my sincere thanks for its generous permission to quote
from translations in the Loeb Classical Library; I have indicated

in the notes the full extent of this indebtedness. To the University
of Illinois warm thanks are given for a variety of favors: to the
Classics Department for secretarial assistance, to the University
Press for the use of a special typewriter in composing the pages for
the lithoprint process, and to Professor John L. Heller, Head of
the Department of the Classics, for his happy suggestion that I
make use of such assistance to hasten the completion of my book.
During the past two years of intensive work I have been under deep
obligation to the University of Cincinnati for the privilege of using
freely and conveniently the remarkable collection of volumes in its
Classical Library. To Mr. W. W. Parker, Director of the University of Cincinnati Library, and to Mrs. Mildred Smith, Classics
Librarian, my special thanks are given for assistance in biblio-
graphical matters. It is a pleasure here to thank Professors
Blegen, Boulter, Bradeen, Cameron, and Trahman of the University of Cincinnati Classics Department for helpful information on
matters touching their special fields of interest.

To my two editors at the University of Illinois, Professor
Heller and Dr. Eleanor G. Huzar, formerly in charge of the course
"Greek and Roman Sports," but now Associate Professor of History
in Southeast Missouri State College, my grateful thanks are here
expressed for their many hours of unselfish work in the supervision of the production of copy. Besides all this, I am deeply indebted to them for many critical observations, by reason of which
my final manuscript was improved in content and style.

Finally, however much my friends have contributed indirectly
to the content of this book, I hasten to absolve them from any
responsibility for the conclusions expressed in it or for the

wording of those translations marked with an asterisk in the Index
of Sources. Such responsibility must rest squarely upon my own
shoulders.

                              R. S. R.

November, 1955
Cincinnati, Ohio

CONTENTS

I. THE INFORMAL AGE OF GREEK ATHLETICS
(before 776 B.C.)

At the beginning of the long journey through the literary records of Greek athletic sports there stands the justly famous description in Homer's Iliad of the funeral games held just outside of Troy by the Thessalian prince, Achilles, in remembrance of his friend, Patroclus. But the games in honor of Patroclus are by no means to be considered the first athletic competitions staged by the Greeks, as will be clearly shown by the body of traditions to be presented in Chapter Two. Agamemnon, Menelaus, Nestor, and other leaders at Troy, it would appear, were descended from a family stock which had long been interested in promoting athletic games in southwestern Greece.

The precise year when Homer wrote has not been clearly determined -- scholars, ancient and modern, offer estimates varying all the way from the tenth to the sixth centuries B.C. -- but, whatever the century, it is clear that Homer was narrating his story for a public that was already athletics-minded. More than two-thirds of one of the longest divisions of this poem was devoted to a recital of recreational sports, and into the background fabric of martial deeds and challenging personalities, Homer chose to weave many a simile drawn from the peacetime realm of sports and even to portray the most stirring combats as being athletic events in essence.

Achilles' men while away leisure moments with discus-throwing, casting of javelins, and archery (Il. II 774) and Penelope's suitors with similar diversions (Od. IV 625 f., XVII 167 f.); Helen, on the wall, looks in vain for her brother, Polydeuces, already known as the "skilful boxer" (Il. III 237); a discus cast and a javelin cast are as familiar measures of distance as a furrow's length or a weaver's rod (Il. X 351; XV 358; XVI 590). The armed combat of Aias and Hector (Il. VII 245 ff.) is described with all the gusto of an athletic event even to the sportsmanlike exchange of gifts at the end, and likewise the capture of Dolon, the spy, resolves itself into a foot race in which Diomedes wins by a final spurt (Il. X 366). But it is in the thrilling pursuit of Hector around the walls of Troy that the comparison with athletics is most clearly stated (Il. XXII 159 ff.):

"For not for beast of sacrifice or for an oxhide were they
striving, such as are prizes for men's speed of foot, but for
the life of horse-taming Hector was their race. And as when
victorious whole-hooved horses run rapidly round the turning-
points, and some great prize lieth in sight, be it a tripod or a
woman, in honour of a man that is dead, so thrice around
Priam's city circled those twain with flying feet and all the
gods were gazing on them."

A. Funeral Games in Honor of Patroclus

In Homer's account of the games for Patroclus we are brought
face to face with a wholly delightful and vivid picture from an early
stage in Greek athletic practises. In those days, on some important occasion and at the invitation of a distinguished host, princes
competed with princes, extemporaneously, in person raced their
expensive chariots, and fought the matches in any convenient
clearing. It did not spoil the fun for such aristocrats if one side
of the track happened to be marred by a "washout", if the turning
post was only an old stump flanked on either side by a pair of
grave stones, or if the audience consisted not of thousands of
spectators enthroned in a marble stadium but of fellow princes,
varying widely in age, each ready in his turn at the next call for
volunteers to enter some event. An Aias and an Odysseus, after
a gruelling wrestling bout, looked for no shower bath or oil flask
but merely brushed the dust off, wrapped their cloaks about them
and waited on the side lines to enter any other event which interested them. In spite of bitter words during the exciting moments,
contestants accepted victory or defeat as courteous friends, and,
in any case, each was presented with a substantial memento of
the occasion donated by a generous host.

With these funeral games there should be compared at all
points the similar accounts of prehistoric funeral games described
by Roman writers, centuries later, Vergil, Statius, and Quintus
Smyrnaeus.* Each of these, though endeavoring to follow the
general Homeric style and order of events, unconsciously adds
many details which clearly reflect the current literary taste and
the practices of his own day.

To the attentive reader the following selection is an encyclopedia of information about contests in the Informal Period,
the equipment, dress and technique of participants, the mental
attitude of the onlookers, and the variety and value of the awards.

Iliad XXIII 256-897*

Then when they had heaped up the barrow they were for going
back. But Achilles stayed the folk in that place, and made them
sit in wide assembly, and from his ship he brought forth prizes,
caldrons and tripods, and horses and mules and strong oxen, and
fair-girdled women, and grey iron.

The Chariot Race

First for fleet chariot-racers* he ordained a noble prize, a
woman skilled in fair handiwork for the winner to lead home,
and an eared tripod that held two-and-twenty measures; these for
the first man; and for the second he ordained a six-year-old mare
unbroke, with a mule foal in her womb; and for the third he gave a
goodly caldron yet untouched by fire, holding four measures,
bright as when first made; and for the fourth he ordained two talents of gold; and for the fifth a two-handled urn untouched of fire.
[Achilles explains that mourning will not permit him to contend
with his own prize-winning horses but he invites all others who
"trust in their horses and firm-jointed cars" to enter the race.]

First of all arose up Eumelos king of men, Admetos' son, a
skilful charioteer; and next to him arose Tydeus' son, valiant
Diomedes, and yoked his horses of the breed of Tros, which on
a time he seized from Aineias, when Apollo saved their lord.
And after him arose Atreus' son, fair-haired, heaven-sprung
Menelaos, and yoked him a swift pair, Aithe, Agamemnon's
mare, and his own horse, Podargos. Her unto Agamemnon did
Anchises' son Echepolos give in fee, that he might escape from
following him to windy Ilios and take his pleasure at home; for
great wealth had Zeus given him, and he dwelt in Sikyon of spacious lawns: -- so Menelaos yoked her, and she longed exceedingly

for the race. And fourth, Antilochos made ready his fair-maned horses, even the noble son of Nestor, high-hearted king, who was the son of Neleus; and fleet horses bred at Pylos drew his car. And his father standing by his side spake counselling him to his profit, though himself was well-advised:

"Antilochos, verily albeit thou art young, Zeus and Poseidon have loved thee and taught thee all skill with horses; wherefore to teach thee is no great need, for thou well knowest how to wheel round the post; yet are thy horses very slow in the race: therefore methinks there will be sad work for thee. For the horses of the others are fleeter, yet the men know not more cunning than thou hast. So come, dear son, store thy mind with all manner of cunning, that the prize escape thee not. By cunning is a woodman far better than by force; by cunning doth a helmsman on the wine-dark deep steer his swift ship buffeted by winds; by cunning hath charioteer the better of charioteer. For whoso trusting in his horses and car alone wheeleth heedlessly and wide at either end, his horses swerve on the course, and he keepeth them not in hand.* But whoso is of crafty mind, though he drive worse horses, he ever keeping his eye upon the post turneth closely by it, neither is unaware how far at first to force his horses by the ox-hide reins, but holdeth them safe in hand and watcheth the leader in the race. Now will I tell thee a certain sign, and it shall not escape thee. A fathom's height above the ground standeth a withered stump, whether of oak or pine: it decayeth not in the rain, and two white stones on either side thereof are fixed at the joining of the track, and all round it is smooth driving ground. Whether it be a monument of some man dead long ago, or has been made their goal in the race by ancient men, this now is the mark fixed by fleet-footed goodly Achilles. Wherefore do thou

drive close and bear thy horses and chariot hard thereon, and lean
thy body on the well-knit car slightly to their left, and call upon
the off-horse with voice and lash, and give him rein from thy hand.
But let the near horse hug the post so that the nave of the well-
wrought wheel seem to graze it -- yet beware of touching the stone,
lest thou wound the horses and break the chariot; so would that be
triumph to the rest and reproach unto thyself. But, dear son, be
wise and on thy guard; for if at the turning-post thou drive past the
rest, there is none shall overtake thee from behind or pass thee
by, not though he drave the goodly Arion in pursuit, the fleet
horse of Adrastos, of divine descent, or the horses of Laomedon,
best of all bred in this land."

Thus spake Neleian Nestor and sate him down again in his
place, when he had told his son the sum of every matter.*

And Meriones was the fifth to make ready his sleek-coated
steeds. Then went they up into their chariots, and cast in the
lots: and Achilles shook them, and forth leapt the lot of Antilochos Nestor's son, and the next lot had lord Eumelos, and next
to him the son of Atreus, spear-famed Menelaos, and next to him
drew Meriones his place; then lastly Tydeides, far the best of all,
drew his lot for his chariot's place. Then they stood side by side,
and Achilles showed to them the turning-post, far off in the
smooth plain; and beside it he placed an umpire, godlike Phoinix,
his father's follower, that he might note the running and tell the
truth thereof.

Then all together lifted the lash above their steeds, and smote
them with the reins, and called on them eagerly with words; and
they forthwith sped swiftly over the plain, leaving the ships behind; and beneath their breasts stood the rising dust like a cloud

or whirlwind, and their manes waved on the blowing wind. And
the chariots ran sometimes on the bounteous earth, and other
whiles would bound into the air. And the drivers stood in the cars,
and the heart of every man beat in desire of victory, and they
called every man to his horses, that flew amid their dust across
the plain.

But when the fleet horses were now running the last part of the
course, back toward the grey sea, then was manifest the prowess
of each, and the horses strained in the race; and presently to the
front rushed the fleet mares of Pheres' grandson, and next to them
Diomedes' stallions of the breed of Tros, not far apart, but hard
anigh, for they seemed ever as they would mount Eumelos' car,
and with their breath his back was warm and his broad shoulders,
for they bent their heads upon him as they flew along. Thus
would Tydeus' son have either outstripped the other or made it a
dead heat, had not Phoebus Apollo been wroth with him and smit-
ten from his hand the shining lash. Then from his eyes ran tears
of anger, for that he saw the mares still at speed, even swiftlier
than before, while his own horses were thrown out, as running
without spur. But Athene was not unaware of Apollo's guile
against Tydeides, and presently sped after the shepherd of hosts,
and gave him back the lash, and put spirit into his steeds. Then
in wrath after the son of Admetos was the goddess gone, and
brake his steeds' yoke, and the mares ran sideways off the
course, and the pole was twisted to the ground. And Eumelos was
hurled out of the car beside the wheel, and his elbows and mouth
and nose were flayed, and his forehead bruised above his eye-
brows; and his eyes filled with tears and his lusty voice was
choked. Then Tydeides held his whole-hooved horses on one side,
darting far out before the rest, for Athene put spirit into his

steeds and shed glory on himself. Now next after him came
golden-haired Menelaos Atreus' son. But Antilochos called to his
father's horses:

"Go ye too in, strain to your fleetest pace. Truly I nowise bid
you strive with those, the horses of wise Tydeides, unto which
Athene hath now given speed, and shed glory on their charioteer.
But overtake Atreides' horses with all haste, and be not outstripped by them, lest Aithe that is but a mare pour scorn on you.
Why are ye outstripped, brave steeds? Thus will I tell you, and
verily it shall be brought to pass --ye will find no tendance with
Nestor shepherd of hosts, but straightway he will slay you with
the edge of the sword if through heedlessness we win but the worse
prize. Have after them at your utmost speed, and I for my part
will devise a plan to pass them in the strait part of the course,
and this shall fail me not."

Thus spake he, and they fearing the voice of the prince ran
swiftlier some little while; and presently did the good warrior
Antilochos espy a strait place in a sunk part of the way. There
was a rift in the earth, where torrent water gathered and brake
part of the track away, and hollowed all the place; there drave
Menelaos, shunning the encounter of the wheels. But Antilochos
turned his whole-hooved horses out of the track, and followed him
a little at one side. And the son of Atreus took alarm and shouted
to Antilochos: "Antilochos, thou art driving recklessly --hold in
thy horses! The road is straitened, soon thou mayest pass me in
a wider place, lest thou foul my chariot and undo us both."

Thus spake he, but Antilochos drave even fiercelier than
before, plying his lash, as though he heard him not. As far as is
the range of a disk swung from the shoulder when a young man

hurleth it, making trial of his force, even so far ran they on; then the mares of Atreus' son gave back, for he ceased of himself to urge them on, lest the whole-hooved steeds should encounter on' the track, and overset the well-knit cars, and the drivers fall in the dust in their zeal for victory. So upbraiding Antilochos spake golden-haired Menelaos: "Antilochos no mortal man is more malicious than thou. Go thy mad way, since falsely have we Achaians called thee wise. Yet even so thou shalt not bear off the prize unchallenged to an oath."

Thus saying he called aloud to his horses: "Hold ye not back nor stand still with sorrow at heart. Their feet and knees will grow weary before yours, for they both lack youth."

Thus spake he, and they fearing the voice of the prince sped faster on, and were quickly close upon the others.

Now the Argives sitting in concourse were gazing at the horses, and they came flying amid their dust over the plain. And the first aware of them was Idomeneus, chief of the Cretans, for he was sitting outside the concourse in the highest place of view, and when he heard the voice of one that shouted, though afar off, he knew it; and he was aware of a horse showing plainly in the front, a chestnut all the rest of him, but in the forehead marked with a white star round like the moon. And he stood upright and spoke among the Argives: "Friends, chiefs, and counsellors of the Argives, is it I alone who see the horses, or do ye also? A new pair seem to me now to be in front, and a new charioteer appear-eth; the mares which led in the outward course must have been thrown out there in the plain. For I saw them turning first the hither post, but now can see them nowhere, though my eyes are gazing everywhere along the Trojan plain. Did the reins escape

the charioteer so that he could not drive aright round the post and
failed in the turn? There, methinks, must he have been cast
forth, and have broken his chariot, and the mares must have left
the course, in the wildness of their heart. But stand up ye too and
look, for myself I discern not certainly, but the first man seemeth
to me one of Aitolian race, and he ruleth among Argives, the son
of horse-taming Tydeus, stalwart Diomedes."

Then fleet Aias Oileus' son rebuked him in unseemly sort:
"Idomeneus, why art thou a braggart of old? As yet far off the
high-stepping mares are coursing over the wide plain. Neither
art thou so far the youngest among the Argives, nor do thy eyes
look so far the keenliest from thy head, yet continually braggest
thou. It beseemeth thee not to be a braggart, for there are here
better men. And the mares leading are they that led before,
Eumelos' mares, and he standeth and holdeth the reins within the
car."

Then wrathfully in answer spake the chief of Cretans: "Aias,
master of railing, ill-counselled, in all else art thou behind other
Argives, for thy mind is unfriendly. Come then let us wager a
tripod or caldron, and make Agamemnon Atreus' son our umpire,
which mares are leading, that thou mayest pay and learn."

Thus said he, and straightway fleet Aias Oileus' son arose
angrily to answer with harsh words; and strife between the twain
would have gone further, had not Achilles himself stood up and
spake a word: "No longer answer each other with harsh words,
Aias and Idomeneus, ill words, for it beseemeth not. Surely ye
are displeased with any other who should do thus. Sit ye in the
concourse and keep your eyes upon the horses; soon they in zeal
for victory will come hither, and then shall ye know each of you

the Argives' horses, which follow, and which lead."

He said, and the son of Tydeus came driving up, and with his lash smote now and again from the shoulder, and his horses were stepping high as they sped swiftly on their way. And sprinklings of dust smote ever the charioteer, and his chariot overlaid with gold and tin ran behind his fleetfooted steeds, and small trace was there of the wheel-tires behind in the fine dust, as they flew speeding on. Then he drew up in the mid concourse, and much sweat poured from the horses' heads and chests to the ground. And Diomedes leapt to earth from the shining car, and leant his lash against the yoke. Then stalwart Sthenelos tarried not, but promptly took the prize, and gave to his proud comrades the woman to lead and the eared tripod to bear away, and he loosed the horses from the yoke.

And next after him drave Neleian Antilochos his horses, by craft, not swiftness, having passed by Menelaos; yet even now Menelaos held his swift steeds hard anigh. As far as a horse is from the wheel, which draweth his master, straining with the car over the plain -- his hindmost tailhairs touch the tire, for the wheel runneth hard anigh nor is much space between, as he speedeth far over the plain -- by so much was Menelaos behind high-born Antilochos, howbeit he was at first a whole disk-cast behind, but quickly he was catching Antilochos up, for the high mettle of Agamemnon's mare, sleek-coated Aithe, was rising in her. And if yet further both had had to run he would have passed his rival nor left it even a dead heat. But Meriones, stout squire of Idomeneus, came in a spear-throw behind famous Menelaos, for tardiest of all were his sleek-coated horses, and slowest he himself to drive a chariot in the race. Last of them all came

Admetos' son, dragging his goodly car, driving his steeds in
front. Him when fleet-footed noble Achilles beheld he pitied him,
and he stood up and spake winged words among the Argives: "Last
driveth his whole-hooved horses the best man of them all. But
come let us give him a prize, as is seemly, prize for the second
place, but the first let the son of Tydeus take."

Thus spake he, and all applauded that he bade. And he would
have given him the mare, for the Achaians applauded, had not
Antilochos, son of great-hearted Nestor, risen up and answered
Peleian Achilles on behalf of his right: "O Achilles, I shall be
sore angered with thee if thou accomplish this word, for thou art
minded to take away my prize, because thou thinkest of how his
chariot and fleet steeds miscarried, and himself withal, good
man though he be. Nay, it behooved him to pray to the Immortals,
then would he not have come in last of all in the race. But if thou
pitiest him and he be dear to thy heart, there is much gold in thy
hut, bronze is there and sheep, handmaids are there and whole-
hooved horses. Thereof take thou and give unto him afterward
even a richer prize, or even now at once, that the Achaians may
applaud thee. But the mare I will not yield; for her let what man
will essay the battle at my hands."

Thus spake he, and fleet-footed noble Achilles smiled, pleased
with Antilochos, for he was his dear comrade; and spake in
answer to him winged words: "Antilochos, if thou wouldst
have me give Eumelos some other thing beside from out my
house, that also will I do. I will give unto him a breastplate that
I took from Asteropaios, of bronze, whereon a casting of bright
tin is overlaid, and of great worth will it be to him." He said,
and bade his dear comrade Automedon bring it from the hut, and
he went and brought it. (Then he placed it on Eumelos' hands,

and he received it gladly).

But Menelaos also arose among them, sore at heart, angered exceedingly against Antilochos; and the herald set the staff in his hand, and called for silence among the Argives; then spake among them that godlike man: "Antilochos, who once wert wise, what thing is this thou hast done? Thou hast shamed my skill and made my horses fail, thrusting thine own in front that are far worse. Come now, ye chiefs and counsellors of the Argives, give judgment between us both and favour neither: lest some one of the mail-clad Achaians say at any time: 'By constraining Antilochos through false words hath Menelaos gone off with the mare, for his horses were far worse, howbeit he hath advantage in rank and power.' Nay, I myself will bring the issue about, and I deem that none other of the Danaans shall reproach me, for the trial shall be just. Antilochos, fosterling of Zeus, come thou hither and as it is ordained stand up before thy horses and chariot and take in thy hand the pliant lash wherewith thou dravest erst, and touching thy horses swear by the Enfolder and Shaker of the earth that not wilfully didst thou hinder my chariot by guile."

Then answered him wise Antilochos: "Bear with me now, for far younger am I than thou, king Menelaos, and thou art before me and my better. Thou knowest how a young man's transgressions come about, for his mind is hastier and his counsel shallow. So let thy heart suffer me, and I will of myself give to thee the mare I have taken. Yea, if thou shouldst ask some other greater thing from my house, I were fain to give it thee straightway, rather than fall for ever from my place in thy heart, O fosterling of Zeus, and become a sinner against the gods."

Thus spake great-hearted Nestor's son, and brought the mare
and put her in the hand of Menelaos. And his heart was gladdened
as when the dew cometh upon the ears of ripening harvest-corn,
what time the fields are bristling. So gladdened was thy soul,
Menelaos, within thy heart. And he spake unto Antilochos and
uttered winged words: "Antilochos, now will I of myself put away
mine anger against thee, since nowise formerly wert thou flighty
or light-minded, howbeit now thy reason was overcome of youth-
fulness. Another time be loth to outwit better men. Not easily
should another of the Achaians have persuaded me, but thou hast
suffered and toiled greatly, and thy brave father and brother, for
my sake: therefore will I hearken to thy prayer, and will even
give unto thee the mare, though she is mine, that these also may
know that my heart was never overweening or implacable."

He said, and gave the mare to Noëmon Antilochos' comrade to
lead away, and then took the shining caldron. And Meriones took
up the two talents of gold in the fourth place, as he had come in.
So the fifth prize was left unclaimed, a two-handled cup; to Nestor
gave Achilles this, bearing it to him through the concourse of
Argives, and stood by him and said: "Lo now for thee too, old
man, be this a treasure, a memorial of Patroklos' burying; for
no more shalt thou behold him among the Argives. Now give I
thee this prize unwon, for not in boxing shalt thou strive, neither
wrestle, nor enter on the javelin match, nor race with thy feet;
for grim old age already weigheth on thee."

Thus saying he placed it in his hand, and Nestor received it
gladly, and spake unto him winged words: "Ay, truly all this,
my son, thou hast meetly said; for no longer are my limbs,
friend, firm, nor my feet, nor do my arms at all swing lightly

from my shoulders either side. Would that my youth were such
and my force so firm as when the Epeians were burying lord
Amarynkes at Buprasion, and his sons held the king's funeral
games. Then was no man found like me, neither of the Epeians
nor of the Pylians themselves or the great-hearted Aitolians. In
boxing I overcame Klytomedes, son of Enops, and in wrestling
Ankaios of Pleuron, who stood up against me, and in the foot-race
I outran Iphiklos, a right good man, and with the spear outthrew
Phyleus and Polydoros; only in the chariot race the two sons of
Aktor beat me (by crowding their horses in front of me, jealous
for victory, because the chief prizes were left at home). Now
they were twins -- one ever held the reins, the reins he ever
held, the other called on the horses with the lash. Thus was I
once, but now let younger men join in such feats; I must bend to
grievous age, but then was I of mark among heroes. But come
hold funeral for thy comrade too with games. This gift do I accept with gladness, and my heart rejoiceth that thou rememberest
ever my friendship to thee -- (nor forget I thee) -- and the honor
wherewith it is meet that I be honored among the Achaians. And
may the gods for this grant thee due grace."

The Boxing Match*

Thus spake he, and Peleides (Achilles) was gone down the full
concourse of Achaians, when he had hearkened to all the thanks
of Neleus' son. Then he ordained prizes of the violent boxing
match; a sturdy mule he held forth and tethered amid the assembly, a six-year mule unbroken, hardest of all to break; and for
the loser set a two-handled cup. Then he stood up and spake a
word among the Argives: "Son of Atreus and ye other well-
greaved Achaians, for these rewards we summon two men of the
best to lift up their hands to box amain. He to whom Apollo shall

grant endurance to the end, and all the Achaians acknowledge it, let him take the sturdy mule and return with her to his hut; and the loser shall take with him the two-handled cup."

Thus spake he, and forthwith arose a man great and valiant and skilled in boxing, Epeios son of Panopeus, and laid his hand on the sturdy mule and said aloud: "Let one come nigh to bear off the two-handled cup; the mule I say none other of the Achaians shall take for victory with his fists, for I claim to be the best man here. Sufficeth it not that I fall short of you in battle? Not possible is it that in all arts a man be skilled. Thus proclaim I, and it shall be accomplished: I will utterly bruise mine adversary's flesh and break his bones, so let his friends abide together here to bear him forth when vanquished by my hands."

Thus spake he, and they all kept deep silence. And alone arose against him Euryalos, a godlike man, son of king Mekisteus the son of Talaos, Mekisteus, who came on a time to Thebes when Oedipus had fallen, to his burial, and there he overcame all the sons of Kadmos. Thus Tydeides famous with the spear made ready Euryalos for the fight, cheering him with speech, and greatly desired for him victory. And first he cast about him a girdle, and next gave him well-cut thongs* of the hide of an ox of the field. And the two boxers being girt went into the midst of the ring, and both lifting up their stalwart hands fell to, and their hands joined battle grievously. Then was there terrible grinding of teeth, and sweat flowed from all their limbs. And noble Epeios came on, and as the other spied for an opening, smote him on the cheek, nor could he much more stand, for his fair limbs failed straightway under him. And as when beneath the North Wind's ripple a fish leapeth on a tangle-covered beach, and

then the black wave hideth it, so leapt up Euryalos at that blow.
But great-hearted Epeios took him in his hands and set him upright, and his dear comrades stood around him, and led him
through the ring with trailing feet, spitting out clotted blood,
drooping his head awry, and they set him down in his swoon among
them and themselves went forth and fetched the two-handled cup.

The Wrestling Match*

Then Peleus' son ordained straightway the prizes for a third
contest, offering them to the Danaans, for the grievous wrestling
match: for the winner a great tripod for standing on the fire,
prized by the Achaians among them at twelve oxen's worth; and
for the loser he brought a woman into the midst, skilled in mani-
fold work, and they prized her at four oxen. And he stood up and
spake a word among the Argives: "Rise, ye who will essay this
match."

Thus said he, and there arose great Aias son of Telamon, and
Odysseus of many wiles stood up, the crafty-minded. And the
twain being girt went into the midst of the ring, and clasped each
the other in his arms with stalwart hands, like gable rafters of a
lofty house which some famed craftsman joineth, that he may
baffle the wind's force. And their backs creaked, gripped firmly
under the vigorous hands, and sweat ran down in streams, and
frequent weals along their ribs and shoulders sprang up, red with
blood, while ever they strove amain for victory, to win the
wrought tripod. Neither could Odysseus trip Aias and bear him to
the ground, nor Aias him, for Odysseus' strength withheld him.
But when they began to irk the well-greaved Achaians, then said
to Odysseus great Aias, Telamon's son: "Heaven-sprung son of
Laertes, Odysseus of many wiles, or lift thou me, or I will thee,
and the issue shall be with Zeus."

Having thus said he lifted him, but Odysseus was not unmindful of his craft. He smote deftly from behind the hollow of Aias'
knee, and loosed his limbs, and threw him down backward, and
Odysseus fell upon his chest, and the folk gazed and marvelled.
Then in his turn much-enduring noble Odysseus tried to lift, and
moved him a little from the ground, but lifted him not, so he
crooked his knee within the other's and both fell to the ground
nigh to each other, and were soiled with dust. And now starting
up again a third time would they have wrestled, had not Achilles
himself arisen, and held them back: "No longer press each the
other, nor wear you out with pain. Victory is with both; take
equal prizes and depart, that other Achaians may contend."

Thus spake he, and they were fain to hear and to obey, and
wiped the dust from them and put their doublets on.

The Foot Race*

Then straightway the son of Peleus set forth other prizes for
fleetness of foot; a mixing-bowl of silver, chased; six measures
it held, and in beauty it was far the best in all the earth, for
artificers of Sidon wrought it cunningly, and men of the Phoeni-
cians brought it over the misty sea, and landed it in harbour, and
gave it a gift to Thoas; and Euneos son of Jason gave it to the
hero Patroklos a ransom for Lykaon Priam's son. Now this cup
did Achilles set forth as a prize in honor of his friend, for whoso
should be fleetest in speed of foot. For the second he set an ox
great and very fat, and for the last prize half a talent of gold.
And he stood up and spake a word among the Argives: "Rise, ye
who will essay this match."

Thus spake he, and straightway arose fleet Aias Oileus' son,
and Odysseus of many wiles, and after them Nestor's son Anti-

lochos, for he was best of all the youth in the foot race. Then they stood side by side, and Achilles showed to them the goal. Right eager was the running from the start, but Oileus' son forthwith shot to the front, and close behind him came noble Odysseus, as close as is a weaving rod to a fair-girdled woman's breast when she pulleth it deftly with her hands, drawing the spool along the warp, and holdeth the rod nigh her breast -- so close ran Odysseus behind Aias and trod in his footsteps or ever the dust had settled there, and on his head fell the breath of noble Odysseus as he ran ever lightly on, and all the Achaians applauded his struggle for the victory and called on him as he laboured hard. But when they were running the last part of the course forthwith Odysseus prayed in his soul to bright-eyed Athene: "Hearken, goddess, come thou a good helper of my feet."

Thus prayed he, and Pallas Athene hearkened to him, and made his limbs feel light, both feet and hands. But when they were now nigh darting on the prize, then Aias slipped as he ran, for Athene marred his race, where filth was strewn from the slaughter of loud-bellowing oxen that fleet Achilles slew in honour of Patroklos: and Aias' mouth and nostrils were filled with that filth of oxen. So much-enduring noble Odysseus, as he came in first, took up the mixing bowl, and famous Aias took the ox. And he stood holding in his hand the horn of the ox of the field, sputtering away the filth, and spake among the Argives: "Out on it, it was the goddess who marred my running, she who from of old like a mother standeth by Odysseus' side and helpeth him."

So spake he, but they all laughed pleasantly to behold him. Then Antilochos smiling bore off the last prize, and spake his

word among the Argives: "Friends, ye will all bear me witness
when I say that even herein also the immortals favour elder men.
For Aias is a little older than I, but Odysseus of an earlier generation and earlier race of men. A green old age is his, they say,
and hard were it for any Achaian to rival him in speed, save only
Achilles."

Thus spake he, and gave honour to the fleet son of Peleus.
And Achilles answered him and said: "Antilochos, not unheeded
shall thy praise be given; a half-talent of gold I will give thee over
and above." He said, and set it in his hands, and Antilochos
received it gladly.

Contest in Armor*

Then Peleus' son brought a long-shadowed spear into the ring
and laid it there, and a shield and helmet, the arms of Sarpedon
whereof Patroklos spoiled him. And he stood up and spake a word
among the Argives: "To win these arms we bid two warriors of
the best put on their armour and take flesh-cleaving bronze to
make trial of each other before the host whether of the two shall
first reach the other's fair flesh and touch the inward parts
through armour and dark blood. To him will I give this silver-
studded sword, a goodly Thracian sword that I took from Asteropaios; and these arms let both bear away to hold in common, and
a fair feast will we set before them in the huts."

Thus spake he, and then arose Telamon's son great Aias, and
up rose Tydeus' son, stalwart Diomedes. So when on either side
the assembly they had armed them, they met together in the
midst eager for battle, with terrible gaze; and wonder fell on all
the Achaians. But when they were now nigh in onset on each
other, thrice they came on and thrice drew nigh to smite. Then

Aias smote on the round shield, but pierced not to the flesh, for the breast-plate within kept off the spear. But the son of Tydeus over his great shield kept ever aiming at the neck with the point of his bright spear. Then fearing for Aias the Achaians bade them cease and each take equal prize. But to Tydeus' son the hero gave the great sword, bringing it with its scabbard and well-cut belt.

The Discus Throw*

Then the son of Peleus set an unwrought metal mass which anciently the mighty Eëtion was wont to hurl; but him fleet noble Achilles slew, and brought the mass in his ships with his other possessions. And he stood up and spake a word among the Argives: "Rise, ye who will essay this match. The winner of this, even though his rich fields be very far remote, will have it for use five rolling years, for his shepherd or ploughman will not for want of iron have to go into the town, but this will give it them."

Thus said he, and then arose warlike Polypoites, and the valiant strength of godlike Leonteus, and Aias son of Telamon and noble Epeios. And they stood in order, and noble Epeios took the weight, and whirled and flung it; and all the Achaians laughed to see it. Then next Leonteus, of the stock of Ares, threw; and thirdly great Aias Telamon's son hurled it from his stalwart hand, and overpassed the marks of all. But when warlike Polypoites took the mass he flung it as far as a herdsman flingeth his staff, when it flieth whirling through herds of kine; -- so far cast he beyond all the space, and the people shouted aloud. And the comrades of strong Polypoites arose and bare the king's prize to the hollow ships.

Archery Contest*

Then for the archers he set a prize of dark iron -- ten double-headed axes he set, and ten single; and set up the mast of a dark-prowed ship far off in the sands, and bound a pigeon thereto by the foot with a fine cord, and bade shoot thereat; -- "Whosoever shall hit the pigeon let him take all the double axes home with him, and whoso shall miss the bird but hit the cord, he shall take the single, since his shot is worse."

Thus spake he, and then arose the strength of the chief Teukros, and Meriones arose, Idomeneus' brave brother in arms. And they took lots and shook them in a brazen helm, and Teukros drew the first place by lot. Forthwith he shot an arrow with power, but made no vow to offer a famous hecatomb of firstling lambs to the Lord of archery. The bird he missed -- Apollo grudged him that -- but struck the cord beside its foot, where the bird was tied, and the keen dart cut the cord clear away. Then the bird shot up toward heaven, and the cord hung loose toward earth; and the Achaians shouted. Then Meriones made haste and took from Teukros' hand the bow; -- an arrow he had ready, while the other aimed -- and vowed withal to far-darting Apollo a famous hecatomb of firstling lambs. High up under the clouds he saw the pigeon; there, as she circled round, he struck her in the midst beneath her wing, and right through her went the dart, and fell back and fixed itself in the ground before Meriones' foot; but the bird lighting on the mast of the dark-prowed ship hung down her neck, and her feathered pinions drooped. And quickly life fled from her limbs, and she fell far down from the mast; and the folk looked on and marvelled. And Meriones took up all the ten axes, and Teukros bare the single to the hollow ships.

Spear Casting Contest*

Then Peleus' son brought and set in the ring a far-shadowing
spear and a caldron that knew not the fire, an ox's worth, em-
bossed with flowers; and men that were casters of the javelin
arose up. There rose Atreus' son wide-ruling Agamemnon, and
Meriones, Idomeneus' brave squire. And swift-footed noble
Achilles spake among them: "Son of Atreus, for that we know
how far thou excellest all, and how far the first thou art in the
might of thy throw, take thou this prize with thee to the hollow
ships, and to the hero Meriones let us give the spear, if thou art
willing in thy heart; thus I at least advise."

Thus spake he, nor disregarded him Agamemnon king of men.
So to Meriones he gave the spear of bronze, but to the herald
Talthybios the hero gave the goodliest prize.

B. After-dinner Games Among the Phaeacians

The following selection from Homer's Odyssey describes the
impromptu athletic sports arranged by the Phaeacians after a
dinner in honor of Odysseus who had come by accident to their
shore after years of wandering over the seas. Just who the
mysterious Phaeacians were and where they lived is still a matter of conjecture; but all are agreed that they were not Achaeans
(i.e., Greeks). The importance of the passage quoted lies in the
difference stressed by the poet between the practical Greek recreational sports of this Informal Period, and the aesthetic type
in vogue among this fabled race of Phaeacians which seems to be
similar to those reported for the early Cretans.* The visiting
Greek hero was impressed by their speed of foot, agility, acrobatic dancing, and music, but in turn the Phaeacians were filled
with amazement at the Greek Odysseus' superior prowess in
hurling the discus-like stone, and his evident aptitude for boxing,
wrestling, and archery.

Odyssey VIII 97-384*

"Hearken, ye captains and counsellors of the Phaeacians, now have our souls been satisfied with the good feast, and with the lyre, which is the mate of the rich banquet. Let us go forth anon and make trial of divers games, that the stranger may tell his friends, when home he returneth, how greatly we excel all men in boxing, and wrestling, and leaping, and speed of foot."

He spake, and led the way, and they went with him. And the henchman hung the loud lyre on the pin, and took the hand of Demodocus, and led him forth from the hall, and guided him by the same way, whereby those others, the chiefs of the Phaeacians, had gone to gaze upon the games. So they went on their way to the place of assembly, and with them a great company innumerable; and many a noble youth stood up to play. [Sixteen young men are named.] From the very start they strained at utmost speed; and all together they flew forward swiftly, raising the dust along the plain. And noble Clytoneus was far the swiftest of them all in running, and by the length of the furrow that mules cleave in a fallow field, so far did he shoot to the front, and came to the crowd by the lists, while those others were left behind. Then they made trial of strong wrestling, and here in turn Euryalus excelled all the best. In leaping Amphialus was far the foremost, and Elatreus in weight-throwing, and in boxing Laodamas, the good son of Alcinous. Now when they had all taken their pleasure in the games, Laodamas, the son of Alcinous, spake among them:

"Come, my friends, let us ask the stranger whether he is skilled or practised in any sport. Ill-fashioned,at least, he is not in his thighs and sinewy legs and hands withal, and his stalwart neck and mighty strength: yea and he lacks not youth, but is crushed by many troubles. For I tell thee there is nought else worse than the sea to confound a man, how hardy soever he be." And Euryalus in turn made answer, and said: "Laodamas, verily thou hast spoken this word in season. Go now thyself and challenge him, and declare thy saying."

Now when the good son of Alcinous heard this, he went and stood in the midst, and spake unto Odysseus: "Come, do thou too, father and stranger, try thy skill in the sports, if haply thou art practiced in any; and thou art like to have knowledge of games, for there is no greater glory for a man while yet he lives, than that which he achieves by hand and foot. Come, then, make essay, and cast away care from thy soul: thy journey shall not now be long delayed; lo, thy ship is even now drawn down to the sea, and the men of thy company are ready."

And Odysseus of many counsels answered him, saying: "Laodamas, wherefore do ye mock me, requiring this thing of me? Sorrow is far nearer my heart than sports, for much have I endured and laboured sorely in time past, and now I sit in this your gathering, craving my return, and making my prayer to the king and all the people."

And Euryalus answered, and rebuked him to his face: "No truly, stranger, nor do I think thee at all like one that is skilled in games, whereof there are many among men, rather art thou such an one as comes and goes in a benched ship, a master of sailors that are merchantmen, one with a memory for his freight, or that hath the charge of a cargo homeward bound, and of greedily gotten gains; thou seemest not a man of thy hands."*

[Odysseus stung to the quick explains why he happens not to look more physically fit. He concludes:] "Yet even so, for all my affliction, I will essay the games, for thy word hath bitten to the quick, and thou hast roused me with thy saying."

He spake, and clad even as he was in his mantle leaped to his feet, and caught up a weight larger than the rest, a huge weight heavier far than those wherewith the Phaeacians contended in casting. With one whirl he sent it from his stout hand, and the stone flew hurtling; and the Phaeacians of the long oars, those mariners renowned, crouched to earth beneath the rushing of the stone. Beyond all the marks it flew, so lightly it sped from his hand, and Athene in the fashion of a man marked the place, and spake and hailed him:

"Yea, even a blind man, stranger, might discern that token if he groped for it, for it is in no wise lost among the throng of the others, but is far the first; for this bout then take heart; not one of the Phaeacians shall attain thereunto or overpass it."

So spake she; and the steadfast goodly Olysseus rejoiced and was glad, for that he saw a true friend in the lists. Then with a lighter heart he spake amid the Phaeacians:

"Now reach ye this throw, young men, if ye may; and soon, methinks, will I cast another after it, as far or yet further. And whomsoever of the rest his heart and spirit stir thereto, hither let him come and try the issue with me, in boxing or in wrestling or even in the foot race, I care not which, for ye have greatly angered me; let any of all the Phaeacians come save Laodamas alone, for he is mine host: who would strive with one that entreated him kindly? Witless and worthless is the man, whoso

challengeth his host that receiveth him in a strange land, he doth
but maim his own estate. But for the rest, I refuse none and
hold none lightly, but I fain would know and prove them face to
face. For I am no weakling in all sports, even in the feats of
men. I know well how to handle the polished bow, and ever the
first would I be to shoot and smite my man in the press of foes,
even though many of my company stood by, and were aiming at
the enemy. Alone Philoctetes in the Trojan land surpassed me
with the bow in our Achaean archery. But I avow myself far more
excellent than all besides, of the mortals that are now upon the
earth and live by bread. Yet with the men of old time I would not
match me, neither with Heracles nor with Eurytus of Oechalia,
who contended even with the deathless gods for the prize of archery. Wherefore the great Eurytus perished all too soon, nor did
old age come on him in his halls, for Apollo slew him in his
wrath, seeing that he challenged him to shoot a match. And with
the spear I can throw further than any other man can shoot an
arrow. Only I doubt that in the foot race some of the Phaeacians
may outstrip me, for I have been shamefully broken in many
waters, seeing that there was no continual sustenance on board;
wherefore my knees are loosened."

So spake he and all kept silence; and Alcinous alone answered
him, saying:

"Stranger, forasmuch as these thy words are not ill-taken in
our gathering, but thou wouldest fain show forth the valour which
keeps thee company, being angry that yonder man stood by thee
in the lists, and taunted thee, in such sort as no mortal would
speak lightly of thine excellence, who had knowledge of sound
words; nay now, mark my speech; so shalt thou have somewhat

to tell another hero, when with thy wife and children thou suppest
in thy halls, and recallest our prowess, what deeds Zeus bestow-
eth even upon us from our fathers' days even until now. For we
are no perfect boxers, nor wrestlers, but speedy runners, and
the best of seamen; and dear to us ever is the banquet, and the
harp, and the dance, and changes of raiment, and the warm bath,
and love, and sleep. Lo, now arise, ye dancers of the Phaeacians,
the best in the land, and make sport, that so the stranger may
tell his friends, when he returneth home, how far we surpass all
men besides in seamanship, and speed of foot, and in the dance
and song. And let one go quickly, and fetch for Demodocus the
loud lyre which is lying somewhere in our halls."

[After a much-appreciated song by the minstrel, Alcinous bade
his two sons Halius and Laodamas dance alone "for none ever
contended with them."]

So when they had taken in their hands the goodly ball* of
purple hue, that cunning Polybus had wrought for them, the one
would bend backwards, and throw it towards the shadowy clouds;
and the other would leap upward from the earth, and catch it
lightly in his turn, before his feet touched the ground. Now after
they had made trial of throwing the ball straight up, the twain set
to dance upon the bounteous earth, tossing the ball from hand to
hand, and the other youths stood by the lists and beat time, and
a great din uprose.

Then it was that goodly Odysseus spake unto Alcinous: "My
lord Alcinous, most notable among all the people, thou didst
boast thy dancers to be the best in the world, and lo, thy words
are fulfilled; I wonder as I look on them."

C. An Impromptu Boxing Match

This familiar account, also from Homer's Odyssey, of the boxing match fought on the spur of the moment between Irus, the professional beggar, and the returning Odysseus is an important contribution to the picture of the Informal Era in Greek Athletics. Irus, tall, heavy, and possessing the advantage of youth, and Odysseus, disguised in beggar's rags, were quarrelling for first place on Odysseus' own door-step, and were goaded on by the delighted suitors. That even in such a sudden brawl the Greek was supposed to exhibit some technique if he hoped to win is indicated by Odysseus' scientific knock-out blow.

"The tactics adopted," to quote Professor Frost (216), "were exactly those which a modern professor would employ against a heavier but unskilled opponent, namely, drawing and countering ... It is clear that such encounters were of common occurrence from the readiness with which the challenge was given and taken, the easy but strictly orthodox manner in which the preliminaries were arranged, and the sporting spirit of the nobles."

Odyssey XVIII 66-101

Then Odysseus girt his rags about his loins, and let his thighs be seen, goodly and great, and his broad shoulders and breast and mighty arms were manifest. And Athene came nigh and made greater the limbs of the shepherd of the people. Then the wooers were exceedingly amazed, and thus would one speak looking to his neighbor:

"Right soon will Irus, unIrused, have a bane of his own bringing, such a thigh as that old man shows from out his rags!"

So they spake, and the mind of Irus was pitifully stirred; but even so the servants girded him and led him out perforce in great fear, his flesh trembling on his limbs. Then Antinous chid him, and spake and hailed him:

"Thou lubber, better for thee that thou wert not now, nor ever hadst been born, if indeed thou tremblest before this man, and art so terribly afraid; an old man too he is, and foredone with the travail that is come upon him. But I will tell thee plainly, and it shall surely be accomplished. If this man prevail against thee and prove thy master, I will cast thee into a black ship, and send thee to the mainland to Echetus the king, the maimer of all mankind, who will cut off thy nose and ears with the pitiless steel, and draw out thy vitals and give them raw to dogs to rend."

So he spake, and yet greater trembling gat hold of the limbs of Irus, and they led him into the ring, and the twain put up their hands. Then the steadfast goodly Odysseus mused in himself whether he should smite him in such wise that his life should leave his body, even there where he fell, or whether he should strike him lightly, and stretch him on the earth. And as he thought thereon, this seemed to him the better way, to strike lightly, that the Achaeans might not take note of him, who he was. Then the twain put up their hands, and Irus struck at the right shoulder, but the other smote him on his neck beneath the ear, and crushed in the bones, and straightway the red blood gushed up through his mouth, and with a moan he fell in the dust, and drave together his teeth as he kicked the ground. But the proud wooers threw up their hands, and died outright for laughter. Then Odysseus seized him by the foot, and dragged him forth through the doorway.

D. Funeral Games for Pelias
(One generation before Troy)

Besides the hint of a general athletic background throughout Homer's works there is definite mention of previous funeral games. The oldest hero in the Greek army fighting at Troy,

Nestor, refers to funeral games for Lord Amarynceus in Bupras-
ium (near Elis) in which he participated as a youth (Il. XXIII 625
ff.) and to other games for which his father, Neleus, sent prize-
winning horses (Il. XI 700).

The names of thirty-three heroes* for whom, according to
tradition, funeral games were held in the period before recorded
Greek history begins are known to us from surviving works of art
and from allusions in the ancient writers. Particularly famous
were the games for Pelias portrayed on the now lost Cypselus
chest,* probably the work of an artist of the seventh century B.C.
Pausanias saw this chest, or a replica of it, in the temple of Hera
at Olympia in 174 A.D. and has left us a description of its pictured contests.

Pausanias V (Elis) 17, 5-11*

There is also a chest, made of cedar, with figures on it, some

of ivory, some of gold, others carved out of the cedar-wood itself.

On most of the figures on the chest there are inscriptions, written

in the ancient characters. In some cases the letters read straight

on, but in others the form of the writing is what the Greeks called

bustrophedon. It is like this: at the end of the line the second

line turns back, as runners do when running the double race.

Moreover the inscriptions on the chest are written in winding

characters difficult to decipher. ...

After the house of Amphiaraüs come the games at the funeral

of Pelias, with the spectators looking at the competitors.

Heracles is seated on a throne, and behind him is a woman.

There is no inscription saying who the woman is, but she is play-

ing on a Phrygian, not a Greek, flute. Driving chariots drawn by

pairs of horses are Pisus, son of Perieres, and Asterion, son of

Cometas (Asterion is said to have been one of the Argonauts),

Polydeuces, Admetus and Euphemus. The poets declare that the

last was a son of Poseidon and a companion of Jason on his

voyage to Colchis. He it is who is winning the chariot-race.
Those who have boldly ventured to box are Admetus and Mopsus,
the son of Ampyx. Between them stands a man playing the flute,
as in our day (i.e. 174 A.D.) they are accustomed to play the flute
when the competitors in the pentathlum are jumping. The wres-
tling-bout between Jason and Peleus is an even one. Eurybotas is
shown throwing the quoit; he must be some famous quoit-thrower.
Those engaged in a running-race are Melanion, Neotheus and
Phalareus; the fourth runner is Argeius, and the fifth is Iphiclus.
Iphiclus is the winner, and Acastus is holding out the crown to
him. He is probably the father of the Protesilaüs who joined in
the war against Troy. Tripods too are set here, prizes of course
for the winners; and there are the daughters of Pelias, though the
only one with her name inscribed is Alcestis. Iolaüs, who
voluntarily helped Heracles in his labours, is shown as a victor
in the chariot race. At this point the funeral games of Pelias
come to an end.

II. THE LEGENDARY ORIGINS OF THE GAMES AT OLYMPIA

In the Funeral Games for Patroclus quoted in Chapter I it is
evident that the poet of the Iliad was depicting princes who were
in no wise novices at such impromptu matches. In fact all
through the corpus of ancient writers there are allusions to
traditions which concern athletic gatherings attended by the
forefathers of those who fought at Troy. Athletic competitions
held at the shrine of Zeus in Olympia, a district between Elis
and Pisa in Southwestern Greece, figure prominently in such
legendary accounts.

When did the age-old religious rites at Olympia first become
linked with athletic games--games that were destined to become
so important that Greek athletic history revolved around them
for a dozen centuries? No definite answer at present can be
given to this question. Even the ancient writers could reach no
thorough-going agreement on the matter since there remained
for them from the earliest times only the uncertain echoes of
a folk memory. But an analysis and a comparison of the varying
ancient accounts about early Olympia will reveal to the painstak-
ing reader that the authors often supplement rather than contra-
dict each other. Such a study will also show what, in the opinion
of the ancient Greeks, were the nature and the importance of
prehistoric athletic competitions at Olympia.

The ancient literary evidence to be cited begins with a poem
by Pindar in the fifth century before Christ and extends through
the chronology compiled by Eusebius in the fourth century of
the Christian era. It clearly shows that the ancient Greeks
thought that those misty centuries of Olympic history before the
official records began in 776 B.C. fell into three distinct periods.

In the first era, according to the accounts, athletic games
were held at Olympia at irregular intervals on the invitation
of some neighboring prince. The shrine of Olympia appears
to have been under some sort of supervision by Pisa. Writers
agree that on three occasions in this period certain famous
personages increased the importance of Olympia by holding
athletic festivals more brilliant than ever before. These
sponsors are mentioned by name: a Pelops, two or three
generations before Troy; a younger Heracles, possibly a long
generation before Troy; an Oxylus who was pictured as returning

to Elis with the Dorians eighty years after Troy. With so much
smoke of detail among the writers perhaps it is not unreasonable
to assume a little fire of truth. If we leave out of consideration
those conjectures which reach back to the far horizons of fancy,
the first era, as the writers picture it, may be conservatively
estimated as embracing the years 1370-1104 B.C.* However
one hesitates to affix precise dates for times whose boundaries
are subject to change as often as new evidence is analyzed.

The second era in the history of early Olympia is less distinctly described by the ancient writers. It is vaguely referred
to as a period, lasting some two centuries, when the shrine at
Olympia was neglected. There are statements that migrations,
disease, and political frictions caused such unsettled conditions
in the Peloponnesus that the games at Olympia were well-nigh
forgotten.

At the beginning of the third era, which is called either the
Period of Revival or the Period of Reorganization, the festival
of Olympia was said to have been restored to more than its
original magnitude by three leaders: Lycurgus of Sparta,
Iphitus of Elis and Cleisthenes of Pisa. Their object, it is
claimed, was to restore political harmony; in this purpose they
found an enthusiastic supporter in Delphi, when they consulted
the Oracle there. Ancient opinion leans heavily to the view that
the Reorganization (or Revival) of the Olympic festival took
place about 884 B.C.

Today, the finds of archaeology in the general region of
Olympia begin to lend color to the legendary stories and to the
statements in the chronographers. Perhaps it is not too much
to hope that at no very distant date evidence will be forthcoming,
as did happen in the case of Homer's Troy, to prove that the
literary traditions about Olympia and environs rest on a coherent
and trustworthy folk-memory.

A.   Pindar (518?--446 B.C.)

From Pindar comes the earliest surviving ancient account, a
masterpiece in succinct delineation, of the founding of the Olympic Games. Throughout his odes, these are described as held
"in Pisa." Pindar passes by the rumors of an earlier century
and a half of activities at Olympia under both Pisa and Elis and
awards the honor of founding formal Olympic Games, regularly
recurring at four year intervals, to Heracles of Argos, who was,

supposedly, celebrating a victory over Augeas a half century befor Troy. This account reflects early fifth century opinion as to what contests were included at Olympia before the Trojan War (that is, before 1193-83 B.C. --to use, as is the general practice, the average one of all the varying ancient estimates of the date of that event).

How general among the Greeks was the popular acceptance of this tradition about the younger Heracles as the founder of the Olympic Games is revealed by Lysias, the orator, a century later than Pindar. In his opening paragraph before that critical audience in Olympia where an unacceptable statement could have cost him dearly, he did not hesitate to stress Heracles' part in originating the games (Olymp. XXXIII 1). Aristotle, too, is credited with having called Heracles the founder of Olympic Games in honor of Pelops (Frag. Gr. Hist. [Müller] II 282).

Olympian Ode X 29-92*

But the laws of Zeus prompt me to sing that famous scene of contest, founded by Heracles* with its altars six in number, near the olden tomb of Pelops*; for Heracles slew Cteatus, the blameless son of Poseidon, and slew Eurytus too, that he might forthwith exact from the unwilling and over-weening Augeas the wage for his menial service; ----and, verily, not long after, the faithless king of the Epeians saw his rich country, aye, his own city, sinking into the deep gulf of ruin beneath the remorseless fire and the iron blows. . . .*

Then did the brave son of Zeus gather all the host, with the whole of the spoil, in Pisa, and measured out a holy precinct for his sire supreme; and, fencing around the Altis, he marked if off in the open, and the soil around he set apart as a resting-place for the evening banquet, thus doing honour to the stream of the Alpheus, among the twelve rulers divine. And he gave a name to the hill of Cronos, for aforetime it was nameless, while Oenomaüs was king, and it was besprent with many a shower of

snow. But, in this rite primaeval, the Fates were standing near
at hand, and Time, the sole declarer of the very truth. And Time,
in passing onward, clearly told the plain story, how Heracles
divided the spoils that were the gift of war, and offered sacrifice,
and how he ordained the four years' festival along with the first
Olympic games and with contests for victors.*

Tell me who it was that won the primal crown with hands or
feet or chariot, when he had set before his mind the glory of the
games and had attained that glory in very deed?*   In the stadium
the bravest in running a straight course with his feet was Oeonus,
son of Licymnius who had come from Midea at the head of his host.
And in wrestling, it was Echemus who got glory for Tegea. And
the prize in boxing was won by Doryclus, who dwelt in the city of
Tiryns; and, in the car of four horses, the victor was Samos of
Mantinea, the son of Halirothius. Phrastor it was who hit the
mark with the javelin, and Niceus, who, with a circling sweep of
his hand, excelled all the others in flinging afar the weight of
stone; and all the friendly host raised a mighty cheer, while the
lovely light of the fair-faced moon lit up the evening, and, in the
joyous festival, all the precinct rang with song, like banquet-
music.

B. Strabo (63 B.C. -- A.D. 21)

After Pindar many another author, as we know from brief
quotations in the later writers, wrote on the early origins of
Olympia; but no consecutive account is preserved until Strabo's
slightly fuller account four hundred years later in the days of the
Roman Augustus.

Strabo does not deny the possibility that some sort of Olympic
festival may have been in existence in the thirteenth century B.C.,

but he emphasizes that it was at the end of the twelfth century that Olympic Games of any note were established. Accepting the claims of the Priests of Elis, he emphatically names Oxylus as the founder, who, with such other Aetolians as were Elean in early origin, returned to Elis (? 1104 B.C.).

The learned and widely travelled Strabo should rightly be considered an important witness on almost any ancient problem; but on the subject of early Olympia there are serious gaps in his statements, if what has been preserved is his whole account. His treatment of events before the end of the 12th century is inconclusive compared with that in the historians still to be cited, while he telescopes the events of later centuries, failing to separate the activities of an Oxylus and an Iphitus by any mention of a time interval and abruptly introducing a Coroebus who belonged to a century later than Iphitus. Further, his discussion of Augeas and the race horses of Neleus reveals so little first-hand study of the context of Homer's words that it shakes one's confidence in the historical value of his pronouncement, often quoted by scholars, that stories about earlier days of Olympia should all be rejected as untrustworthy. A self-admitted dependence on the fourth century historian Ephorus (whose account, if Diodorus [IV 1, 3] is to be trusted, expressly stated disinterest in traditions before the Dorian invasion), is perhaps sufficient to explain the omissions and the tenor of Strabo's account for the period before Oxylus.

<u>Geography</u> VIII 3, 30*

It remains for me to tell about Olympia, and how everything fell into the hands of the Eleians. The temple is in Pisatis* less than three hundred stadia (i.e. about 34 miles) distant from Elis. In front of the temple is situated a grove of wild olive trees, and the stadium is in this grove. Past the temple flows the Alpheius which, rising in Arcadia, flows between the west and the south into the Triphylian Sea. At the outset the temple got fame on account of the Olympian Zeus; and yet, after the oracle failed to respond, the glory of the temple persisted none the less, and it received all that increase of fame of which we know, on account both of the festal assembly and of the Olympian Games, in which the prize was a crown and which were regarded as sacred, the greatest games in the world.

The Eleians above all others are to be credited both with the magnificence of the temple and with the honour in which it was held. In the times of the Trojan war, it is true, or even before those times, they were not a prosperous people, since they had been humbled by the Pylians, and also, later on, by Heracles when Augeas their king was overthrown. The evidence is this: the Eleians sent only forty ships to Troy, whereas the Pylians and Nestor sent ninety*. But later on, after the return of the Heracleidae (sons and grandsons of Heracles), the contrary was the case, for the Aetolians, having returned with the Heracleidae under the leadership of Oxylus, and on the strength of ancient kinship having taken up their abode with the Epeians, enlarged Coele Elis, and not only seized most of Pisatis but also got Olympia under their power. What is more, the Olympian Games are an invention of theirs; and it was they who celebrated the first Olympiads, for one should disregard the ancient stories both of the founding of the temple and of the establishment of the games -- some alleging that it was Heracles one of the Idaean Dactyli, who was the originator of both, and others, that it was Heracles the son of Alcmene and Zeus, who also was the first to contend in the games and win the victory; for such stories are told in many ways, and not much faith is to be put in them. It is nearer the truth to say that from the first Olympiad (776 B.C.), in which the Eleian Coroebus won the stadium-race, until the twenty-sixth Olympiad, the Eleians had charge both of the temple and of the games.

But in the times of the Trojan War either there were no games in which the prize was a crown or else they were not famous,

neither the Olympian* nor any other of those that are now famous.
In the first place, Homer does not mention any of these, though he
mentions another kind -- funeral games. And yet some think that
he mentions the Olympian Games when he says that Augeas depriv-
ed the driver of "four horses, prize-winners that had come to win
prizes."*   And they say the Pisatans took no part in the Trojan
War because they were regarded as sacred to Zeus. But neither
was the Pisatis in which Olympia is situated subject to Augeas at
that time, but only the Eleian country, nor were the Olympian
Games celebrated even once in Eleia, but always in Olympia.
And the games which I have just cited from Homer clearly took
place in Elis where the debt was owing: "for a debt was owing to
him in goodly Elis, four horses, prize-winners." And these were
not games in which the prize was a crown (for the horses were to
run for a tripod) as was the case of Olympia. After the twenty-
sixth Olympiad, when they got back their home-land, the Pisatans
themselves went to celebrating the games because they saw that
these were held in high esteem. But in later times Pisatis again
fell into the power of the Eleians and thus again the direction of
the games fell to them.

Geography VIII 3, 33

Ephorus* (4th century B.C.) says that Aetolus, after he had
been driven by Salmoneus, the king of the Epeians and the Pisatans, out of Eleia into Aetolia, named the country after himself
and also united the cities there under one metropolis; and Oxylus,
a descendant of Aetolus and a friend of Temenus and the Heracleidae who accompanied him, acted as their guide on their way
back to the Peloponnesus, and apportioned among them that part
of the country which was hostile to them, and in general made
suggestions regarding the conquest of the country; and in return

for all this he received as a favour the permission to return to
Eleia, his ancestral land; and he collected an army and returned
from Aetolia to attack the Epeians who were in possession of Elis
... and the Aetolians drove out the Epeians and took possession of
the land; and they also assumed the superintendence, then in the
hands of the Achaeans, of the temple of Olympia; and because of
the friendship of Oxylus with the Heracleidae, a sworn agreement
was promptly made by all that Eleia should be sacred to Zeus, and
that whoever invaded that country with arms should be under a
curse, and that whoever did not defend it to the extent of his power
should be likewise under a curse; consequently those who later
founded the city of the Eleians left it without a wall, and those who
go through the country itself with an army give up their arms and
then get them back again after they have passed out of its borders;
and Iphitus* celebrated the Olympian Games, the Eleians now being a sacred people.

C. Phlegon (circa A.D. 138)

Very fortunately there have been preserved fragments of some
length from the historical introduction to a register of Olympic
victors in sixteen books written by Phlegon of Tralles, a freedman
of Hadrian. These come from a period one hundred years later
than Strabo. From allusions in the ancient writers it is clear
that many other research students published Victor Lists with a
similar historical introduction. The earliest of whom we have
definite knowledge was Hippias of Elis of the fifth century B.C.
whose work was expanded and revised a century later by no less
a scholar than the great Aristotle.*

Phlegon's Historical Introduction is of unusual importance, because, in contrast to Strabo and Pausanias, who leaned heavily
on the records of the Priests of Elis, his story seems to be based
upon reports from a Pisatan source.*

The clear statement that funeral games were the occasion of
the very earliest athletic games at Olympia and the story of

Delphi's role as adviser in the days of the Revival of the Games
are of significance, but Phlegon's most important contribution to
the history of early Olympia is the fact that he included a Cleisthenes of Pisa on the committee for reorganization, whereas other
writers mention only an Iphitus of Elis and/or a Lycurgus of
Sparta. As will be seen, this author gives a brief outline of events
at Olympia before the twelfth century B.C., mentioning a Peisos,
a Pelops, and a Heracles. Omitting altogether the events of the
Trojan War century, though its closing years included the important story of Oxylus and Elis, he plunges directly into what is our
most detailed story of a revival and reorganization of the games
after an indefinite period of neglect. Phlegon's statement about
Lycurgus' descent and his cryptic clause about the length of time
the games were neglected up to the time of Coroebus indicate that
this author joins other ancient scholars in putting the date of this
revival of Olympic Games more than one hundred years earlier
than the 776 B.C. when official records began.

History of Olympia*

I now think that I should explain the reason why the Olympic
Games came to be organized. This is the story. After Peisos*
and Pelops and then Heracles* who were the first to establish the
festival and the contest at Olympia, the Peloponnesians omitted
the observance of them for a while until beginning with Iphitus,
twenty eight Olympic festivals are reckoned to Coroebus the
Elean. After neglect of the games had set in a condition of strife
prevailed throughout the Peloponnesus.

(2) Lycurgus the Lacedaemonian (the son of Prytanis, the son
of Eurypon, the son of Sous, the son of Procles, the son of
Aristodemus, the son of Aristomachus, the son of Cleodaeus, the
son of Hyllus, the son of Heracles* and Deaneira) and Iphitus*,
the son of Haemon, but as some say of Praxonides, a descendant
of Heracles and an Elean, and Cleosthenes, son of Cleonicus, a
Pisatan, desirous of bringing the people back to a state of harmony and peace resolved to restore the Olympic Festival

according to its original pattern and to celebrate athletic games.
(3) They undertook a mission to Delphi to inquire whether the god
approved of their undertaking. The god answered in the affirm-
ative and directed them to announce a truce for the cities wishing
to take part in the athletic contest. (4) After this had been
announced by messenger throughout Greece it was also inscribed
on a discus* for the Hellanodicae (i.e. controlling judges) to
use as a law for the Olympic games.

(5) Now at that very time the Peloponnesians* who were not
promoting the games enthusiastically and in fact were full of ran-
cor were visited by disease and a blight on their crops which
caused them distress. So they sent back Lycurgus and his associates and inquired how to stop the pestilence and how to cure it.
(6) The priestess gave the following oracle:*

"O reverend sirs, and best of all mortals, who dwell in the
citadel of Pelops famous in every land, you are requesting of me
an oracle of the god which I may perchance express.

"Zeus is angry at you for sacred rites which he revealed by
oracles because you fail to honor the Olympic games of all-ruling
Zeus which as an honor to him first Peisos founded and arranged;
and after him Pelops, when he trod the soil of Greece was the
next to set up a festival and the contest prizes for Oenomaüs, de-
ceased; then third after these Heracles, Amphitryo's son, ordained a festival and games for his late uncle, Pelops, descendant of Tantalus, which games you somehow are neglecting along
with the sacred rites. Wroth at this in his heart Zeus has launch-
ed a dreadful famine in their households and a pestilence which
it is possible to stop by restoring the festival for him again."

(7) They reported to the Peloponnesians what they had heard. Some, skeptical about the oracle, by common consent themselves sent persons again to question the god more in detail about the oracle and the Pythian priestess replied:

"O inhabitants of Peloponnesus . . . go to the altar,

Sacrifice and hearken to whatever the priests (i. e. Elean) enjoin."

(8) Due to this oracle the Peloponnesians turned over to the men of Elis the superintending* of the Olympic Games and the announcing of the truce to the cities. (9) And after this the Eleans were willing to help the Lacedaemonians when they were besieging Helos but first they sent to inquire of the Delphic Oracle. And the Pythian replied as follows: "Eleans, strictly keeping to the law of your fathers -- defend your own country -- keep away from war, treating Greeks with impartial friendship whenever the genial quinquennial arrives." Due to this oracle they refrained from going to war and devoted themselves to the Olympic Games.

(10) And no one was given a wreath* for five Olympiads. In the sixth they voted to ask the oracle whether they should put wreaths on the victors and they sent their king, Iphitus,* to the god's temple. The god spoke as follows:

"Iphitus, do not put on for victory what grows on an apple tree but wreathe around the fruitful wild olive branch which is now encircled with gossamer spider webs."

(11) Arriving then at Olympia where there were many wild olives in the precinct he found one hung with cobwebs, fenced it round about and from this tree the wreath was given to victors.

Daicles of Messenia was the first man given a wreath who won in
the seventh Olympiad (752 B.C.)

D. Pausanias (A.D. 174)

From Pausanias, author of a guide book to Greece written
about fifty years later than Phlegon's work, comes our fullest
account of the traditions about the early centuries of Olympia and
its athletic observances, compiled from an on-the-spot examination of temple exhibits and from conferences with the Priests
of Elis, custodians of the records. If Pausanias' statements in
his chapters on the history of Olympia are combined with those in
his history of Elis and supplemented by the remarks of the other
writers quoted in this chapter, the resulting synthesis will reveal
a story of considerable unity about early Olympia, and important
gaps in the story can be closed, especially in the decades after
Pelops and in the years just before and after the Trojan War.*

On the subject of the remote origins of the festival, Pausanias
dutifully rehearses the views of the "learned antiquarians of Elis"
though it cannot be believed that he was ever convinced of their
credibility. Next -- Pausanias now treads on a little firmer ground
-- a Cretan Clymenus "fifty years after Deucalion and the flood"
is said to have held games at Olympia in honor of his ancestor,
the Cretan Heracles. The name of the peoples over whom
Clymenus ruled is noticeably omitted in this story, which throughout emphasizes the Elean viewpoint, but in date he corresponds
with Phlegon's Peisos, and it is presumed that Pisa is the district.

Through the fourteenth century B.C., and into the thirteenth,
rulers of Elis begin, in Pausanias' account, what seems like a
see-saw struggle with Pisa for the control of Olympia. The
first Elean mentioned is an Aethlius, "Sir Contest," furnished
with an ancestry outdating Clymenus by one generation. Pisa's
part is very indistinct -- an Endymion of Elis deposed Clymenus,
and an Epeius of Elis won the kingship as a result of a foot race
at Olympia but lost the Olympia district to Pelops, ruler of Pisa.
Under Pelops' direction -- and on this point Pausanias is in complete harmony with writers reporting Pisatan traditions -- games
on a more magnificent scale than ever before were celebrated
to honor Zeus.

During the next decades of Pausanias' story, when Pelops' sons had left Pisa and were scattered through the Peloponnesus and when in Elis, also, there was a break in the line of succession, occasional celebrations of games at Olympia by neighboring princes are mentioned -- by an Amythaon, a Pelias, a Neleus -- followed by those of Augeas, the extraordinarily wealthy ruler of Elis. Heracles' famous games at Olympia to celebrate his triumph over Augeas, already familiar to readers of the Pindar and Phlegon selections above, are duly listed by Pausanias.*

After the games attributed to Heracles in the 13th century there is no mention of athletic activities at Olympia by Pausanias or the other writers until the days of Oxylus (?1104 B.C.). The reasons for this omission are not difficult to find if one studies Pausanias' lines. Elis, for the moment weakened, was in the hands of a governing committee at the close of Augeas' long lifetime. Princes of neighboring districts, round about Olympia, who were still wealthy and important enough to find occasion for holding athletic games, apparently had more pressing matters to consider. An overseas expedition to Asia (the Trojan War) requiring close attention to recruiting and equipment was in the air, sponsored by kinfolk on the Eastern seaboard. Pausanias, accepting Homer's statements (Il. II 615 ff.), cites the forty ships and the four commanding princes sent to Troy as a contribution from Elis. If the ninety ships from Pylos and the sixty from Arcadia also listed by Homer (Il. II 602,610), filled with "many men ... well-skilled in battle," are to be taken as reflecting a degree of reality (and this Catalog of Ships despite some opinion to the contrary is seriously regarded by the majority of scholars as "a genuine relic of the Bronze Age"*), then plainly many potential athletes along with their possible sponsors were removed for more than a decade from the scene at Olympia. These men would, in normal times, have been interested, physically or financially, in participating in athletic festivals at the shrine of Zeus.* But the passages quoted from the Iliad in Chapter I have shown that their love for athletic competitions did not languish even in the midst of a foreign war, if Homer's account is accepted as a faithful picture of those times. It was there on the plain before Troy and not at Olympia that the West Greeks and their associates were working off their athletic enthusiasms, perhaps with some homesickness for the green meadows of Elis, as is hinted by Nestor's nostalgic reminiscences (cf. p. 14 above).

In the general confusion and shiftings of folk once the Trojan expedition was over (Thucyd. I 12), it is no wonder that there is

no mention for nearly three generations of any noteworthy festival
at Olympia. But with the "Return of the Sons of Heracles" guided
by Oxylus, the grandson of the Trojan War veteran Thoas,
Pausanias resumes his chronicle of events at Olympia. Though
Pausanias does not go as far as does Strabo who calls Oxylus the
Founder of the Olympic Games, he does contribute many worthwhile details to the general background of the story. Oxylus, described as being an Elean eighth in descent from old Aetolus, and
apparently resembling that ancestor in the two respects of being
active in sports and "accident prone" (V 1, 8), is pictured as having, with unusual finesse, reconciled the older inhabitants to
sharing their lands and ceremonial observances with his followers
from Aetolia. Under such a leader, it would be natural to assume
a period of great brilliance for the athletic meetings at Olympia.
Whether or not Oxylus' son, Laias, who inherited the kingdom of
Elis, carried on in the athletic tradition of his family is not mentioned by Pausanias.

  With the passing of Laias, there follows, as in all the writers,
a period of almost complete silence about events at Olympia,
lasting through the rest of the eleventh century B.C. and the
tenth. We learn from other sources that, aside from unsettled
conditions in the Peloponnesus, migrations eastward to Asia were
keeping the folk excited. But Pausanias does leave one remark
(V 4, 5), exasperating to one who would learn more about that
Dark Age, which indicates that he had perhaps seen some sort of
records (or heard some traditions) at Elis covering that period:
"His (Laias') descendants, however, I find did not reign, and so
I pass them by, though I know who they were; my narrative must
not descend to men of common rank."

  The story of the revival and reorganization of the almost forgotten Olympic Games, which has already been described by
Phlegon, is related very briefly by Pausanias and, like Strabo,
with a definite bias toward claims made by Elis, For, unlike
Phlegon, he gives the credit for all the executive work on the
promotion of Olympia to one man alone -- to Iphitus of Elis. In
what century an Iphitus accomplished those reforms in the games
at Olympia is a problem which Pausanias has left for his readers
to solve since his comments on that point are hardly clear and
consistent. An Iphitus (V 4, 5), contemporary of a Lycurgus
whom he dates (9th cent. B.C.) in the reign of Agesilaus (III 2, 4),
an Iphitus listed with three possible lines of descent (V 4, 6), an
Iphitus (V 8, 5) who might possibly be understood by the context
to have lived in 776 B.C. at the time of Coroebus (though the information in the rest of that same paragraph about the contests'

having been forgotten and recalled gradually as Olympiads went
past is generally regarded by scholars as unacceptable), and lastly an Iphitus (VIII 26,4) who revived the games definitely mentioned in the same breath with Coroebus of 776 B.C. as though
contemporary with him --all these are present in Pausanias'
pages.

In Pausanias' chapters on the history of Elis, an Eleius (I) and
an Eleius (II) appear with no comment on the similarity of the name
but, luckily, to neither one was accredited such outstanding
achievements that posterity was likely to merge the personality
and the deeds of the one with those of the other. However, in the
case of the puzzling Iphitus it seems natural to assume, as one or
two scholars have half-heartedly suggested, that the deeds of the
famous Iphitus of the ninth century B.C. and those of an Iphitus
(called King) of the eighth century B.C. (see Phlegon page 42
above) were in the passage of time erroneously merged.*

Description of Greece, V (Elis) 7*

By the time you reach Olympia the Alpheius is a large and
very pleasant river to see, being fed by several tributaries, including seven very important ones. . . . (6) As for the Olympic
Games, the most learned antiquaries of Elis say that Cronus was
the first king of heaven, and that in his honour a temple was
built in Olympia by the men of that age, who were named the
Golden Race. When Zeus was born, Rhea entrusted the guard-
ianship of her son to the Dactyls of Ida, who are the same as
those called Curetes.* They came from Cretan Ida --Heracles,
Paeonaeus, Epimedes, Iasius and Idas. (7) Heracles, being the
eldest, matched his brothers, as a game, in a running race, and
crowned the winner with a branch of wild olive, of which they had
such a copious supply that they slept on heaps of its leaves while
still green. It is said to have been introduced into Greece by
Heracles from the land of the Hyperboreans, men living beyond
the home of the North wind. . . . (9) Heracles of Ida, therefore,
has the reputation of being the first to have held, on the occasion

I mentioned, the games, and to have called them Olympic. So he
established the custom of holding them every fifth year, because
he and his brothers were five in number. (10) Now some say that
Zeus wrestled here with Cronus himself for the throne, while
others say that he held the games in honour of his victory over
Cronus. The record of victors include Apollo, who outran Hermes
and beat Ares at boxing. It is for this reason, they say, that the
Pythian flute-song is played while the competitors in the pentathlum are jumping; for the flute-song is sacred to Apollo, and
Apollo won Olympic victories.

V, 8: (1) Later on there came (they say) from Crete Clymenus,
the son of Cardys, about fifty years after the flood came upon the
Greeks in the time of Deucalion.* He was descended from Heracles of Ida; he held the games at Olympia and set up an altar in
honour of Heracles, his ancestor, and the other Curetes, giving
to Heracles the surname of Parastates (assistant). And Endymion, the son of Aëthlius, deposed Clymenus, and set his sons a
race in Olympia with the kingdom as the prize. (2) And about a
generation later than Endymion, Pelops held the games in honor
of Olympian Zeus in a more splendid manner than any of his
predecessors. When the sons of Pelops were scattered from
Elis over all the rest of Peloponnesus, Amythaon, the son of
Cretheus, and cousin of Endymion on his father's side (for they
say that Aëthlius too was the son of Aeolus though supposed to be
a son of Zeus) held the Olympian games, and after him Pelias
and Neleus in common. (3) Augeas too held them, and likewise
Heracles,* the son of Amphitryon, after the conquest of Elis.
The victors crowned by Heracles include Iolaüs, who won with
the mares of Heracles. . . . (4) So Iolaüs won the chariot-race,

and Iasius, an Arcadian, the horse-race; while of the sons of
Tyndareus one won the foot-race and Polydeuces the boxing match.
Of Heracles himself it is said that he won victories at wrestling
and the pancratium.* (5) After the reign of Oxylus, who also
celebrated the games, the Olympic festival was discontinued until the reign of Iphitus.*

V, 1: (3) The Eleans we know crossed over from Calydon and
Aetolia generally. Their earlier history I found to be as follows.
The first to rule in this land, they say, was Aëthlius, who was
the son of Zeus and of Protogeneia, the daughter of Deucalion, and
the father of Endymion. . . . (4) . . . all agree that Endymion
begat Paeon, Epeius, Aetolus, and also a daughter Eurycyda.
Endymion set his sons to run a race at Olympia for the throne;
Epeius won, and obtained the kingdom, and his subjects were then
named Epeans for the first time. . . . (6) Epeius married
Anaxiroë, the daughter of Coronus, and begat a daughter Hyrmina,
but no male issue. In the reign of Epeius the following events also occurred. Oenomaüs--while lord of the land of Pisa--was
put down by Pelops the Lydian, who crossed over from Asia.*
(7) On the death of Oenomaüs Pelops took possession of the land
of Pisa and its bordering country Olympia, separating it from the
land of Epeius. . . . (8) Aetolus, who came to the throne after
Epeius, was made to flee from Peloponnesus, because the children of Apis tried and convicted him of unintentional homicide.
For Apis, the son of Jason, from Pallantium in Arcadia, was run
over and killed by the chariot of Aetolus at the games held in hon-
or of Azan. Aetolus, son of Endymion, gave to the dwellers
around the Acheloüs their name, when he fled to this part of the
mainland. But the kingdom of the Epeians fell to Eleius, the son of

Eurycyda, daughter of Endymion and, believe the tale who will, of
Poseidon. It was Eleius who gave the inhabitants their present
name of Eleans in place of Epeans. (9) Eleius had a son Augeas.
Those who exaggerate his glory give a turn to the name "Eleius"
and make Helius (the sun) to be the father of Augeas. This Augeas
had so many cattle and flocks of goats that actually most of his
land remained untilled because of the dung of the animals. Now he
persuaded Heracles to cleanse for him the land from dung, either
in return for a part of Elis or possibly, for some other reward.
(10) Heracles accomplished this feat too, turning aside the stream
of the Menius into the dung. But, because Heracles had accomplished the task by cunning, without toil, Augeas refused to give
him his reward, and banished Phyleus, the elder of his two sons,
for objecting that he was wronging a man who had been his bene-
factor. He made preparations himself to resist Heracles, should
he attack Elis; more particularly he made friends with the sons of
Actor and with Amarynceus. Amarynceus, besides being a good
soldier, had a father, Pyttius, of Thessalian descent, who came
from Thessaly to Elis. To Amarynceus, therefore, Augeas also
gave a share in the government of Elis; Actor and his sons had a
share in the kingdom and were natives of the country. For the
father of Actor was Phorbas, son of Lapithus, and his mother was
Hyrmina, daughter of Epeius.

V, 3 : (1) Heracles afterwards took Elis and sacked it, with
an army he had raised of Argives, Thebans and Arcadians. The
Eleans were aided by the men of Pisa and of Pylus in Elis. The
men of Pylus were punished by Heracles, but his expedition
against Pisa was stopped by an oracle from Delphi to this effect:
- My father cares for Pisa, but to me in the hollows of Pytho. . . .

This oracle proved the salvation of Pisa. To Phyleus Heracles gave up the land of Elis and all the rest, more out of respect for Phyleus than because he wanted to do so; he allowed him to keep the prisoners, and Augeas to escape punishment.

(3) When Phyleus had returned to Dulichium after organizing the affairs of Elis, Augeas died at an advanced age, and the kingdom of Elis devolved on Agasthenes, the son of Augeas, and on Amphimachus and Thalpius. For the sons of Actor married two sisters -- Amphimachus was born to one -- Thalpius to her sister. (4) However, neither Amarynceus himself nor his son Diores remained common people. Incidentally this is shown by Homer (<u>Il.</u> II 622) in his list of the Eleans; he makes their whole fleet to consist of forty ships,* half of them under the command of Amphimachus and Thalpius and of the remaining twenty he puts ten under Diores, the son of Amarynceus, and ten under Polyxenus, the son of Agasthenes. Polyxenus came back safe from Troy and begat a son, Amphimachus. This name I think Polyxenus gave his son because of his friendship with Amphimachus, the son of Cteatus, who died at Troy. (5) Amphimachus begat Eleius, and it was while Eleius was king in Elis that the assembly of the Dorian army under the sons of Aristomachus took place, with a view to returning to the Peloponnesus. To their kings was delivered this oracle, that they were to choose the "one with three eyes" to lead them on their return. When they were at a loss as to the meaning of the oracle, they were met by a man driving a mule, which was blind in one eye. (6) Cresphontes inferred that this was the man indicated by the oracle, and so the Dorians made him one of themselves. He urged them to descend upon the Peloponnesus in ships, and not to attempt to go across the Isthmus with a land army. Such was his

advice, and at the same time he led them on the voyage from Nau-
pactus to Molycrium. In return they agreed to give him at his request the land of Elis. The man was Oxylus, son of Haemon, the
son of Thoas. This was the Thoas who helped the sons of Atreus
to destroy the empire of Priam and from Thoas to Aetolus the son
of Endymion are six generations.   (7) There were the ties of kindred between the Heracleidae and the kings of Aetolia; in particular the mothers of Thoas, the son of Andraemon, and of Hyllus,
the son of Heracles, were sisters. It fell to the lot of Oxylus to
be an outlaw from Aetolia. The story goes that as he was throwing the quoit he missed the mark and committed unintentional homicide.

   V, 4: (2) . . . He (Oxylus) allowed the old inhabitants, the
Epeans, to keep their possessions, except that he introduced
among them Aetolian colonists, giving them a share in the land.
He assigned privileges to Dius, and kept up after the ancient manner the honours paid to heroes, especially the worship of Augeas
to whom even at the present day hero-sacrifice is offered. (3) He
is also said to have induced to come into the city the dwellers in
the villages near the wall, and by increasing the number of inhabitants to have made Elis larger and generally more prosperous.
There also came to him an oracle from Delphi, that he should
bring in as co-founder "the descendant of Pelops". Oxylus made
diligent search, and in his search he discovered Agorius, son of
Damasius, son of Penthilus, son of Orestes. He brought Agorius
himself from Helice in Achaia, and with him a small body of
Achaeans.

   (5) After Oxylus the kingdom devolved on Laïas, son of Oxylus.
His descendants,* however, I find did not reign, and so I pass

them by, though I know who they were; my narrative must not descend to men of common rank.   Later on Iphitus, of the line of
Oxylus and contemporary with Lycurgus, who drew up the code of
laws for the Lacedaemonians, arranged the games of Olympia and
re-established afresh the Olympic festival and truce, after an interruption of uncertain length.   The reason for this interruption
I will set forth when my narrative deals with Olympia.   (6) At this
time Greece was grievously worn by internal strife and plague,
and it occurred to Iphitus to ask the god at Delphi for deliverance
from these evils.   The story goes that the Pythian priestess ordained that Iphitus himself* and the Eleans must renew the Olympic
games.   Iphitus also induced the Eleans to sacrifice to Heracles
as to a god, whom hitherto they had looked upon as their enemy.
The inscription at Olympia calls Iphitus the son of Haemon, but
most of the Greeks say that his father was Praxonides and not
Haemon, while the ancient records of Elis traced him to a father
of the same name.*

E. Eusebius (circa A.D. 324)

Five generations later than Pausanias, Eusebius of Caesarea,
"a man of many notebooks," had finished his <u>Chronology,</u> one of
his several immense research projects.   In this there was included the Olympic Register of Victors from the first Olympiad
776 B.C. to the 249th Olympiad A.D. 217, based on the compilation made by Sextus Julius Africanus of the preceding century.
The historical preface to this Register contains an account of
early Olympia with tentative dates which agree with the gist of the
reports from the other writers on this subject.   As will be seen,
this Africanus-Eusebius chronology follows Phlegon's account in
the matter of dating the renewal of the games in the early ninth
century B.C., though only two committee members, Lycurgus and
Iphitus, are mentioned.

Chronology I col. 190*

The above dates in the section on early Athens are recorded just as they are preserved in the ancient and more accurate histories. But since the years previous to the capture of Troy and the important events therein did not meet with accurate listing we have made our excerpts as best we could from the differing accounts. The events from the capture of Troy up to the first Olympiad also, it seems, were not considered worthy of a complete recording. However Porphyrius (3rd cent. A.D.) in the first book of the "History of Philosophy" writes this summary:

"From the capture of Troy to the Return of the Heracleidae to the Peloponnesus was eighty years according to Apollodorus (1st cent. A.D.?); from the Return to the Founding of Ionia was sixty years; from that point to Lycurgus, one hundred and fifty nine years. In all from the capture of Troy to the first Olympiad, four hundred and seven years."

At this point I have decided to add on to my account the "Olympic Register" compiled by the Greeks.*

Col. 192: For it was beginning with this Register that Greek chronology seems to have met with accurate recording. What happened before that was set forth according to each man's fancy.

The Founding of the Olympic Games

A few remarks are necessary about the Games to explain that some authorities pushing back their founding to the earliest times assert they were founded before Heracles by one of the Idaean Dactyls; next they were held by Aethlios as a proving ground for his sons; from his name the contestants were called 'athletes'; after him, his son Epeius, next Endymion and then Alexinos (?),

then Oinomaos presided over the sacred rites; after him Pelops
held them to honor his father Zeus; next Heracles, son of Alcmena
and Zeus from whom ten generations elapsed ... (text uncertain) ...
until Iphitus and the renewal of the games. Iphitus was from Elis
and had the welfare of Greece at heart so with a desire to stop the
wars between cities he sent an official group from all the Peloponnesus (i. e. to Delphi) to inquire how to effect a release from
the prevailing feuds. The god replied as follows to the Peloponnesians:*

"O inhabitants of Peloponnesus go to the altar,

Sacrifice and hearken to what the priests enjoin."

To the Eleans the god bade the following:

"Citizens of Elis keep straight to the law of your fathers

Defend your own country and refrain from war

Leading the Greeks in impartial friendship

Whenever the genial year returns [? in your ways]."

Col. 194: Because of this Iphitus announced the truce (text is
uncertain) and ordained the games with the help of Lycurgus the
Lacedaemonian who happened to be his relative, both being descended from Heracles. At that time the foot race was the only
contest but later the other contests were added.*

Aristodemus of Elis (3rd cent. B. C.?) and his school claim that
it was after the 27th Olympiad [gap in text] athletes began to be
listed, that is, whoever were victors of course; before that no one
was listed, no attention being paid to earlier victors. In the 28th,
Coroebus of Elis won the stade race and was the first to be listed;
and this was recorded in writing as the first Olympiad. From
this event the Greeks date their years. And Polybius (2nd cent.
B. C.) leaves the same report as Aristodemus.* Callimachus

(3rd cent. B.C.) says that thirteen Olympiads* elapsed after Iphitus without any victories being listed; in the fourteenth Coroebus won. Many assert that from the founding of the games.by Heracles, the son of Alcmena, to the first officially recorded Olympiad was 419 years. The Eleans hold the games every fifth year--after a four year interval.

III. THE RISE OF ORGANIZED ATHLETICS (776-510 B.C.)

A. Introduction

Literary documents before the fifth century B.C. are scant in number but those that exist do afford a glimpse of the athletic situation in the eighth and seventh centuries. It is probably safe to assert from their evidence that athletic games continued to be the usual feature of the day wherever and whenever Greeks met in recreational assembly, whether it was to worship gods or to honor departed heroes.

The Homeric Hymn to Delian Apollo, perhaps written by an Asia Minor or Island poet of the eighth century before Christ, mentions long-robed Ionians gathering at Delos to delight the god with boxing as well as with song and dance (see also Thucyd. III 104.)

From Hesiod and the Hesiodic corpus of poems come a few glimpses of early athletic sports as held on the mainland of Greece in Boeotia:

Theogony 435-8*: Good is she (i.e. Hecate) also when men contend at the games, for there too the goddess is with them and profits them: and he who by might and strength gets the victory wins the rich prize easily with joy, and brings glory to his parents.

In a poem which describes the Shield of Heracles, scenes of athletic contests take their place beside those of commerce, agriculture, war, marriage, and crafts. The poet quite naturally, as though they were a typical feature, includes them in that panorama of ancient life which Hephaestus was supposed to have wrought in concentric circles as a decoration for the shield.

Scutum 301-13*: Also there were men boxing and wrestling, and huntsmen chasing swift hares with a leash of sharp-toothed dogs before them, they eager to catch the hares, and the hares eager to escape.

Next to them were horsemen hard set, and they contended and laboured for a prize. The charioteers standing on their well-woven cars urged on their swift horses with loose rein; the jointed cars flew along clattering and the naves of the wheels shrieked loudly. So they were engaged in an unending toil, and the end with victory came never to them, and the contest was ever unwon. And there was set out for them with-

in the course a great tripod of gold, the splendid work of
cunning Hephaestus.

In the seventh century, Tyrtaeus voiced the official policy of
Sparta when he stated in a poem that excellence in athletics was
not to be compared with excellence in military matters (Frag. 9
Diehl). We do not know whether he actually convinced "the man in
the street" of that fact for Sparta had long taken pride in her victories at Olympia. Many a man then living had of course helped
celebrate some of the seven victories in the foot-race won by their
famous Chionis (see the note below).

The information on athletics in the few contemporary literary
sources may be supplemented with reliable information from a
variety of other sources. First and foremost are the tangible remains from these two centuries and a half, which have been gathered and analyzed by the archaeologists: black-figured vases with
their athletic scenes, coins, the so-called "Apollo" statues, inscriptions and carved scenes on monument bases, and some inscribed athletic equipment. Next in importance are the statements
on early Greek athletic practices to be found in the writers of the
two centuries immediately following the sixth. Other secondary
sources rich in information are the portions of the Olympic Victor Lists still in existence, papyrus fragments, learned notes
(scholia) of scholars in Alexandria, and the more elaborate accounts of athletics written by research students of the later Roman
period. The finds of archaeology act as a check, of course, on
the credibility of the later accounts and in many instances clearly
support the written statements.

An examination of all the evidence will reveal that the age-old
practice of casual, informal athletic competitions developed gradually in the course of these eight generations into a system of
organized athletics. Undirected exercise and chance advice from
experienced relatives, such as Nestor's counsel to his son mentioned above in Homer's Iliad, no longer sufficed for the contestant in the national or even the local games. Regular training
under experienced teachers enforcing well-formulated rules became, during these centuries, a part of the regular life of every
Greek community.

From the eighth century B.C., however, through most of the
sixth it was still, for the most part, the young man of means and
social distinction who could afford to spend his time training for
the national festivals. Besides, in those days when skill in athletics was in such high social repute, there was no easier step-

ping stone to an advantageous marriage or to a prominent place in
affairs of state for an ambitious man than a victory in the games
before the eyes of distinguished spectators gathered from all over
Greece. The list of persons recorded as victors at the festival of
Olympia, in the two centuries after official lists began to be kept,
reads like a page from the Social Register.* It is to be expected
that wealthy aristocrats and tyrants would be entering four horse
chariots in contests (see "Cimon" below); but in these centuries
future statesmen, generals, sons-in-law of wealthy tyrants and
the like were also fighting hard pancratium matches of a far from
gentle type of boxing and wrestling and were sprinting in the foot
races at Olympia during the stifling heat of August.* Such was the
social and political prestige of that festival in the early seventh
century B.C. that the powerful and rich king of Argos, Pheidon,
wantonly usurped control of it for a season.*

A glimpse of the social importance of proficiency in sports for
a young man of fashion in the early sixth century is left by Herodotus in his account (VI 126 f.) of the year-long house party held
at the home of Cleisthenes, a hundred years before the historian's
day. That wealthy tyrant of Sicyon, just after receiving a wreath
for the chariot race victory at Olympia in the 570's, announced to
the youths assembled there a "Son-in-Law Contest" to begin at his
home within sixty days. From Greece and Italy came prominent
young men (one of them brother of the Strong Man, Titormus,
cited in the section on Milo, below) willing to be observed for a
year in the hope of winning the hand of Agariste. "Whom, having
that end in view" remarks Herodotus "Cleisthenes made to contend
in running and wrestling". So, apparently, athletic skill was
checked along with general deportment. When the choice had nar-
rowed to two Athenian youths of impeccable social connections, it
was Hippocleides who lost because of an utterly non-Greek athletic exhibition of acrobatic dancing! Megacles, the winner of
Agariste's hand, it is hardly necessary to add in view of Cleisthenes taste in sports, was the son of that immensely wealthy
Alcmaeon (Herodot. VI 125) who had won for Athens her first recorded victory in the chariot race at Olympia. And Herodotus
adds a final detail which is of importance in connection with the
Solon selection to be cited just below: "To those of you whose
suit is rejected (said Cleisthenes) I make a gift of a talent of silver to each, for his desire to take a wife from my house and his
sojourn away from his home (130)."*

By the end of the sixth century B.C., the four major national
"wreath" festivals on the mainland together with the hundreds of

local ones* held in every corner of Greece proper and in the wide
reaches of the Greek colonies -- from Olbia in the Cimmerian Bos-
porus far to the northeast, all the way to western Sicily -- must
have kept the public interest in athletics at fever point. Greek
colonists seem to have converted even their non-Greek neighbors
into ardent "fans" of Greek sports. Anacharsis of Scythia and his
visit to Athens to learn more in detail about the subject of athletics
(to be quoted below from Lucian) are testimony to this effect, also
the story of the physician, Democedes, and his message to King
Darius. For Dr. Democedes, leading specialist of his day, sent
a special message to the Persian King, according to Herodotus
(III 137), announcing his engagement to the daughter of Milo, the
famous Croton wrestler (below). And the historian adds the comment: "For Darius held the name of Milo the wrestler in great
honor; and, to my thinking,the reason of Democedes' seeking this
match and paying a great sum for it was to show Darius that he
was a man of estimation in his own country as well as Persia."*

B. Solon and the Subsidizing of Athletes
(just after 594 B.C.)

From Plutarch, a native of Boeotia and sound scholar of the
first century A.D., comes a statement of great importance in the
history of Greek athletics, namely that the famous Solon passed a
law awarding sums of cash to victors in major festivals.

Commercial prosperity for his city was the goal for which the
far-sighted Solon aimed in much of his legislation.* These athletic awards seem to have been in line with that policy, as of
course great prestige could come to Athens (and her manufactured
products) if victories, always so publicly proclaimed, should become more numerous for her at Olympia and at the Isthmus, where
important persons from every section of the Greek trade world
were regularly in the audience.

The sums of money allotted were very large, as may be seen
by a comparison with the price of staple articles mentioned in the
same paragraph and with prices mentioned in inscriptions of the
following century.* An Athenian, victor at Olympia, would have
been able with the prize money to purchase five hundred bushels
of grain and thereby to enter the class of topmost financial rating
for that one year. According to Solon's division of citizens (Plut.
Solon 18) an income of five hundred bushels a year entitled a citi-

zen to be rated in the millionaire group, "pentacosio-medimni."

One of the immediate results of Solon's law must have been that competition in the national festivals became less exclusively the privilege of the wealthy few. With such an inducement a person could afford to leave his gainful occupation long enough for the journey to Olympia and the month of training there. The Isthmus, being nearer, entailed less expense. The investment by the city of such sums, possibly provided by the state-owned silver mines at Laurium, must have paid dividends far exceeding Solon's expectations, for Athens from that time began her rise to first place in Greece on all matters athletic.

Plutarch, Solon 23,3*: In the valuations of sacrificial offerings, at any rate, a sheep and a bushel of grain are reckoned at a drachma; the victor in the Isthmian games was to be paid a hundred drachmas, and the Olympic victor five hundred; the man who brought in a wolf was given five drachmas, and for a wolf's whelp, one; the former sum, according to Demetrius the Phalerian, was the price of an ox, the latter that of a sheep. For although the prices which Solon fixes in his sixteenth table are for choice victims, and naturally many times as great as those for ordinary ones, still, even these are low in comparison with present prices.

C. An Egyptian View of the Rules at Olympia
(between 592-589 B.C.)

An account left by Herodotus makes it clear that the management of the Olympia festival was doing a bit of critical self-examination in the early decades of the sixth century. A delegation, with some advance publicity, was sent to Egypt at that time to consult with her wise men on the subject of the rules of the Games at Olympia. Those in control evidently wanted to make sure that there were no loop-holes in Olympia's claim of being the "games with the finest and fairest of rules". A complete endorsement of this slogan would have been the best possible advertisement throughout Greece; as it was, the limited one received from the Wise Men was not too bad.

A brief look at what was going on elsewhere in Greece will help explain what may have been causing concern to the Dorian management at Olympia. The Pythian Games of Apollo at Delphi, a festival of very ancient origins, were being expanded into a

regularly recurring Panhellenic gathering in the early sixth century B.C. Athletic events were added to the customary musical ones
and a wreath was introduced as the sole prize, all with the helping
hands of Athens and Sicyon. At about the same time the old Isthmian Games in honor of Poseidon, promoted by Corinth, were
undergoing the same sort of expansion, quite clearly with a nod of
approval from Athens. A wreath was adopted as the award and to
the sober Olympic list of events there were added novel and attractive features. The work of reorganization into national festivals for both the Isthmian and the Pythian Games was completed
by 582 B.C. Such rise to importance of competitive festivals may
have worried the officials at Olympia, especially as the lively
Isthmian Games were held twice as often as the Olympic and in a
spot near the Isthmus of Corinth, more accessible to the population centers of the Eastern Greek world. Some scholars therefore trace to the fine hand of Olympia the sudden emergence of the
old Nemean festival into the ranks of the Panhellenic group in
573 B.C. Celebrated in simple surroundings between Argos and
Sicyon and on a strictly Dorian plan always, this festival, held in
the same years as the Isthmian, may have been reorganized with
the help of Elis for the express purpose of curtailing a bit the influence of the Ionian festival near Corinth.*

Herodotus II 160 : While this Psammis was king of Egypt he was
visited by ambassadors from Elis, the Eleans boasting that
they had ordered the Olympic games with all the justice and
fairness in the world, and claiming that even the Egyptians,
albeit the wisest of all men, could not better it. When the
Eleans came to Egypt and told the purpose of their coming,
Psammis summoned an assembly of those who were said to be
the wisest men in Egypt. These assembled, and inquired of
the Eleans, who told them of the rules of the games which they
must obey, and, having declared these, said they had come
that if the Egyptians could invent any juster way they might
learn this too. The Egyptians consulted together, and then
asked the Eleans if their own townsmen took part in the contests. The Eleans answered that this was so: all Greeks from
Elis or elsewhere might contend. Then the Egyptians said
that this rule was wholly wide of justice: "For," said they,
"it cannot be but that you will favour your own townsmen in the
contest and deal unfairly by a stranger. Nay, if you will indeed make just rules and have therefore come to Egypt, you
should admit only strangers to the contest, and not Eleans."
Such was the counsel of the Egyptians to the Eleans.

D. Solon and Anacharsis
(about 560 B. C.)

A Syrian Greek named Lucian (A. D. 125-180), who spent twenty years in Athens, living some seven hundred and fifty years later than Solon, has left a pleasant dialogue on the subject of physical education in the days of Solon. With due allowance for his marked journalistic temperament and for a few anachronisms, Lucian shows himself to have been, on the whole, a careful research student. This account, even if idealized, is no doubt essentially correct for a gymnasium scene of the sixth century B.C., especially for the days of Pisistratus when Solon was a retired onlooker of the Athenian scene. It is even more a faithful picture of athletic practices of the fifth century B.C., for which there is much more contemporary evidence to serve as a check.

The conversation is supposed to have taken place in the Lyceum* at Athens between Solon and that legendary figure, Anacharsis of Scythia (Southern Russia), whose reported visit to Greece in quest of wisdom gripped the imagination of both ancient and modern writers.*

Lucian, Anacharsis*

(1) ANACHARSIS: And why are your young men doing all this, Solon? Some of them, locked in each other's arms, are tripping one another up, while others are choking and twisting each other and grovelling together in the mud, wallowing like swine. Yet, in the beginning, as soon as they had taken their clothes off, they put oil on themselves, and took turns at rubbing each other down very peacefully -- I saw it. Since then, I do not know what has got into them that they push one another about with lowered heads and butt their foreheads together like rams. And see there! That man picked the other one up by the legs and threw him to the ground, then fell down upon him and will not let him get up, shoving him all down into the mud; and now, after winding his legs about his middle and putting his forearm underneath his throat, he is choking the poor fellow, who is slapping him sidewise on the

shoulder, by way of begging off, I take it, so that he may not be strangled completely. Even out of consideration for the oil, they do not avoid getting dirty; they rub off the ointment, plaster themselves with mud, mixed with streams of sweat, and make themselves a laughingstock, to me at least, by slipping through each other's hands like eels.

(2) Another set is doing the same in the uncovered part of the court, though not in mud. They have a layer of deep sand under them in the pit, as you see, and not only besprinkle one another but of their own accord heap the dust on themselves like so many cockerels, in order that it may be harder to break away in the clinches, I suppose, because the sand takes off the slipperiness and affords a firmer grip on a dry surface.

(3) Others, standing upright, themselves covered with dust, are attacking each other with blows and kicks. This one here looks as if he were going to spew out his teeth, unlucky man, his mouth is so full of blood and sand; he has had a blow on the jaw, as you see. But even the official there does not separate them and break up the fight -- I assume from his purple cloak that he is one of the officials; on the contrary, he urges them on and praises the one who struck the blow.

(4) Others in other places are all exerting themselves; they jump up and down as if they were running, but stay in the same place; and they spring high up and kick the air.

(5) I want to know, therefore, what good it can be to do all this, because to me at least the thing looks more like insanity than anything else, and nobody can easily convince me that men who act in that way are not out of their minds.

(6) SOLON: It is only natural, Anacharsis, that what they are doing should have that appearance to you, since it is unfamiliar and very much in contrast with Scythian customs. In like manner you yourselves probably have much in your education and training which would appear strange to us Greeks if one of us should look in upon it as you are doing now. But have no fear, my dear sir; it is not insanity, and it is not out of brutality that they strike one another and tumble each other in the mud, or sprinkle each other with dust. The thing has a certain usefulness, not unattended by pleasure, and it gives much strength to their bodies. As a matter of fact, if you stop for some time, as I think you will, in Greece, before long you yourself will be one of the muddy and dusty set; so delightful and at the same time so profitable will the thing seem to you.

ANACH. Get out with you, Solon! You Greeks may have those benefits and pleasures. For my part, if one of you should treat me like that, he will find out that we do not carry these daggers at our belts for nothing!

(7) But tell me, what name do you give to these performances? What are we to say they are doing?

SOL. The place itself, Anacharsis, we call a gymnasium, and it is consecrated to Lyceian Apollo; you see his statue -- the figure leaning against the pillar, with the bow in his left hand; his right arm bent back above his head indicates that the god is resting, as if after long exertion. As for these forms of athletics, that (8) one yonder in the mud is called wrestling; and the men in the dust are wrestling too. When they stand upright and strike one another, we call it the pancratium. We have other such athletic exercises, too -- boxing, throwing the discus, and jumping -- in all of which

we hold contests, and the winner is considered best in his class
and carries off the prizes.

(9) ANACH. And these prizes of yours, what are they?

SOL. At the Olympic games, a wreath made of wild olive, at
the Isthmian one of pine, and at the Nemean one of parsley, at the
Pythian some of the apples sacred to Apollo, and with us at the
Panathenaea, the oil from the holy olive. What made you laugh,
Anacharsis? Because you think these prizes trivial?

ANACH. No, the prizes that you have told of are absolutely
imposing, Solon; they may well cause those who have offered them
to glory in their munificence and the contestants themselves to be
tremendously eager to carry off such guerdons, so that they will
go through all these preliminary hardships and risks, getting
choked and broken in two by one another, for apples and parsley,
as if it were not possible for anyone who wants them to get plenty
of apples without any trouble, or to wear a wreath of parsley or of
pine without having his face bedaubed with mud or letting himself
be kicked in the belly by his opponent!

(10) SOL. But, my dear fellow, it is not the bare gifts that we
have in view! They are merely tokens of the victory and marks
to identify the winners. But the reputation that goes with them is
worth everything to the victors, and to attain it, even to be kicked
is nothing to men who seek to capture fame through hardships.
Without hardships it cannot be acquired; the man who covets it
must put up with many unpleasantnesses in the beginning before at
last he can expect the profitable and delightful outcome of his exertions.

ANACH. By this delightful and profitable outcome, Solon, you mean that everybody will see them wearing wreaths and will applaud them for their victory after having pitied them a long time beforehand for their hard knocks, and that they will be felicitous to have apples and parsley in compensation for their hardships!

SOL. You are still unacquainted with our ways, I tell you. After a little you will think differently about them, when you go to the games and see that great throng of people gathering to look at such spectacles, and amphitheatres* filling that will hold thousands, and the contestants applauded, and the one among them who succeeds in winning counted equal to the gods.

(11) ANACH. That is precisely the most pitiable part of it, Solon, if they undergo this treatment not before just a few but in the presence of so many spectators and witnesses of the brutality, who no doubt felicitate them on seeing them streaming with blood or getting strangled by their opponents; for these are the extreme felicities that go with their victory! With us Scythians, Solon, if anyone strikes a citizen, or assaults him and throws him down, or tears his clothing, the elders impose severe penalties upon him, even if the offence takes place before just a few witnesses, not to speak of such great assemblies as that at the Isthmus and that at Olympia which you describe. I assure you, I cannot help pitying the contestants for what they go through, and I am absolutely amazed at the spectators, the prominent men who come, you say, from all sides to the games, if they neglect their urgent business and fritter their time away in such matters. I cannot yet conceive what pleasure it is to them to see men struck, pummelled, dashed on the ground, and crushed by one another.

(12) SOL. If it were the time, Anacharsis, for the Olympic or the Isthmian or the Panathenaic games, what takes place there would itself have taught you that we had not spent our energy on all this in vain. Just by talking about the delightfulness of the doings there, one cannot convince you of it as thoroughly as if you yourself, sitting in the midst of the spectators, were to see manly perfection, physical beauty, wonderful condition, mighty skill, irresistible strength, daring, rivalry, indomitable resolution, and inexpressible ardour for victory. I am very sure that you would never have stopped praising and cheering and clapping.

(13) ANACH. No doubt, Solon; and laughing and gibing, into the bargain; for I see that all these things which you have enumerated -- the perfection, the condition, the beauty, the daring -- are being wasted for you without any great object in view, since your country is not in peril, nor your farmlands being ravaged, nor your friends and kinsmen insolently carried off. So the competitors are all the more ridiculous if they are the flower of the country, as you say, and yet endure so much for nothing, making themselves miserable and defiling their beautiful, great bodies with sand and black eyes to get possession of an apple and an olive-branch when they have won! You see, I like to keep mentioning the prizes, which are so fine! But tell me, do all the contestants get them?

SOL. Not by any means; only one among them all, the victor.

ANACH. Then do so many undergo hardships upon the uncertain and precarious chance of winning, Solon, knowing too that there will surely be but one winner and very many losers, who, poor fellows, will have received blows and in some cases even wounds for nothing?

(14) SOL. It seems, Anacharsis, that you have never yet done any thinking about the proper way to direct a state; otherwise you would not disparage the best of institutions. If ever you make it your object to find out how a state is to be organized in the best way possible, and how its citizens are to reach the highest degree of excellence, you will then praise these exercises and the rivalry which we display in regard to them, and you will know that they have much that is useful intermingled with the hardships, even if you now think our energy is spent on them for nothing.

ANACH. I assure you, Solon, I had no other object in coming to your country from Scythia, over such a vast stretch of land and across the wide and tempestuous Euxine, than to learn the laws of the Greeks, to observe your institutions, and to acquaint myself with the best form of polity.* That is why I selected you in particular out of all the Athenians for my friend and host, in deference to your reputation, for I used to hear that you were a maker of laws, an inventor of excellent institutions. ...

(15) SOL. To describe everything, my friend, in brief compass is not an easy task... And I shall now tell you what we think about our young men, and how we deal with them from the time when they begin to know good from bad, to be physically mature, and to bear hardships, in order that you may learn why we prescribe these exercises for them and compel them to train their bodies. It is not simply on account of the contests, in order that they may be able to take the prizes -- very few out of the entire number have the capacity for that -- but because we seek a certain greater good from it for the entire state and for the young men themselves . . . that is to say, freedom for each individual singly and for the state in general, wealth, glory, enjoyment of

ancestral feast-days, safety for one's family, and in short, the
fairest blessings that one could pray to receive from the gods. All
these things are interwoven in the wreath that I speak of and ac-
crue from the contest to which these exercises and hardships lead.

(16) ANACH. Then, Solon, you amazing person, when you had
such magnificent prizes to tell of, you spoke of apples and parsley
and a sprig of wild olive and a bit of pine?

SOL. But really, Anacharsis, even those prizes will no longer
appear trivial to you when you understand what I mean. They orig-
inate in the same purpose, and are all small parts of that greater
contest and of the wreath of complete felicity which I mentioned. ...

(24) As to their bodies -- for that is what you were especially
eager to hear about -- we train them as follows. When, as I said,
they are no longer soft and wholly strengthless, we strip them,
and think it best to begin by habituating them to the weather, making them used to the several seasons, so as not to be distressed
by the heat or give in to the cold. Then we rub them with olive
oil and supple them in order that they may be more elastic, for
since we believe that leather, when softened by oil, is harder to
break and far more durable, lifeless as it is, it would be extraordinary if we should not think that the living body would be put in
better condition by the oil.

After that, having invented many forms of athletics and appointed teachers for each, we teach one, for instance, boxing and
another the pancratium, in order that they may become accustomed to endure hardships and to meet blows, and not recoil for
fear of injuries. This helps us by creating in them two effects

that are most useful, since it makes them not only spirited in fac-
ing dangers and unmindful of their bodies, but healthy and strong
into the bargain.

Those of them who put their bent heads together and wrestle
learn to fall safely and get up easily, to push, grip and twist in
various ways, to stand being choked, and to lift their opponent
high in the air. They too are not engaging in useless exercises;
on the contrary, they indisputably acquire one thing, which is first
and greatest: their bodies become less susceptible and more vigorous through being exercised thoroughly. There is something
else, too, which itself is not trivial: they become expert as a result of it, in case they should ever come to need what they have
learned in battle. Clearly such a man, when he closes with an
enemy, will trip and throw him more quickly, and when he is
down, will know how to get up again most easily. For we make
all these preparations, Anacharsis, with a view to that contest,
the contest under arms, and we expect to find men thus disciplined far superior, after we have suppled and trained their bodies
naked, and so have made them healthier and stronger, light and
elastic, and at the same time too heavy for their opponents.

(25) You can imagine, I suppose, the consequences -- what they
are likely to be with arms in hand when even unarmed they would
implant fear in the enemy. They show no white and ineffective
corpulence or pallid leanness, as if they were women's bodies
bleached out in the shade, quivering and streaming with profuse
sweat at once and panting beneath the helmet, especially if the
sun, as at present, blazes with the heat of noon. What use could
one make of men like that, who get thirsty, who cannot stand dust,
who break ranks the moment they catch sight of blood, who lie

down and die before they get within a spear's cast and come to grips with the enemy!

But these young men of ours have a ruddy skin, coloured darker by the sun, and manly faces; they reveal great vitality, fire, and courage; they are aglow with such splendid condition; they are neither lean and emaciated nor so full-bodied as to be heavy, but symmetrical in their lines;* they have sweated away the useless and superfluous part of their tissues, but what made for strength and elasticity is left upon them uncontaminated by what is worthless, and they maintain it vigorously. In fact, athletics do in our bodies just what winnowers do to wheat; they blow away the husks and the chaff, but separate the grain out cleanly and accumulate it for future use.

(26) Consequently a man like that cannot help keeping well and holding out protractedly under exhausting labours; it would be long before he would begin to sweat, and he would rarely be found ill. ...

(27) Furthermore, we train them to be good runners, habituating them to hold out for a long distance, and also making them light-footed for extreme speed in a short distance. And the running is not done on hard, resisting ground but in deep sand, where it is not easy to plant one's foot solidly or to get a purchase with it, since it slips from under one as the sand gives way beneath it. We also train them to jump a ditch, if need be, or any other obstacle, even carrying lead weights as large as they can grasp. (see Sect. H below) Then, too, they compete in throwing the javelin for distance. And you saw another implement in the gymnasium, made of bronze (see Sect. H below), circular, resembling a little shield without handle or straps; in fact, you tested it as it lay there, and thought it heavy and hard to hold on account of its

smoothness. Well, they throw that high in the air and also to a distance, vying to see who can go the farthest and throw beyond the rest. This exercise strengthens their shoulders and puts muscle into their arms and legs.

(28) As for the mud and the dust, which you thought rather ludicrous in the beginning, you amazing person, let me tell you why it is put down. In the first place, so that instead of taking their tumbles on a hard surface they may fall with impunity on a soft one; secondly, their slipperiness is necessarily greater when they are sweaty and muddy. This feature, in which you compared them to eels, is not useless or ludicrous; it contributes not a little to strength and muscle when both are in this condition and each has to grip the other firmly and hold him fast while he tries to slip away. And as for picking up a man who is muddy, sweaty, and oily while he does his best to break away and squirm out of your hands, do not think it a trifle! All this, as I said before, is of use in war, in case one should need to pick up a wounded friend and carry him out of the fight with ease, or to snatch up an enemy and come back with him in one's arms. So we train them beyond measure, setting them hard tasks that they may manage smaller ones with far greater ease.

(29) The dust we think to be of use for the opposite purpose, to prevent them from slipping away when they are grasped. After they have been trained in the mud to hold fast what eludes them because of its oiliness, they are given practice in escaping out of their opponent's hands when they themselves are caught, even though they are held in a sure grip. Moreover, the dust, sprinkled on when the sweat is pouring out in profusion, is thought to check it; it makes their strength endure long, and hinders them

from being harmed by the wind blowing upon their bodies, which are then unresisting and have the pores open. Besides, it rubs off the dirt and makes the man cleaner. I should like to put side by by side one of those white-skinned fellows who have lived in the shade and any one you might select of the athletes in the Lyceum, after I had washed off the mud and the dust, and to ask you which of the two you would pray to be like. I know that even without testing each to see what he could do, you would immediately choose on first sight to be firm and hard rather than delicate and mushy and white because your blood is scanty and withdraws to the interior of the body.

(30) That, Anacharsis, is the training we give our young men, expecting them to become stout guardians of our city, and that we shall live in freedom through them, conquering foes if they attack us and keeping our neighbors in dread of us, so that most of them will cower at our feet and pay tribute. In peace, too, we find them far better, for nothing that is base appeals to their ambitions and idleness does not incline them to arrogance, but exercises such as these give them diversion and keep them occupied. The chief good of the public and the supreme felicity of the state, which I mentioned before, are attained when our young men, striving at our behest for the fairest objects, have been most efficiently prepared both for peace and for war.

(31) ANACH. Then if the enemy attack you, Solon, you yourselves will take the field rubbed with oil and covered with dust, shaking your fists at them, and they, of course, will cower at your feet and run away, fearing that while they are agape in stupefaction you may sprinkle sand in their mouths, or that after jumping behind them so as to get on their backs, you may wind

your legs about their bellies and strangle them by putting an arm under their helmets. Yes, by Zeus, they will shoot their arrows, naturally, and throw their spears, but the missiles will not affect you any more than as if you were statues, tanned as you are by the sun and supplied in abundance with blood. You are not straw or chaff, so as to give in quickly under their blows; it would be only after long and strenuous effort, when you are all cut up with deep wounds, that you would show a few drops of blood. This is the gist of what you say, unless I have completely misunderstood your comparison.

(32) ... No, I am afraid that all these clever tricks of yours are silliness, nothing but child's play, amusements for your young men who have nothing to do and want to lead an easy life. If you wish, whatever betides, to be free and happy, you will require other forms of athletics and real training, that is to say, under arms, and you will not compete against each other in sport, but against the enemy, learning courage in perilous conflict. So let them give up the dust and the oil; teach them to draw the bow and throw the spear; and do not give them light javelins that can be deflected by the wind, but let them have a heavy lance that whistles when it is hurled, a stone as large as they can grasp, a double axe, a target in their left hand, a breastplate, and a helmet.

(33) In your present condition, it seems to me that you are being saved by the grace of some god or other, seeing that you have not yet been wiped out by the onfall of a handful of light-armed troops. Look here, if I should draw this little dirk at my belt and fall upon all your young men by myself, I should capture the gymnasium with a mere hurrah, for they would run away and not one would dare to face the steel; no, they would gather about the stat-

ues and hide behind the pillars, making me laugh while most of
them cried and trembled. Then you would see that they were no
longer ruddy-bodied as they are now; they would all turn pale on
the instant, dyed to another hue by fright. Profound peace has
brought you to such a pass that you could not easily endure to see
a single plume of hostile helmet.

(34) SOL. The Thracians who campaigned against us with
Eumolpus did not say so, Anacharsis, nor your women who marched against the city with Hippolyta, nor any others who have tested
us under arms. It does not follow, my unsophisticated friend,
that because our young men's bodies are thus naked while we are
developing them, they are therefore undefended by armour when
we lead them out into dangers. When they become efficient in
themselves, they are then trained with arms and can make far better use of them because they are so well conditioned.

ANACH. Where do you do this training under arms? I have
not seen anything of the sort in the city, though I have gone all
about the whole of it.

SOL. But you would see it, Anacharsis, if you should stop with
us longer, and also arms for every man in great quantity, which
we use when it is necessary, and crests and trappings and horses,
and cavalrymen amounting to nearly a fourth of our citizens. But
to bear arms always and carry a dirk at one's belt is, we think,
superfluous in time of peace; in fact, there is a penalty prescribed
for anyone who carries weapons unnecessarily within the city
limits or brings armour out into a public place. As for your people, you may be pardoned for always living under arms. Your
dwelling in unfortified places makes it easy to attack you, and
your wars are very numerous, and nobody knows when someone

may come upon him asleep, drag him down from his wagon, and kill him. Besides, your distrust of one another, in as much as your relations with each other are adjusted by individual caprice and not by law, makes steel always necessary, so as to be at hand for defence if anyone should use violence.

(35) ANACH. Then is it possible, Solon, that while you think it superfluous to carry weapons without urgent reason, and are careful of your arms in order that they may not be spoiled by handling, keeping them in store with the intention of using them some day, when need arises; yet when no danger threatens you wear out the bodies of your young men by mauling them and wasting them away in sweat, not husbanding their strength until it is needed but expending it fruitlessly in the mud and dust?

SOL. Apparently, Anacharsis, you think that strength is like wine or water or some other liquid. Anyhow, you are afraid that during exertions it may leak away unnoticed as if from an earthen jar, and then be gone, leaving our bodies empty and dry, since they are not filled up again with anything from within. As a matter of fact, this is not the case, my friend: the more one draws it out by exertions, the more it flows in, like the fable of the Hydra, if you have heard it, which says that when one head was cut off, two others always grew up in its place. ...

(36) ANACH. I do not understand this at all, Solon; what you have said is too subtle for me, requiring keen intellect and penetrating discernment. But do by all means tell me why it is that in the Olympic and Isthmian and Pythian and the other games, where many, you say, come together to see the young men competing, you never match them under arms but bring them out naked* and show them receiving kicks and blows, and when they have won you

give them apples and parsley. It is worth while to know why you do so.

SOL. We think, Anacharsis, that their zeal for the athletic exercises will be increased if they see those who excel in them receiving honours and having their names proclaimed before the assembled Greeks. For this reason, expecting to appear unclothed before so many people, they try to attain good physical condition so that they may not be ashamed of themselves when they are stripped, and each makes himself as fit to win as he can. Furthermore, the prizes, as I said before, are not trivial -- to be praised by the spectators, to become a man of mark, and to be pointed at with the finger as the best of one's class. Therefore, many of the spectators, who are still young enough for training, go away immoderately in love with manfulness and hard work as a result of all this. Really, Anacharsis, if the love of fame should be banished out of the world, what new blessing should we ever acquire, or who would want to do any glorious deed? But as things are, even from these contests they give you an opportunity to infer what they would be in war, defending country, children, wives and fanes with weapons and armour, when contending naked for parsley and apples they bring into it so much zeal for victory.

(37) What would your feelings be if you should see quail-fights and cock-fights here among us, and no little interest taken in them? You would laugh, of course, particularly if you discovered that we do it in compliance with law, and that all those of military age are required to present themselves and watch the birds spar to the uttermost limit of exhaustion. Yet this is not laughable, either; their souls are gradually penetrated by an appetite for dangers, in order that they may not seem baser and more cowardly

than the cocks, and may not show the white feather early on account of wound or weariness or any other hardship.

As for testing them under arms, and watching them get wounded
-- no! It is bestial and terribly cruel and, more than that, unprof-
itable to kill off the most efficient men who can be used to better
advantage against the enemy.

(38) As you say that you intend to visit the rest of Greece,
Anacharsis, bear it in mind if ever you go to Sparta* not to laugh
at them, either, and not to suppose that they are exciting themselves for nothing when they rush together and strike one another
in the theatre over a ball, or when they go into a place surrounded
by water, divide into companies and treat one another like enemies, naked as with us, until one company drives the other out of
the enclosure, crowding them into the water -- the Heraclids driving out the Lycurgids, or the reverse -- after which there is peace
in future and nobody would think of striking a blow. Above all, do
not laugh if you see them getting flogged at the altar and dripping
blood while their fathers and mothers stand by and are so far from
being distressed by what is going on that they actually threaten to
punish them if they should not bear up under the stripes, and be-
seech them to endure the pain as long as possible and be staunch
under the torture.

E. A Famous Pancratium Match of 564 B.C.

In the <u>Imagines</u> (Pictures) of Philostratus (early third century
A.D.) which is a work containing sprightly and detailed descrip-
tions of sixty-four paintings, presented in the surprisingly modern
style of the explanatory voice and picture of any movie theatre of
today, there happens to be the fullest account extant of a pancratium contest. Whether the painting described actually existed in a

portico in Naples, as seems likely, or, as has been argued, was merely a word picture created by Philostratus as a result of his imagination and wide reading, is of no consequence here.

The physical setting of a pancratium match, the enthusiasm of the spectators and the permissible holds are vividly described and are in accord with other evidence for such contests in the sixth century B.C.

The hero of this story, Arrhichion (or Arrhachion), from the simple mountain town of Phigalia in Arcadia, was a vivid personality to the ancient world. As will be seen from the second selection below, Pausanias, a few years earlier than Philostratus, had described this athlete's statue and the victory for which he was famous. Even today he is the subject of discussion among modern scholars* who have not yet agreed whether or not the rigid, "Apollo-type" stone statue belonging to the early half of the sixth century B.C. and found in two portions in a pasture at Phigalia is actually the statue seen and described by Pausanias.

Had Anacharsis, the Scythian of Lucian's story, accepted Solon's suggestion and visited Olympia, he could have seen the winner of this contest, in person. Both were probably of the same period.

Philostratus, Imagines II 6*

[Philostratus* presumably is explaining the picture gallery to a ten year old boy and his friends].

Next you come to Olympia itself and to the noblest of the contests there; for this right here is the pancratium for men. Arrhichion is being crowned in it, the man who died at the very moment of victory, and this man who is placing the wreath on him is one of the Olympic officials -- he can be called that without question for he is actually in charge and besides he is pictured just like those men over there [i.e., other officials] -- the country here provides a natural stadium in an open valley extending just the distance of a stadium [i.e., 600 feet], and the waters of the Alpheius are moving past lightly -- this is the only river which floats on the surface of the sea -- and wild olives grow thick around here in bright shimmering beauty, with foliage curly like parsley. This part over here behind the stadium we will examine presently and many other details, too, but let us now inquire into Arrhichion's deed before it is all over. For he seems to have overpowered not only his adversary but the Greek audience as well. At any rate they have jumped up from their seats and are shouting, some of them waving their hands, some are leaping up from the ground, while others are good-naturedly sparring with each other. The really astonishing feat has left the spectators beside themselves. Who is so stolid as not to shriek aloud at the athlete? This present achievement is greater than his great record of winning twice at Olympia for he has gained this victory at the cost of his life and he is being sent down to the land of the blessed with the dust [see Anacharsis 29 above] still on him. Don't consider this an accident. Very cleverly he thought out the victory beforehand.

And what about the wrestling technique? Well, my boy, people who contend in the pancratium use the dangerous type of wrestling for they have to employ falls backward* which are not safe for the wrestler, and holds by which one who has fallen can still win, and they must have skill in strangling various ways at various times, and they also use wrestling strokes against the ankle and twist the hand of the person preparing to strike them or to jump upon them. All such, then, is the business of the pancratium, with the exception only of biting and gouging.* The Lacedaemonians allow even this practice, training themselves hard, I suppose, for war, but the Elean contests (i.e., the Olympic Games) prohibit this but do approve of strangling.

Wherefore the opponent seizing Arrhichion around the waist
thought to kill him and he had already thrust his arm around his
throat to cut off his breath. Fitting his legs close around his groin
and gripping the ends of his feet in the bend of his knees, he did get
ahead of Arrhichion in the matter of choking, with the sleep of death
stealing over his senses, but he did not get ahead of Arrhichion's
reasoning powers for at the moment he happened to relax the pressure of his legs, Arrhichion kicked away the ball of his opponent's
foot beneath which his own right side was imperilled, leaving the
leg bent at the knee, dangling there. Then Arrhichion seized his
opponent at the groin so that he could no longer resist and sank
down on him toward the left. Gripping the end of the useless foot
in the crook of his knee, he did not leave the ankle joint in place
such was the force of his sharp wrench outwards. Arrhichion himself was becoming weak as consciousness was leaving him but his
body could all the more forcibly fall against an object.

The man who did the strangling is painted in the picture to look
like a corpse and is the one indicating defeat by his upraised hand;
whereas Arrhichion is painted as victors always are, for his color
is fresh, perspiration is still dripping, and he is smiling just as
living men do when they become aware of victory.

Pausanias VIII 40, 1-2*

The Phigalians have on their market-place a statue of the pancratiast Arrhachion; it is archaic, especially in its posture. The
feet are close together, and the arms hang down by the side as far
as the hips. The statue is made of stone, and it is said that an
inscription was written upon it. This has disappeared with time*,
but Arrhachion won two Olympic victories at Festivals before the
fifty-fourth, while at this Festival (564 B.C.) he won one due part-

ly to the fairness of the Umpires (Hellanodicae) and partly to his own manhood. For when he was contending for the wild olive with the last remaining competitor, whoever he was, the latter got a grip first, and held Arrhachion, hugging him with his legs, and at the same time he squeezed his neck with his hands. Arrhachion dislocated his opponent's toe, but expired owing to suffocation; but he who suffocated Arrhachion was forced to give in at the same time because of the pain in his toe.

F. Cimon and his Prize-Winning Horses
(532-524 B.C.)

Long after Solon in 593 B.C. had opened the way for Athenians of moderate means to enter competitions in the major festivals, chariot racing with four horses still remained everywhere the one event exclusively the privilege of the wealthy. Rulers and aristocrats of every city realized that they could increase the prestige of their cities and themselves in no more noteworthy manner than by a victory at the games with the high-bred horses. It seems to have been a peculiarly gratifying way to flaunt their power and wealth. From the records of Olympic victors comes an imposing list of such notable persons who won victories in the seventh and sixth centuries B.C.*

Pisistratus, the immensely wealthy tyrant of Athens (560-527 B.C.) was so eager, it seems, to gain credit for a victory at Olympia in chariot racing that he willingly effected a trade with a personal enemy in order to obtain it.

The Cimon in this story came of a family well-known in racing circles, as Herodotus expressly states (VI 35); and his half-brother, Miltiades, had won a notable chariot victory a quarter of a century earlier.

Miltiades' handsome horses perhaps still survive in representations on the coins which their owner issued soon after reaching his colony in the Thracian Chersonese.* Cimon's horses, besides being given the extraordinary burial honors indicated, were said to have been set up in bronze in Athens by an artist who achieved an astonishingly lifelike representation of them (Aelian, Var. Hist. IX 32).

Herodotus VI 103*: Cimon, son of Stesagoras, had been, as fate
would have it, banished from Athens by Pisistratus, son of Hippocrates. Being an exile, he had the luck to win the prize for
four-horse chariots at Olympia, by this victory gaining the same
honour as his mother's son Miltiades had won. At the next
Olympiad he was a winner again with the same team of mares,
but suffered Pisistratus to be proclaimed victor, for which surrender of his victory he returned to his home under treaty. A
third Olympic prize he won with the same team. ... Cimon lies
buried outside the city, beyond the road that is called Through
the Hollow; and the mares that won him the three Olympic prizes
are buried over against his grave. None others save the mares
of the Laconian Evagoras had ever achieved the same.

G. Popular Athletes of the Sixth Century B.C.

The rise of star athletes, who were able to win wreaths at the
four major festivals over a long span of years, and the public acclaim they evoked were outstanding features in the development of
Greek athletic history during the last half of the sixth century B.C.
These heroes of the public, however, were not a small group of
over-trained, full-time professional athletes, as was true in the
later centuries of athletic history. They were, rather, intelligent
citizens who, possessing a natural flair for some certain athletic
sport, trained themselves diligently in it, sometimes with the help
of teachers who were ex-athletes, until a peak of perfection was
reached. Their routine exercises in weight lifting and the like,
their habit of eating abundantly and living in a simple, healthful
manner developed in them a robust physique which was the envy of
their public.

In those days the idols of the spectators seem to have been the
men who excelled in wrestling, boxing or in the pancratium, a
combination of the first two. The names and records of several
such athletes have been preserved in the ancient writers.* Besides Arrhichion, already mentioned as a champion in the pancratium, there was a famous boxer from Aegina, Praxidamas, with
eight "wreath" victories after his first one at Olympia in 544 B.C.
With him the custom began of honoring athletes with statues in the
precinct (Altis) of Olympia (Pausan. VI 18, 7). Pindar's ode in
praise of this man's grandson (Nemean VI, see below) recounts
the noble ancestry and athletic achievements of Praxidamas' clan.
A Tisandros of Naxos, 540-524 B.C., who was said to have kept him-

self fit by swimming around the promontories of his island (Philost. Gymn. 43 [IX D]) is credited with four victories in boxing at Olympia, four at Delphi, and an uncertain number at the Nemean and Isthmian games since "at this time neither the Corinthians nor the Argives kept complete records of the victors at Nemea* and the Isthmus" (Pausan. VI 13, 8). When the career of Tisandros, who came from the Euboean colony of Naxos, was drawing to a close, audiences were beginning to be thrilled by the performance of Glaucus, a spectacular young Greek boxer direct from Euboea itself.

1. Glaucus of Carystus

Such was the public adulation of champions by this time that not only was a statue accorded Glaucus but the first Greek lyric poet to charge money (Schol. Aristoph. Pax 697) for writing odes in praise of victors was hired to sing of his achievements. Further, this poet, Simonides, dared to rank Glaucus above the god Pollux and even above Heracles: "The strength of Polydeuces would not have held out against him nor would the hands of that man of iron, son of Alcmene (Lyr. Gr. [Edmonds] II 30)." And what is more revealing is that the poem was enthusiastically accepted by the Greeks with no attention paid to its impiety (Lucian, Pro Imag. 19).

The story of Glaucus' debut as a boxer, told by Pausanias, is in harmony with the traditions of natural aptitude and absence of elaborate training in the athletes of that day.

Description of Greece VI 10, 1-4*: (Glaucus of Carystus) ...
This Carystian was a son of Demylus, and they say that to begin with he worked as a farmer. The ploughshare one day fell out of the plough, and he fitted it into its place, using his hand as a hammer; Demylus happened to be a spectator of his son's performance, and thereupon brought him to Olympia to box. There Glaucus, inexperienced in boxing, was wounded by his antagonists, and when he was boxing with the last of them he was thought to be fainting from the number of his wounds. Then they say that his father called out to him, "Son, the plough touch" (cf. Philostr. Gymn. 20, below). So he dealt his opponent a more violent blow which forthwith brought him the victory. He is said to have won other crowns besides, two at Pytho, eight at the Nemean and eight at the Isthmian games. The statue of Glaucus was set up by his son, while Glaucias of Aegina made it. The statue represents a figure sparring

["shadow boxing" is the Greek word], as Glaucus was the best
exponent of the art of all his contemporaries.

2. Milo of Croton

Of all the athletic heroes of the sixth century B.C., no one was
as celebrated in his own day and even in later times as was Milo
of Croton, the famous wrestler.* After winning the junior wrestling match at Olympia in 536 B.C., he was wreathed six times at
Olympia, six times at the Pythian Games, ten times at the Isthmian and nine times at the Nemean (Euseb. Chron. I Col. 202).
He seems to have remained first in popularity over a period of
nearly thirty years until in his seventh try for the Olympic wreath
he was forced to yield to a younger man.

As the centuries rolled by, tales about this marvelous wrestler
became longer and more precisely detailed. The number of pounds
of meat he ate each day, the quarts of wine he drank, his feats of
strength, his manner of death were favorite subjects until "Milo"
became a household word and in some instances became, unfairly,
a symbol of unintelligent brawn and gluttony (Cic. de Senectute 9,
27; 10; Galen, Exhort. 13, below, VIII D). But it should be remembered that there is only one remark which comes directly
from the years of Milo's lifetime and only one from a period as
near as the next generation to him and that both of these mention
him with the greatest personal respect.

From the lyric poet Simonides, Milo's contemporary, there
survives a fragment of the epigram written for Milo's statue:

"This is the noble statue of the noble Milo who at Pisa won
six times never falling to his knees" (Lyr. Gr. [Edmonds] II,
186).

Herodotus, whose father and grandfather could have seen Milo
in action, indicates the prestige of the Milo family in Croton and
hints at this wrestler's high reputation even in a foreign land with
the story about Democedes and the King of Persia, quoted above
(p. 59).

In a short fragment preserved from Aristotle, who, two hundred years later than Milo's time, was doing extensive research
in athletics, there is the comment: "Milo was a huge eater* ...
and a real man" (Frag. Hist. Gr. [Müller] 2, 183).

But it is from the researches of writers, centuries later, that
the colorful details of Milo's life come. Diodorus Siculus, in a

history published in 30 B.C., tells of Milo's spectacular success as a general. The psychological effect of his costume and demeanour was no doubt shrewdly planned by him in an advance strategy session with the great Pythagoras, who had been the one to persuade the Croton folk to undertake this campaign against their neighbors.

Library of History, XII, 9: The men from Croton numbering one hundred thousand were arrayed opposite the three hundred thousand men from Sybaris who had taken the field against them; Milo, the athlete, was their leader who by his superlative physical vigour was the first to turn to rout those in the line opposite him. For this man had won six times at Olympia and, possessing courage corresponding to his physique, is said to have advanced to battle wearing his Olympic wreaths and fitted out in the fashion of Heracles with a lionskin and a club. He was given credit for the victory and was an object of admiration on the part of his fellow citizens.

Ten years later than Diodorus, Strabo published an account of Milo with some facts about his home town. Croton had been founded in 710 B.C. by Greek colonists coming from that strip along the Corinthian Gulf called Achaea. Those early settlers had evidently brought with them from the homeland an enthusiastic interest in athletic competitions and seem always to have welcomed the opportunity of returning to Olympia to a festival so conveniently located by sea for the colonies of Southern Italy.

Geography VI 1, 12*: And the city (Croton) is reputed to have cultivated warfare and athletics; at any rate, in one Olympian festival the seven men who took the lead over all others in the stadium-race were all Crotoniates, and therefore the saying "The last of the Crotoniates was the first among all other Greeks" seems reasonable. And this, it is said, is what gave rise to that other proverb "more healthful than Croton," the belief being that the place contains something that tends to health and bodily vigour, to judge by the multitude of its athletes. And its fame was increased by the large number of its Pythagorean philosophers, and by Milo, who was the most illustrious of athletes, and also a companion of Pythagoras, who spent a long time in the city. It is said that once, at the common mess of the philosophers, when a pillar began to give way, Milo slipped in under the burden and saved them all, and then drew himself from under it and escaped. And it is probably because he relied upon this same strength that he brought on himself the end of his life as reported by some writers; at any rate, the story is told that once, when he was travelling through a deep forest, he strayed rather far from the road, and then, on finding a large log cleft with wedges, thrust his hands and feet at the same time into the cleft and strained to split the log completely asunder; but he was only strong enough to make the wedges fall out, whereupon the two parts of the log instantly snapped together; and caught in such a trap as that, he became food for wild beasts.*

The fullest account of Milo comes from information gathered by Pausanias at Olympia in A.D. 174.

Descrip. of Greece VI 14, 5-9*: The statue* of Milo the son of Diotimus was made by Dameas, also a native of Crotona. ... It is further stated that Milo carried his own statue into the Altis. His feats with the pomegranate and the quoit are also remembered by tradition. He would grasp a pomegranate* so firmly that nobody could wrest it from him by force, and yet he did not damage it by pressure. He would stand upon a greased quoit, and make fools of those who charged him and tried to push him from the quoit. He used to perform also the following exhibition feats. He would tie a cord round his forehead as though it were a ribbon or a crown. Holding his breath and filling with blood the veins on his head, he would break the cord by the strength of these veins. It is said that he would let down by his side his right arm from the shoulder to the elbow, and stretch out straight the arm below the elbow turning the thumb upwards, while the other fingers lay in a row. In this position, then the little finger was lowest, but nobody could bend it back by pressure. ...[Then follows the story of Milo's death.]

A description of Milo's statue and an explanation of its accessories is given by the early third century writer Philostratus in his "Life of Apollonius of Tyana". Apollonius, a roving philosopher and sage of the first century A.D., is represented as haranguing an audience at Olympia.

Apollonius of Tyana IV 28*: And he also gave them an account of the brazen statue of Milo and explained the attitude of this figure. For this Milo is seen standing on a disk with his two feet close together, and in his left hand he grasps a pomegranate, while of his right hand the fingers are extended and as it were stringing together. Now among the people of Olympia and Arcadia the story told about this athlete is, that he was so inflexible and firm that he could never be induced to leave the

spot on which he stood; and this is the meaning of the clenched
fingers as he grasps the pomegranate, and of the look as if they
could never be separated from one another, however much you
struggled with any of them, because the intervals between the
extended fingers are very close; and they say that the fillet
with which his head is bound is a symbol of temperance and so-
briety .... [Apollonius interprets Milo's statue as representing
him a Priest of Hera] .... As for the artist's way of rendering
the fingers between which he has left no interval, that you may
ascribe to the antique style of the sculpture.

Aelian, who wrote a generation later than Pausanias, leaves an
account of the famous trial of strength between Titormus and Milo.
Huge stones with inscriptions coming from this era lend plausi-
bility to such contests between the strong men of the sixth century
B.C.

Various History XII 22: They say that Milo, who was arrogant
      because of his physical strength, chanced to meet the herdsman,
      Titormus.* Noticing that Titormus was large to look at, he de-
      sired to make trial of his strength. But Titormus kept saying
      that he was not very strong. However, he went down to the
      Evenus River (Arcadia) and, taking off his cloak, he grasped a
      huge rock, at first dragging it toward himself and then thrusting
      it away. After he had done this two or three times he raised it
      to his knees and finally raising it in his arms he carried it some
      fifty feet and hurled it. But Milo of Croton could scarcely roll
      the stone. ... [Titormus then as an exhibition of strength caught
      and held two wild steers by the hoof--one in each hand!].

In the course of seven and a half centuries of anecdotes Milo
was transformed from the strong man of good appetite, at home in
the circle of that foremost philosopher who preached restraint in
diet, to the type of professional athlete that could be encountered
anywhere in the second and third centuries of the Christian era.
Athenaeus, a contemporary of Aelian, sums up the gastronomic
feats which tradition pinned to the name of Milo.

Doctors at Dinner X 412*: Milon of Croton, as Theodorus of
      Hierapolis says in his work On Athletic Contests, used to eat
      twenty pounds of meat and as many of bread, and he drank
      three pitchers of wine. And at Olympia he put a four-year-old
      bull on his shoulders and carried it around the stadium; after
      which he cut it up and ate it all alone in a single day. Titormus
      of Aetolia ate an ox in competition with him at breakfast, as
      Alexander of Aetolia records. And Phylarchus, in the third

book of the Histories, says that Milon devoured a bull reclining in front of the altar of Zeus.

H.   Inscribed Implements Used by Athletes in the Sixth Century B.C.

1.   Halter of Epaenetus

At Eleusis, near Athens, was found the oldest known halter* (jumping weight) made of lead weighing about five pounds and with an inscription on it dating from the late seventh or early sixth century B.C.   Greek contestants carried in their hands metal or stone weights to give more impetus to their jumps (Philost. Gymn. 55 [IX D]).   This victor had probably fastened the halter to a temple wall as a dedication in thanksgiving to some god for his success.

I G I ed. minor, 802: Epaenetus won in jumping because of this.

2.   Discus of Exoidas

A bronze discus now in the British Museum, a votive offering of the sixth century B.C., was found in Cephallenia.   The inscription is legible enough, but the implement itself has posed a difficult problem.   It is not the type of discus which was actually thrown in that period according to the other evidence.

Jüthner seems to have solved the puzzle in a scientific manner.*   After analyzing the drawings of discuses on vase paintings of the different epochs, after estimating the size and weight of metal and stone discuses from casts which were specially made for the purpose, after weighing, critically, the literary evidence, he has reached the plausible conclusion that Exoidas did not dedicate the actual discus which he had used in the contests, but, for dedication purposes, had had a smaller one made of bronze.   This was at that time still a precious metal.   What he actually hurled, Jüthner suggests, was a larger circular stone discus, such as was customary from Homer's time until near the end of the sixth century B.C.*

The words of the inscription support this conclusion if, as Jüthner suggests, the word "chalkeon" is translated as a predicate adjective instead of as an attributive.

I G IX[1] 649: Exoidas dedicated me in bronze* to the twin sons of
mighty Zeus, the discus with which he won from the noble-heart-
ed Cephallenians.

3. Inscribed Boulders

Weight lifting was a favorite form of exercise for athletes in the
early days, as has been seen in the stories about Milo. Archaeological evidence has come to light to confirm the literary evidence.

An unworked block of sandstone weighing, it is said, about three
hundred and fifteen pounds has been found at Olympia. Its inscription, cut in a spiral fashion and lettering which date it in the sixth
century B.C. and reading from the inside of the spiral outwards,
proclaims a feat which almost exactly parallels what Titormus
did in the contest with Milo.

Inschriften von Olympia (Dittenberger-Purgold) 717: Bybon (? the
son of Phocion*) with one hand threw me over his head.

On an oval boulder of black volcanic material on the island of
Thera there is cut an inscription in large letters which has been
dated by scholars as of the sixth century B.C. The block weighs
some 1056 pounds.

I G XII[3] 449: Eumastos, the son of Critobulus, lifted me from the
earth.

I. A Protest against Over-Attention to Athletes
(last half of 6th century B.C.)

During the period when the triumphal homecomings of a
Tisandros, a Glaucus, or a Milo from the Panhellenic games were
being celebrated with a deluge of honors and awards, there was
travelling through Greece and Southern Italy a brilliant philosopher and satirist from Colophon in Asia Minor. This man, named
Xenophanes, did not hesitate to speak out in denunciation of omi-
nous current trends whether in religion or in athletics.

To Xenophanes we are indebted for the one piece of writing
from the sixth century B.C. which contains a dissenting vote a-
gainst all the hue and cry over athletic champions. In his estimation, winning athletes were being accorded honors and awards entirely out of harmony with their accomplishments. It is significant that there is no hint in his remarks that he means to belittle

the athletes themselves or the character of their performances, and that he makes no reference to the over-training and to the over-in-dulgence in eating so commonly listed as grievances in later dia-tribes against athletics.* How many other persons shared his views in those days it is not safe to estimate, but very probably, as would be the case today, they were very few.

Xenophanes (Frag. 2)*

But even if one should win a victory by swiftness of foot, or in the pentathlon, there where is the precinct of Zeus beside the streams of the fountain of Pisa in Olympia, or in wrestling, or in painful boxing, or in the dread struggle which men call the pancra-tium, and should become a more glorious spectacle for his fellow citizens to behold, and should win a conspicuous seat of honor in athletic contests, and should receive his food at public expense, and a gift which would be a treasure to him; yes, even if he won a victory with racehorses...though he should gain all this, yet would he not be as worthy as I. For our wisdom is a better thing than strength of men and of horses. But this is a most unreasonable custom, and it is not right to honor strength above excellent wis-dom. For even if there should be a good boxer among the folk, or a champion in the pentathlon, or in wrestling, or in swiftness of foot, which is the most honored exhibiton of strength among all the contests of men in games, the state would not on that account be any the more law-abiding. But little would be the state's joy, if a man should win a victory in athletics by the banks of Pisa; for these things do not make rich the store chambers of a state.

IV. THE AGE OF THE YOUTHFUL IDEAL

(circa 510-410 B.C.)

In the closing years of the sixth century B.C., when sculptors and vase painters were beginning to fashion a more life-like athlete in their victor statues and on their vase scenes, and when poets were breathing youth, beauty, and deportment befitting noble ancestry into the subjects of their victory odes, a significant modification in Greek athletic ideals began to appear. The short, stocky Heracles type of athlete (Pindar, Isthmian Ode IV 89 f.) was being replaced gradually by the graceful young Theseus type. The more or less self-developed, weight-lifting champion of the pancratium match, ideal of the sixth century B.C., was changing into the ideal of the fifth century -- a youth, harmoniously developed by scientific training to excel in all the five contests of the pentathlon.

Many of the basic elements, however, remained unchanged in the picture as described in Chapter III. The same prominent and wealthy families from all over the Greek world continued to be interested in chariot racing and in having sons, nephews, grandsons trained to be winners of the wreath.* The number of years such champions could successfully compete continued to remain extraordinary. But there are hints in the evidence that those scions of noble families were not the only ones winning Olympic victories. A more general participation in the major games by other classes of society is indicated. Aristotle (Rhet. I 7, 1365a) quotes a line attributed to Simonides (556-466 B.C.) which gives the clue. A victor at Olympia, it seems, had had the poet compose for his monument the sentence: "Formerly with a scratchy basket on my shoulders I used to carry fish from Argos to Tegea."

Wreaths were the only awards, it is true, at the four major festivals, but the valuable prizes offered at the many local festivals may have been an ever-increasing inducement for entries from all walks of life. Simonides' poem about Nicoladas (quoted below) mentions sixty jars of oil won at Athens. Pindar (Nemean Ode X) lists the astonishing variety of prizes won before 460 B.C. by the Theaeus family of Argos: heirloom vases filled with olive oil, silver cups, virgin wool cloaks, bronze objects too numerous to mention.

An important military engagement at the beginning of the fifth century B.C. also provided a stimulus to interest in Greek athletics. The success of the Athenians and their allies in grappling with the Persian hordes in the famous Battle of Marathon in 490 B.C. was attributed by a grateful public to the physical fitness of the soldiers who had undergone the system of training described by Lucian (above, Chapter III).

To judge from a few statements in Herodotus (VI 111-117), the battle of Marathon was begun and was fought through by the Greek soldiers with all the verve of an athletic contest. The men charged forward as if running the long foot race and then, apparently, had breath enough to tackle, each his opposite foe, with all the tricks learned in the wrestling schools. The flabby, untanned Persians were objects of scorn. No other army except one in the peak of physical condition would have been able, after defeating such superior numbers, to speed back over the road immediately toward Athens to save it from a surprise attack. Pindar, in consequence, though a citizen of Thebes, a city at odds with Athens, boldly named Athens "the bulwark of Greece" in a hymn of praise (frag. 76,2).*

It is no wonder that after 479 B.C., when the Persian menace had been completely removed from Greece by a series of victories, a resurgence of enthusiasm in athletic competitions brought grateful and united Greeks from all directions to witness the brilliant performances of the next festival at Olympia (476).*

It is generally agreed that Greece from the last quarter of the sixth century B.C. through most of the fifth, reached the highest point of excellence in its athletic system which any nation has yet attained. Fortunately, abundant primary evidence exists for depicting the history of Greek athletics of this period. Black-figured and red-figured vases* picture animated scenes from palaestras where youths are exercising in the shadow of a trainer's rod or are busied removing the grime from a hard day in the sand or mud. Sculptors*, lyric poets, dramatists and historians have left vivid evidence.

A. The Lyric Poets

From about 530 to 430 the custom flourished among the Greeks of including a hymn in the festivities for an athlete's victory. This was composed especially for the occasion by a professional writer and was chanted to a musical accompaniment. The victor himself, his friends or sponsoring town, assumed the expense for such Epinikia, as they were called. Stone tablets were also inscribed on occasion with the athlete's record summarized briefly by a well-known writer.

From three great lyric poets portions of such commissions
which they executed have survived.

1. Simonides of Ceos (circa 556-466 B.C.)

Only short fragments remain from the poems of Simonides of
Ceos, oldest of the trio of lyric poets, who was retained at Athens
by Hipparchus, eldest son of the tyrant Pisistratus (Plato, Hipparchus 228c), with high pay and valuable presents. Known for his
sense of humor, his thrift, his invention of a system of memory
aids (Cicero de Oratore 2, 86), he is said also to have been the first
poet to have written for pay.* His brief sentences phrased with an
economy in words matching his economy in money matters are in
sharp contrast to the fulsome inscriptions set up by the vain, professional athletes of later centuries.

One of Simonides' inscriptions to be quoted below neatly sets
forth the events of the pentathlon in an order easy to remember,
because of their Greek initials (A-P--D--A-P, using the English
equivalents of the Greek letters). With the added jingle of the line
it is tempting to think that this was a simple example of his memory aid system. Cicero emphasizes that effective arrangement
was the chief feature of Simonides' mnemonic devices.

Lyr. Gr. II 181* (=Pausan. VI 9, 9): Country Corcyra, Philon my
name, I am Glaucus' son and I won twice at Olympia in boxing.

Lyr. Gr. II 182 (=Anth. Plan. 3): At the Isthmus and at Delphi
Diophon, son of Philon won: Jumping, the swift Foot-race,
Discus, Javelin and Wrestling embrace*.

Lyr. Gr. II, 183 (=Anth. Plan. 23): Tell what is your name,
family, country, victory: Kasmylus, Evagoras family, Rhodes,
boxing at Delphi.

Lyr. Gr. II 184 (=Anth. Pal. 13, 19): This statue, a Corinthian,
Nicoladas, dedicated who won the foot-race at Delphi and took
prizes in five Panathenaic games, sixty jars of oil; at sacred
Isthmus three times his opponents did not get as far as the
oath offerings; at Nemea three times victor, four other times
at Péllene, two times at Lycaeus, and at Tegea, Aegina and
rocky Epidaurus and in the towns of Thebes and Megara. At
Phlius by winning the foot-race and pentathlon he gladdened
great Corinth.

Lyr. Gr. II 178 (=Anth. Plan. 2): Know that you are looking at
Theognetus, Junior Olympic victor in the wrestling art, a
driver adept, very handsome to look at, his athletics ability

equal to his looks, the boy who hung a wreath on his fine family's city.

Lyr. Gr. II 154 (=Anth. Pal. 13, 14): Here lies Dandes* of Argos runner in the stade (200 yd.) race who brought victories to his horse-breeding land, two at Olympia, three at Pytho, two at the Isthmus, fifteen at Nemea besides other victories not simple to list.

2. Pindar* (518? -438 B.C.)

From Pindar "reared by famous Thebes as no stranger nor as ignorant of the Muses (frag. 198)," there are extant fourteen odes for Olympic victors, twelve for Pythian, eleven for Nemean, and seven for Isthmian. These forty-four poems, famous for their originality and perfection of form, contain many a golden nugget of information about the athlete of the poet's own day. Pindar's songs are of a complicated structure and, as he admits, "clear to the wise but for the crowd needing an interpreter" (Olymp. II 150-2). The figure of an athlete flashing through a victorious performance is at times nearly lost in the lush background of myths, proper names, learned geographical allusions, and trills of lyre and flute.

"No sculptor am I that I should carve statues doomed to linger only on the pedestal where they stood" (Nemean V 1) is Pindar's boast, but even so he has left a clear, sharply-cut ideal athlete in his pages: a youthful figure, descended from a distinguished athletic family, competing over long years at many festivals, showered with gifts and honors, handsome, one whose natural flair for sports has been trained amid toil by a competent teacher.

Whether the comparatively few athletes hymned by Pindar are a fair cross section of the many hundreds of men competing in games during the poet's life time is a problem still to be investigated.

Pythian Ode X*
[for Hippocleas of Thessaly, winner in the
double-stade (400 yards) foot-race, 498 B.C.]

...(5-10) I am summoned by Pytho and Pelinna and the sons of Aleuas, who desire to bring to Hippocleas the ringing voices of a triumphant band of men. For he is making trial of contests, and the gorge of Parnassus hath proclaimed him to the host of them that dwell around as foremost of the boys in the double course. ...

(12-18) And his inborn valor hath trodden in the foot-prints of his father, who was twice victor at Olympia in the armour of Ares that bears the brunt of war, and the contest in the deep meadow stretching beneath the rock of Cirrha made Phricias victorious in the race. Even in the days to come may good fortune attend them, so that their noble wealth may flourish. ...

(22-29) By poets wise that man is held happy, and is a theme for their song, whosoever, by being victorious with his hands or with the prowess of his feet, gaineth the greatest prizes by courage or by strength, and who, while still living, seeth his youthful son happily win two Pythian crowns. The brazen heaven he cannot climb; but as for all the bright achievements which we mortals attain, he reacheth the utmost limit of that voyage. ...

(55-59) But I trust that, while the Ephyraeans pour forth my sweet strain beside the Peneius, I may, with my strains of minstrelsy, cause Hippocleas to be admired still more for his crowns among his fellows and his elders, and to be looked upon with a sweet care by the young maidens.

Nemean Ode V
[for Pytheas of Aegina, winner in the
Junior Pancratium 485 B.C.]

(3-10) I would bid my sweet song speed from Aegina, in every argosy, and in every skiff, spreading abroad the tidings that the stalwart Pytheas, son of Lampon, hath won the crown for the pancratium at the Nemean games, or ever he showed on his cheeks the hue of summer, the soft harbinger of youthful bloom. ....

(40-53) It is the natal star that ruleth over every deed; and thou, Euthymenes from Aegina (Pytheas' uncle), twice falling in the lap of victory, didst win thee a varied strain of song. Verily

even now, O Pytheas, thine eme (uncle) doth glorify that hero's
kindred race, for following in his steps*.   Nemea is linked with
thee, and Aegina's festal month beloved of Apollo, and thou wast
victorious over thy comrades who entered the lists, both at home
and in the fair dells of the hill of Nisus (Megara).   I rejoice that
all the State striveth for glory.

Bear in mind that, by the good fortune of Menander, thou didst
win a sweet requital for thy toils.   Meet it is that a fashioner of
athletes should come from Athens; but if thou art come to sing the
praises of Themistius (Pytheas' grandfather), away with cold reserve.   Lift up thy voice, and hoist the sails to the top-most yard;
proclaim him as a boxer, and tell that he hath won a double victory in the pancratium by his conquest in Epidaurus.

Olympian Ode IX
[for Epharmostus of Opus, winner in the
wrestling match, 468 B.C.]

(1-10) The chant of Archilochus that was vocal at Olympia, the
song of victory swelling with its thrice repeated refrain*, sufficed
to welcome Epharmostus when, with his dear comrades, he
marched in triumph to the hill of Cronus.   But now, from the bow
of the far-darting Muses, do thou shoot a shower of such shafts of
song as these ... while trilling the lyre in honour of the wrestling
of the hero from famous Opus. ...

(83-102) I have come at virtue's bidding , and in friendship for
the folk, to pay the further honour due to the Isthmian wreath of
Lampromachus (friend of Epharmostus), for that the twain were
victors in the events on the self-same day; and, afterwards, there
were two gladsome victories at the portals of Corinth (Isthmus),
and others won by Epharmostus in the vale of Nemea, while at
Argos he gained glory in a contest of men, and as a boy at Athens.

And, when reft from the beardless company, what a glorious contest for the prize of silver cups did he maintain at Marathon among the men! And, having vanquished those wights by the cunning skill that swiftly shifts its balance but never falls, amid what loud applause did he pass round the ring, a victor in life's prime, nobly fair, and one who had wrought most noble deeds! Then again he seemed marvellous to look upon, amid the Parrhasian people, at the festival of the Lycaean Zeus, and also on that day when, at Pellana, he carried off as his prize a warm remedy* against the chilly blasts; and the tomb of Iolaus beareth witness to him, and the shore of Eleusis telleth of his glorious prowess.

That which cometh of nature is ever best, but many men have striven to win their fame by means of merit that cometh from mere training.

Olympian Ode VII
[for Diagoras of Rhodes, winner in the
boxing match, 464 B.C.]

(13-16) And now, to the music of flute and lyre alike, have I come to land, while singing of the daughter of the sea, the child of Aphrodite, the bride of the Sun, even Rhodes; that so I may honor, for his fairness in fight and his skill in boxing, that giant form which won the crown beside the Alpheus (Olympia) and the stream of Castalia   (Delphi).

(80-95) With flowers from that contest (i. e. in Rhodes), twice hath Diagoras* crowned himself, and at the famous Isthmus four times, in his good fortune; and, again and again, at Nemea and at rocky Athens; while he is not unknown to the shield of bronze in Argos,* and the works of art given as prizes in Arcadia and at Thebes, and to the duly ordered contests amid the Boeotians, and to Pellana, and to Aegina, where he was six times victor, while in Megara the reckoning on the tablet of stone telleth no other tale.

But do thou, O father Zeus, that rulest over the height of Ata-
byrium, grant honour* to the hymn ordained in praise of an Olympian victor, and to the hero who hath found fame for his prowess
as a boxer; and do thou give him grace and reverence in the eyes
of citizens and of strangers too. For he goeth in a straight course
along a path that hateth insolence; he hath learnt full well all the
lessons prompted by the prudence which he inheriteth from goodly
ancestors. Suffer not the common glory of the seed of Callianax
to be buried in obscurity. Whenever the Eratidae are victorious,
the city also holdeth festivities; but, in one single space of apportioned time, the breezes swiftly change from day to day.

Olympian Ode XIII
[for Xenophon of Corinth, winner of both
200 yard race and the pentathlon, 464 B.C.]

(24-46) Lord supreme of Olympia! that reignest far and wide,
O Father Zeus! never, for all time, be thou jealous of our language, but, ruling this people in all security, grant a straight
course to the fair breeze of Xenophon's good fortune, and accept
from him the duly ordered triumph-band in honour of his crowns,
the band that he bringeth from the plains of Pisa, being victor in
the five events, as well as in the foot-race. He hath thus attained
what no mortal man ever yet attained before. And two wreaths of
wild celery crowned him, when he appeared at the Isthmian festival; and Nemea hath shown no unkindly mood; and, at the stream
of Alpheus, is stored up the glory won by the swift feet of his
father, Thessalus. At Pytho, he hath the fame of the single and
the double foot-race, won within the circuit of the self-same sun;
and in the same month, at rocky Athens did one swift day fling o'er
his hair three fairest crowns of victory, and seven times was he

victorious at the festival of Athene Hellotis. In Poseidon's games
betwixt the seas, too long would be the songs which shall attain to
all the victories won by Terpsias and Eritimus, with their father
Ptoeodorus; and, as for all your prowess at Delphi, and in the
Lion's haunts, (i.e., Nemea) I am ready to contend with many as
to the number of your prizes; for, in truth, I could not have the
skill to tell the number of the pebbles of the sea.*

<u>Nemean Ode</u> VI
[for Alcidamas of Aegina, winner in the
Junior wrestling match, ? 463 B.C.]

(8-15) Even now doth Alcidamas prove to all eyes that the inborn valour of his race resembleth the corn-bearing fields, which
in changing seasons, at one while, give to man abundant sustenance from the plains, and at another while, gather strength by
repose. Lo! from the lovely games of Nemea hath now returned
that athlete boy, who, following this heaven-sent destiny, hath
now shone forth no luckless hunter in the wrestling ring, by plant-
ing his step in the foot-prints of his own true grandsire, Praxidamas*. ...

(33-34) A clan of ancient fame, laden with a goodly cargo of
their own renown, they are well fitted by their gallant deeds to
provide a rich theme of song to those who till the Muses' field. ...

(59-69) But I ... have come as a messenger to proclaim that
thou, Alcidamas, hast won for thy famous family this five and
twentieth triumph, from the games which men call holy. Two
crowns indeed of the Olympic contest beside the sacred precinct
of the hill of Cronus were robbed from thee, the youthful victor,
and from Polytimidas, by a lot at random drawn.* Of Melesias,
as a trainer deft in strength of hands, I would say that in speed he
is a match for the dolphin that darteth through the brine.

Olympian Ode VIII
[for Alcimedon of Aegina, winner in the
Junior Wrestling match, 460 B.C.]

(11-22) O precinct of Pisa, with thy fair trees beside the Alpheus! give welcome to this chorus of triumph, and this crowning of the victor. ... But fate hath allotted thee and thine, Timosthenes, to Zeus, as the god of thy race, Zeus who made thee the observed of all at Nemea and made thy brother, Alcimedon, an Olympian victor beside the hill of Cronus. Comely was he to look upon, and verily he did not belie his beauty of form, when, by his victory in the wrestling-match, he caused Aegina with her long oars to be proclaimed as his fatherland. ...

(53-84) But nothing shall be equally pleasant among all men; and, if I myself have, for Melesias,* rushed up in song to the height of glory won by the training of beardless youths, let not envy cast a rough stone at me; for I could tell of his winning such another victory himself (among boys) at Nemea, and of his later contests among men, even in the pancratium. To teach, as ye know, is easier for him that himself hath knowledge, while it is foolish not to learn betimes (i.e. "not to study beforehand is thoughtless" -- Lattimore). Flighty are the words of them that have made no trial; but he, (Melesias) beyond all others, could speak of those brave deeds telling what manner of training will aid a man that is eager to win from contests in the sacred games the fame that is most yearned for. For himself it is a boon indeed that a thirtieth victory hath been won for him by Alcimedon, who, by heaven-sent good-fortune, but with no slackness in his own prowess, thrust off from himself on the bodies of four boys a most hateful return amid jibes of contempt, while they slink to their homes unseen; and hath inspired his father's sire with strength

that wrestles with old age. Ye know that the grave is forgotten by
him who hath won befitting fame. But meet it is for me to awaken
Memory and to tell of the fruit of the victorious hands of the race
of Blepsias, who have now been wreathed with the sixth garland
won from crowned contests. Even the dead have share in rites
duly paid in their honour, and the noble grace of their kinsmen on
earth is not buried in the dust. But the victor's father, Iphion,
having listened to the Teller of glad tidings, the daughter of Hermes, will haply tell his own brother Callimachus of the bright glory
at Olympia, which Zeus hath given to their race.

3. Bacchylides (507-428 B.C.)

Thirteen Epinikia now remain from the hand of Bacchylides,
described by himself as the "honey-tongued nightingale of Ceos."
He was the grandson of one of the famed athletes of that island and
the nephew of Simonides. Only short fragments of his odes were
known to the modern world until, in 1896, two hundred torn fragments of papyrus containing some 1392 lines were discovered in
Egypt and brought to England, where they were brilliantly edited
by the famous scholar Sir Richard Jebb.

As will be seen from the selections to be quoted, Bacchylides'
odes are simpler in style than those of Pindar and state plain
athletic facts more realistically.

Ode III*
[for Hiero, tyrant of Syracuse, winner of the
chariot race, 468 B.C.]

Sing, O sweet-gifted Clio, of Demeter who rules fair-fruited
Sicily and of her daughter, violet-crowned, and of the swift Olym-
pia-racing mares of Hiero. For they speeded with distinguished
victory and glory by the broad-eddying Alpheus, where they caused
the blessed child of Deinomenes to obtain their crown. And un-
numbered people shouted; "Ah, thrice-happy man, to have obtained from Zeus the widest rule over Grecian men, and to know the

wisdom of not concealing your towered wealth in black-shrouding darkness."

Now teeming are the shrines with holiday sacrifice of oxen, teeming are the streets with hospitality, and shines with glittering light the gold of high-wrought tripods* placed before the temple, where the Delphians manage a very great precinct of Phoebus near the streams of Castalia.

Ode VI
[for Lachon, winner in the
Junior foot race, 452 B.C.]

Through mighty Jove, Lachon has won signal glory in the foot-race near the mouth of the Alpheus, thus augmenting the brilliant victories for which, before this, richly garlanded youths have celebrated in song at Olympia wine-nurturing Ceos, pre-eminent in boxing and the stade race. And now, O wind-footed son of Aristomenes, because of your victory, the hymn of Urania, mistress of song, is honoring you in songs before your door, for you have brought fame to Ceos by winning in the stade race.

Ode II
[for Argeius, winner in the
boxing match, 450 B.C.]

Fame, bestower of distinction, has darted to holy Ceos, bearing the gratifying news that Argeius has gained a victory in the bold-handed boxing match, recalling to our mind how many brilliant exhibitions after leaving our god-favored island of Euxantius, we have given at the famous Isthmus, with our seventy wreaths.

My native Muse is summoning the sweet tones of the flute, honoring the dear son of Pantheides in odes of triumph.

Ode VIII
[for Automedes of Phlius, winner of the
pentathlon, date unknown]

Famous among mortals are those who crown their yellow hair
with the biennial wreath from those glorious contests at Nemea.
To Automedes who won this time the god has given the crown. For
he was conspicuous among the pentathletes as the radiant moon in
the night of her fulness outshines the bright stars. So he appeared
among the numberless throng of Greeks a marvelous form, casting
the circular discus, and as he hurled from his hand high into the
air the branch of the dark-leaved elder tree, he evoked the cheers
of the folk, or as he flashed through the final wrestling.*

Ode IX
[for Aglaus (?) of Athens, winner of
foot-races of unknown date]

In the very famous games of Poseidon straightway you (Aglaus)
showed the Greeks the swift rush of your feet. And a second time
he stood by the rounds of the course, with breath still hot, and
panting, and again he shot away, bespattering with olive oil the
cloaks of the onlookers as he dashed into the arms of the cheering
crowd, after turning the four laps* of the course. Twice the her-
alds of fair-counseling judges proclaimed him Isthmian victor: and
twice at Nemea by the holy altar of Zeus, the son of Cronus; and
famous Thebes gave him a merited welcome and those who dwell
in Pellene and round about Euboea rich in grain and in the holy
island of Aegina.

B. Other Famous Athletes of the Fifth Century B.C.
1. Theagenes of Thasos

A curious omission in the victory odes of the lyric poets as
they have come down to us is the name of Theagenes, of Thasos.
This man was evidently as celebrated for his athletic exploits in
the generation after 480 B.C. as was Milo fifty years earlier. A
statue base with a partial list of his victories has been found at
Olympia (IGA Roehl no. 380). Several later writers mention Theagenes (Plutarch, Lucian, Dio Chrysotomus, Athenaeus) but it is
Pausanias who tells his story in detail. His account includes incidentally a glimpse of Euthymus the boxer from Locris in Italy.

Description of Greece* VI 11: (2) Not far from the kings mentioned stands a Thasian, Theagenes the son of Timosthenes. ...
In his ninth year, they say, as he was going home from school,
he was attracted by a bronze image of some god or other in the
market place; so he caught up the image, placed it on one of
his shoulders and carried it home. (3) The citizens were en-
raged at what he had done, but one of them...bade them not to
kill the lad, and ordered him to carry the image from his home
back again to the market place. This he did, and at once became famous for his strength, his feat being noised abroad
throughout Greece. (4) The achievements of Theagenes at the
Olympian games have already been described (see VI 6,5 just
below). ... At the festival following this, Theagenes was the
winner in the pancratium. (5) He also won three victories at
Pytho. These were for boxing, while nine prizes at Nemea and
ten at the Isthmus were won in some cases for the pancratium
and in others for boxing. At Pythia in Thessaly he gave up
training for boxing and pancratium. He devoted himself to winning fame among the Greeks for his running also, and beat
those who entered for the long race. ... The total number of
crowns that he won was one thousand four hundred. (6) When
he departed this life, one of those who were his enemies while
he lived came every night to the statue of Theagenes and flogged the bronze as though he were ill-treating Theagenes himself. The statue put an end to the outrage by falling on him
[Then follows the tale of the statue prosecuted for murder,
convicted, dropped in the sea, finally fished out and set up to
be worshipped as a god]. ... (9) There are many other places
that I know of, both among Greeks and among barbarians, where
images of Theagenes have been set up, who cures diseases and
receives honours from the natives. The statue of Theagenes
is in the Altis being the work of Glaucias in Aegina.*

Description of Greece VI 6: (5) Euthymus, ... though he won the
  prize for boxing at the seventy-fourth Olympic Festival (484
  B.C.) was not to be so successful at the next. For Theagenes
  of Thasos, wishing to win the prize for boxing and for the pancratium at the same Festival, overcame Euthymus at boxing,
  though he had not the strength to gain the wild olive in the pancratium, because he was already exhausted in his fight with
  Euthymus. (6) Thereupon the umpires fined Theagenes a talent,
  to be sacred to the gods, and a talent for the harm done to
  Euthymus, holding that it was merely to spite him that he entered for the boxing competition. At the seventy-sixth Festival
  Theagenes paid in full the money owed to the god ... and as
  compensation to Euthymus did not enter for the boxing match.
  [Then follows the marvelous tale of Euthymus and the Ghost.]

2. Diagoras and his Family

In connection with his visit to the Altis of Olympia in 174 A.D.,
Pausanias examined the statues of Diagoras and his descendants.
All, beginning with Diagoras himself, were famous boxers (see
Pindar's Olympian Ode VII, above), and their victories covered a
span of seventy-five years (464-388 B.C.).

Description of Greece VI 7: (1) The statues of the Rhodian athletes, Diagoras and his family... were dedicated one after the
  other in the following order. Acusilaus, who received a crown
  for boxing in the men's class; Dorieus, the youngest, who won
  the pancratium at Olympia on three successive occasions (432-
  424 B.C.). Even before Dorieus, Damagetus beat all those who
  had entered for the pancratium. (2) These were brothers, being sons of Diagoras, and by them is set up also a statue of
  Diagoras himself, who won a victory for boxing in the men's
  class. The statue of Diagoras was made by the Megarian Cal-
  licles, the son of Theocosmus who made the image of Zeus at
  Megara. The sons too of the daughters of Diagoras practised
  boxing and won Olympic victories; in the men's class Eucles
  (396 B.C.) son of Callianax and Callipateira, daughter of Diagoras; in the boys' class Peisirodus (388 B.C.), whose mother* dressed herself as a man and a trainer, and took herself
  to the Olympic games. (3) This Peisirodus is one of the statues in the Altis, and stands by the father of his mother. The
  story goes that Diagoras came to Olympia in the company of
  his sons Acusilaus and Damagetus. The youths on defeating
  their father proceeded to carry him through the crowd, while
  the Greeks pelted him with flowers and congratulated him on

his sons. The family of Diagoras was originally, through the
female line, Messenian, as he was descended from the daughter
of Aristomenes. (4) Dorieus, son of Diagoras, beside his
Olympian victories, won eight at the Isthmian and seven at the
Pythian games. ... He is also said to have won a Pythian victory
without a contest. ... Of all men he most obviously showed his
friendship with Sparta, for he actually fought against the Athenians with his own ships, until he was taken prisoner by Attic
men-of-war and brought alive to Athens. (5) Before he was
brought to them the Athenians were wroth with Dorieus and used
threats against him; but when they met in the assembly and beheld a man so great and famous in the guise of a prisoner, their
feelings towards him changed, and they let him go away without doing him any hurt, and that though they might with justice
have punished him severely. (6) The death of Dorieus is told
by Androtion in his Attic history [he was sentenced to death by
the Lacedaemonians].

3. Astylus of Croton

Along with the tendency that apparently gathered momentum in
the early fifth century for groups of spectacular athletes to spend
the major part of their lives in training and in touring the festivals
-- a far cry from the old, informal participation in recreational
sports -- there appeared, especially in the athletics-mad cities of
southern Italy, an unholy eagerness to claim capable athletes as
registered citizens. This sometimes meant stealing them away
from their home towns by financial inducements. Pausanias records the first instance of this and the furore caused by it.

Description of Greece VI 13: (1) The statue of Astylus of Crotona
   is the work of Pythagoras; this athlete won three successive
   victories at Olympia (488-480 B.C.), in the short race and in
   the double race.* But because on the two latter occasions he
   proclaimed himself a Syracusan, in order to please Hiero the
   son of Deinomenes, the people of Crotona for this condemned
   his house to be a prison, and pulled down his statue set up by
   the temple of Lacinian Hera.

C. Administration of the Olympic Games
1. Program Changes in the Fifth Century B.C.

Pausanias, <u>Description of Greece</u> V 9 : (1) Certain contests have
been dropped at Olympia .... The races for mule-carts, and
the trotting race were instituted respectively at the seventieth
Festival (500 B.C.) and the seventy-first (496 B.C.), and were
both abolished by proclamation at the eighty-fourth (444 B.C.).
The trotting race was for mares, and in the last part of the
course the riders jumped off and ran beside the mares, holding
on to the bridle, just as at the present day (174 A.D.) those do
who are called "mounters". The mounters, however, differ
from the riders in the trotting-race by having different badges,
and by riding horses instead of mares. The cart-race was
neither of venerable antiquity nor yet a graceful performance.

(3) The order of the games in our own day, which places the
sacrifices to the god for the pentathlum and chariot-races
second, and those for the other competitions first, was fixed
at the seventy-seventh Festival (472 B.C.). Previously the
contests for men and for horses were held on the same day.
But at the festival I mentioned the pancratiasts prolonged their
contests till night-fall, because they were not summoned to the
arena soon enough. The cause of the delay was partly the
chariot-race, but still more the pentathlum. Callias of Athens
was champion of the pancratiasts on this occasion, but never
afterwards was the pancratium to be interfered with by the
pentathlum or the chariots.

2. Oath Administered to Contestants

<u>Description of Greece</u> V 24: (9) But the Zeus in the Council Cham-
ber is of all the images of Zeus the one most likely to strike
terror into the hearts of sinners. He is surnamed Oath-god and
in each hand he holds a thunderbolt. Beside this image it is the
custom for athletes, their fathers and their brothers, as well
as their trainers to swear an oath upon slices of boar's flesh
that in nothing will they sin against the Olympic games. The
athletes take this further oath also, that for ten successive
months they have strictly followed the regulations for training.
(10) An oath is also taken by those who examine the boys, or
the foals entering for races, that they will decide fairly and
without taking bribes, and that they will keep secret what they
learn about a candidate, whether accepted or not. I forgot to
inquire what it is customary to do with the boar after the oath

of the athletes, though the ancient custom was that no human being might eat of that on which an oath had been sworn.

3. Women at Olympia

Description of Greece V 6: (7) As you go from Scillus along the
road to Olympia, before you cross the Alpheius, there is a
mountain with high, precipitous cliffs. It is called Mount Typa-
eum. It is a law of Elis to cast down it any women who are
caught present at the Olympic games,* or even on the other side
of the Alpheius, on the days prohibited to women. However,
they say that no woman has been caught, except Callipateira
only; some, however, give the lady the name of Pherenice and
not Callipateira [then follows with more details the same story
as in Philostr. Gymn. 17].

Description of Greece VI 20: (8) ... Now the stadium is an embankment of earth, and on it is a seat for the presidents of the
games. Opposite the umpires is an altar of white marble; (9)
seated on this altar a woman looks on at the Olympic games,
the priestess of Demeter Chamyne, which office the Eleans bestow from time to time on different women.* Maidens are not
debarred from looking on at the games.

Description of Greece V 16: (2) Every fourth year there is
woven for Hera a robe by the Sixteen women, and the same also
hold games called Heraea. The games consist of foot-races for
maidens. These are not all of the same age. The first to run
are the youngest; after them come the next in age, and the last
to run are the oldest of the maidens. They run in the following
way: (3) Their hair hangs down, a tunic reaches to a little a-
bove the knee, and they bare the right shoulder as far as the
breast. These too have the Olympic stadium reserved for their
games, but the course of the stadium is shortened for them by
about one-sixth of its length. To the winning maidens they give
crowns of olive and a portion of the cow sacrificed to Hera.
They may also dedicate statues with their names inscribed upon them.* Those who administer to the Sixteen are, like the
presidents of the games, married women. The games of the
maidens too are traced back to ancient times. ...

4. A Starting Device for the Chariot Races

Description of Greece VI 20: (10) When you have passed beyond
the stadium, at the point where the umpires sit, is a place set
apart for the horse-races, and also the starting-place for the

horses. The starting-place is in the shape of the prow of a
ship, and its ram is turned towards the course. At the point
where the prow adjoins the porch of Agnaptus it broadens, and
a bronze dolphin on a rod has been made at the very point of the
ram. (11) Each side of the starting-place is more than four
hundred feet in length, and in the sides are built stalls. These
stalls are assigned by lot to those who enter for the races. Before the chariots or race-horses is stretched a cord as a barrier. An altar of unburnt brick, plastered on the outside, is
made at every Festival as near as possible to the centre of the
prow, and a bronze eagle stands on the altar with his wings
stretched out to the fullest extent. The man appointed to start
the racing sets in motion the mechanism in the altar, (12) and
then the eagle has been made to jump upwards, so as to become visible to the spectators, while the dolphin falls to the
ground. (13) First on either side the barriers are withdrawn
by the porch of Agnaptus, and the horses standing thereby run
off first. As they run they reach those to whom the second
station has been allotted, and then are withdrawn the barriers
at the second station. The same thing happens to all the horses
in turn, until at the ram of the prow they are all abreast. After
this it is left to the charioteers to display their skill and the
horses their speed. (14) It was Cleoetas (middle of 5th cent.)
who originally devised the method of starting. ... It is said
that after Cleoetas some further device was added to the mechanism by Aristeides.

5. Last-Minute Advice to Olympic Contestants

Philostratus (beginning of 3rd Cent. A.D.) represents Apollonius of Tyana as delivering a speech to his followers by which
through an apt allusion to Olympia he managed to discourage ten
of his weaker brethren who had been planning to accompany him
on a sight seeing tour of Egypt.

Life of Apollonius of Tyana V 43:   I need an Olympia-style preface for my speech to you, gentlemen; and an Olympia preface
would be about as follows: The Eleans train the athletes for
thirty days in Elis itself just before each Olympia festival; at
Delphi the management brings the athletes together at the time
of the Pythian games, so does the Corinthian management at
the time of the Isthmian and they say "Go to the stadium and
be man enough to win." But the Eleans on the way to Olympia*
(i.e. from Elis City) harangue the athletes as follows: "You
who have completed the toil of training in a manner worthy of

entering Olympia and have done no loafing and nothing under-
handed, proceed with confident heart; you who have finished the
training otherwise, depart, in whatever direction you choose."

6. The Olympic Truce and its Enforcement

As was indicated by the Theagenes-Euthymus incident quoted a-
bove from Pausanias, the lofty serenity implied by the lyric poets
did not always prevail at Olympia during the contests. Thucydides,
the historian of the Great War between Athens and Sparta, leaves
an account of some happenings in his own day (420 B.C.) at Olympia and shows that the truce, now centuries old (see Chapter II a-
bove), was still being strictly enforced. His story gives a picture
of an Olympic festival during war-time tensions.

Thucydides V 49-50*: This summer the Olympic games were held,
in which Androsthenes an Arcadian won his first victory in the
pancratium.* The Lacedaemonians were excluded from the
sanctuary by the Eleans, and so could neither sacrifice nor contend in the games, as they refused to pay the fine which had
been assessed against them according to Olympic law by the
Eleans, who alleged that they had attacked the Elean fortress of
Phyrcus, and sent a force of their hoplites into Lepraeum during the Olympic truce. The fine was two thousand minas, two
minas* for each hoplite, as the law ordains. The Lacedaemonians sent envoys and urged that the fine had been unfairly
imposed upon them, claiming that the treaty (truce) had not
been announced at Lacedaemon when they sent the hoplites into
Elis. But the Eleans said that the truce was already in force in
their country -- for they proclaim it among themselves first --
and while they were keeping quiet and not expecting any attack,
as in the time of truce, the Lacedaemonians had done the wrong,
taking them by surprise. The Lacedaemonians replied that they
should not have gone on and announced the truce at Lacedaemon
if they were of the opinion that the Lacedaemonians were already wronging them, but they had done this as though they did
not think so, and they themselves had not kept on bearing arms
against them anywhere after the announcement of the truce.
But the Eleans persisted in the same statement, saying that
they could never be persuaded that the Lacedaemonians were
not guilty; if, however, they were willing to restore Lepreum
to them, they would give up their own half of the fine, and what
was due to the gods they would themselves pay on their behalf.

When the Lacedaemonians refused this offer, the Eleans
proposed that they should not restore Lepreum, if they objected

to that, but, as they eagerly desired to have access to the sanctuary, that they should go up to the altar of Olympian Zeus and swear in the presence of the Hellenes that they would assuredly pay the fine later. But as they were unwilling to do even this, the Lacedaemonians were excluded from the temple, from the sacrifice and the contests, and sacrificed at home; while the rest of the Hellenes, except the Lepreates, sent representatives to the festival. Still the Eleans, fearing that the Lacedaemonians would force their way and offer sacrifice, kept guard with young men under arms; and there came to their aid also some Argives and Mantineans, a thousand of each, and some Athenian cavalry that were at Arpina awaiting the festival. And great fear came upon the assembly that the Lacedaemonians might come with arms, especially as Lichas son of Arcesilaus, a Lacedaemonian, received blows from the umpires on the course, because, when his own team won and was proclaimed as belonging to the Boeotian state on account of his having no right to contend, he had come upon the course and crowned the charioteer, wishing to show that the chariot was his. And so everybody was much more afraid, and it seemed that there would be some disturbance. The Lacedaemonians, however, kept quiet, and the festival went through in this way, as far as they were concerned.

D. Chariot Races

1. A Chariot Race Described by Sophocles (420 B.C.)

Praise of athletes was too popular a subject to be left wholly to lyric poets composing odes for pay. Herodotus, without risk of offence, could delay his serious account of the preliminaries to the Battle of Marathon long enough to list for his athletically-minded hearers the Olympic prizes won by Miltiades' father and even to mention the burial spot of his racing-mares (VI 103, cited in Chap. III).

Not only was the living public avid for athletic details but the Greeks could not imagine anyone even in Hades so dead as not to be interested in athletic bulletins (cf. Pindar Olymp. VIII 81; Bacchylides VIII 1-4). Vase-paintings occasionally represent athletic implements* as placed on the graves of departed lovers of sport to enable them to continue the athletic pursuits such as Pindar pictures them as engaging in to while away time in the Elysian fields: "in meadows red with roses... some of them delight themselves with horses and athletic contests" (frag. 129-30, Edmonds ed.).

So it is not surprising that in the time-worn plot of the <u>Electra</u>, Sophocles, the popular and gifted tragic poet, caters to the taste of an Athenian audience* by introducing a messenger's speech which, though purporting to describe the death scene of Orestes not many years after the Trojan War, actually gives a stirring account of a current Pythian festival at Delphi (420 B.C.). With one eye on the drama prize the poet* represents an Athenian as cleverly winning by intelligent driving at the turn.

<u>Electra</u> 680-763*

That was my errand, and I'll tell thee all.
To the great festival of Greece he went,
The Delphic Games, and when the herald's voice
Announced the opening trial, the foot race,
He stepped into the lists, a radiant form,
The admired of all beholders. Like a shaft
He sped from starting point to goal and back,
And bore the crown of glorious victory.
To speak in brief where there is much to tell
I never heard of prowess like to his.
This much I'll add, the judges of the games
Announced no single contest wherein he
Was not the victor, and each time glad shouts
Hailed the award -- "An Argive wins, Orestes,
The son of Agamemnon, King of men,
Who led the hosts of Hellas." So he sped.
But when some angry godhead intervenes
The mightiest man is foiled. Another day,
When at sunsetting chariots vied in speed,
He entered; many were the charioteers.
From Sparta one, and one Achaean, two
From Libya, skilled to guide the yoked team;
The fifth in rank, with mares of Thessaly,
Orestes came, and an Aeolian sixth,
With chestnut fillies, a Megarian seventh,
The eighth, with milk-white steeds, an Aenian,
The ninth from Athens, city built by gods;
Last a Boeotian made the field of ten.
Then, as the appointed umpires signed to each
By lot his place, they ranged their chariots,
And at the trumpet's brazen signal all
Started, all shook the reins and urged their steeds
With shouts; the whole plain echoed with a din
Of rattling cars and the dust rose to heaven.

They drave together, all in narrow space,
And plied their goads, each keen to leave behind
The press of whirling wheels and snorting steeds,
For each man saw his car beflecked with foam
Or felt the coursers' hot breath at his back.
Orestes, as he rounded either goal,
Steered close and shaved the pillar with his nave,
Urging his offside trace-horse, while he checked
The nearer. For a while they all sped on
Unscathed, but soon the Aenian's hard-mouthed steeds
Bolted, and 'twixt the sixth and seventh round
'Gainst the Barcaean chariot headlong dashed.
Then on that first mishap there followed close
Shock upon shock, crash upon crash, that strewed
With wreck of cars all the Crisaean plain.
This the shrewd charioteer of Athens marked,
Slackened and drew aside, letting go by
The surge of chariots running in mid course.
Last came Orestes who had curbed his team
(He trusted to the finish), but at sight
Of the Athenian, his one rival left,
With a shrill holloa in his horses' ears
He followed; and the two abreast raced on,
Now one, and now the other a head in front.
Thus far Orestes, ill-starred youth, had steered
Steadfast at every lap his steadfast team,
But at the last, in turning, all too soon
He loosed the left-hand rein, and ere he knew it
The axle struck against the pillar's edge.
The axle box was shattered, and himself
Hurled o'er the chariot rail, and in his fall
Caught in the rein's grip he was dragged along,
While his scared team dashed wildly o'er the course.
But as the crowd beheld his overthrow,
There rose a wail of pity for the youth --
His doughty deeds and his disastrous end --
Now flung to earth, now bounding to the sky
Feet uppermost. At length the charioteers
Stayed in their wild career his steeds and freed
The corpse all blood-bestained, disfigured, marred
Past recognition of his nearest friend.
Straightway the Phoceans burnt him on a pyre,
And envoys now are on their way to bring
That mighty frame shut in a little urn,

And lay his ashes in his fatherland.
Such is my tale, right piteous to tell;
But for all those who saw it with their eyes,
As I, there never was a sadder sight.*

2. Alcibiades Advertises Athens
in the Chariot Races at Olympia

In a speech delivered during the Great War between Athens and
Sparta   (424 or 416 B.C.), Alcibiades tried to convince his fellow-
Athenians that his recent stunning victories* in the chariot-race at
Olympia merited him the post of general in the Sicilian Expedition
under discussion.

Thucydides VI 16*: He (Alcibiades) now came forward and advised
the Athenians as follows: --

"It belongs to me more than to others, Athenians, to have
command -- for I must needs begin with this, since Nicias has
attacked me -- and I think, too, that I am worthy of command.
For those things for which I am railed at bring glory to my ancestors and myself, as well as advantage to my country. For
the Hellenes, who had previously hoped that our state had been
exhausted by the war, conceived an idea of its greatness that
even transcended its actual power by reason of the magnificence
of my display as sacred deputy at Olympia, because I entered
seven chariots, a number that no private citizen had ever entered before, and won the first prize and the second and the
fourth, and provided everything else in a style worthy of my
victory. For by general custom such things do indeed mean
honour and from what is done, men also infer power."

E. Free Board at Athens for a Victor
at the Major Festivals

The following inscription was discovered on a marble paving
block in Hermes street in Athens. The general character of its
writing and use of words is thought to date it at about 436 B.C.
Socrates (in 399 B.C.) seems to have been making a direct reference to the practice authorized by this inscription when in his appearance before the jury (Plato Apolog. 36d) he advocates giving
a man of his type free board in preference to giving it to a man
who wins any variety of horse race at Olympia, listing the three
kinds exactly as in the inscription. Xenophanes as early as the

sixth century B.C. had grumbled at this favor of free board granted athletes (Chap. III above).

Inscriptiones Graecae I (ed. 2) 77, 11-17: Whoever have won the athletic contests at Olympia or Delphi or the Isthmus or Nemea shall have free board in the town-hall and likewise other honors separately; and likewise they shall secure free board in the town-hall who have won or hereafter shall win in the chariot-race with four horses or with two horses or in horseback riding at Olympia or Delphi or the Isthmus or Nemea.

F. Euripides' Denunciation of Athletes and Athletics

Near the close of the fifth century, Euripides, the youngest of the three great tragic poets, gave utterance to a denunciation of the athletes of his day which was later so often quoted that, like the passage from Xenophanes (see Chap. III), it became a rhetorical commonplace.

A comparison of this selection with Xenophanes will reveal the marked change which had occurred in Greek Athletics during three generations. In the sixth century there had been no acid comments on the appearance of the contestants in their prize-winning days nor any remarks as to their uselessness in later life. Evidence from the sixth century shows a consistent picture of athletic victors serving their state in a distinguished manner, once their festival appearances were over.* By Euripides' time the label "athlete" was not a badge of honor but was apparently applied to a specialized class of persons, so fed and trained for their careers of athletic champions as to set them apart from the body of average citizens.

Only the last paragraph is a direct echo of Xenophanes.

Autolycus, frag. 282 (Nauck)*

Although there are myriads of evils throughout Greece, there is nothing worse than the race of athletes. First of all, they neither learn how to live a good life, nor could they possibly do so. For how could a man who is a slave to his jaw and obedient to his belly acquire wealth to surpass that of his father? Nor, on the other hand, are such men capable of bearing poverty and assisting fortune; for because they have not formed good habits they find things hard for them when they come to face serious difficulties. In their prime they make a brilliant spectacle as they go about and are the pride of the state; but when bitter old age comes upon them, they are gone like coarse cloaks which have lost their nap. Yes, and I blame the Greek custom of assembling to watch these men and of honoring useless pleasures for the sake of a feast. For what good wrestler, what swift runner, or what man who has hurled a discus well, or planted a well delivered blow on another's jaw, has ever defended the city of his fathers because of winning a victor's crown? Do men fight with the enemy holding discuses in their hands, or through the line of shields do they launch blows with their fists, and so drive the enemy out of the fatherland? No one indulges in this folly when he is close to the foeman's steel.

We ought then to crown with garlands the wise and the good, and whatever temperate and upright man best leads the state, and whoever by his counsels rids us of evil deeds, making an end to battles and strife; because such things are good for every state and for all the Greeks.

V. TRENDS IN THE FOURTH CENTURY

By the time of the fourth century B.C. the changes in Greek athletic ideals and practices which had been insidiously developing ever since the Persian Wars, and had been discernible to a few, had reached such a point that they were obvious to all and were the subject of thoughtful discussions by the great thinkers.

A special meat diet introduced about 480 B.C. by Dromeus, "Mr. Runner" ("in name and in fact" Pausan. VI 7, 10) was the first innovation in the training of athletes and it was followed by important consequences. Men aspiring to be artists in boxing, wrestling or pancratium were thereafter subjected by their trainers to a program of heavy eating which aimed at producing bulk and weight. The stream-lined figure of the pentathlete was less often seen on the field of contest. The second innovation occurred some sixty years after Dromeus. A chronic invalid by the name of Herodicus, a gymnastics teacher, had learned from his own personal experience what dieting, massage, and the like could do for one's well-being. Plato (Rep. III 406) gives a caustic account of such new-fangled medical coddling. The principles of Herodicus' system were, shortly afterwards, applied to the training of athletes with the result that the era of Medical Gymnastics was soon in full swing.

Aristotle (Politics II 8) in the middle of the fourth century could quite simply and truthfully remark that in both Medicine and Athletics there had been a departure from the ancestral rules. Another incidental remark of his made in the course of a discussion of the topic "Deliberation," is illuminating: "Athletics is not a subject needing as much deliberation as Navigation, for example, since Athletics has been more completely reduced to a science" (Nicomach. Ethics III 3, 8). The winner in the pentathlon, it is true, might still be the ideal of a great sculptor such as Lysippus* in the fourth century or of a great philosopher: "Beauty varies with each age. In a young man, it consists in possessing a body capable of enduring all efforts, either of the race course or of bodily strength ... This is why the athletes in the pentathlon are most beautiful" (Aristot. Rhet. I 5, 11); but the average athlete of that period, because of his intensive training for a single event, is shown by the realistic scenes on Panathenaic Vases* and by the remarks in the authors to have been far from a symmetrically and harmoniusly developed individual. By Aristotle's time, due to their severe training, few could win victories over a long span of years (Aristol. Polit. V 4) --which was in marked contrast with the "perennial" athlete two centuries before.

Not only had the outward appearance of the athlete suffered a change but his inner spirit and attitude toward competing in the games had undergone a transformation since the sixth century. Flattery by the public and the increasing value of the prizes had had their effect so that, by the fourth century, a class of professional athletes* was finding it a profitable business venture to tour the festivals as contestants.* The extravagances of a celebration for a victor in the foot race returning to his native city of Agrigentum (Southern Sicily) from Olympia in 412 B.C. are reported by Diodorus Siculus (XIII 82) : "Three hundred pairs of white horses, all from Agrigentum, to say nothing of the rest of the parade followed behind Exaenetus as he was driven in a chariot into his home city." Some idea of how attractive the awards had become at one of the hundreds of festivals in the early fourth century can be rather exactly gained from two inscriptions. One lists the prizes given for the athletic events of the Panathenaea festival at Athens in 380 B.C.; the other provides useful information about the price of olive oil for that same period.* Piecing together the information in the two inscriptions we learn that as many as 1300 amphoras of olive oil in prizes varying from sixty to six jars were awarded to victors on that one occasion and that, if he chose to do so, the recipient could have sold his gift of oil at a price of twelve drachmas an amphora. One would naturally expect that the vase holding oil, with its hand-painted picture of Athena in addition to an athletic scene, would be treasured for generations by the victor's family. And such was probably the case since even today more than a hundred of such Panathenaic vases* are still to be seen in the various large museums throughout the world.

A. Displays of Wealth at Olympia

1. Alcibiades' Victories as Told by his Son (397 B.C.)

During the seventh and sixth centuries B.C., in view of the important citizens competing in the games, a contemptuous remark about the social antecedents of contestants at Olympia would have been unthinkable. But specialization and professionalism had become so obvious by 397 B.C. that the orator Isocrates (436-338 B.C.) apparently, as will be seen, had no fear of antagonizing his Athenian audience by referring to athletes as a group low in birth and deficient in culture. The following selection is from a speech written for Alcibiades, the younger.

Isocrates, <u>Team</u> <u>of</u> <u>Horses</u>*: (25) My father on the male side belonged to the Eupatrids (nobles), whose noble birth is apparent
from the very name. On the female side he was of the Alcme-
onidae, who left behind a glorious memorial of their wealth;
for Alcmaeon was the first Athenian to win at Olympia with a
team of horses, and the goodwill which they had toward the
people they displayed in the time of the tyrants (see Chap. III
note). ... (31) After this (battle of Potidaea 432 B.C.) he
married my mother ... a glorious prize of valour. For her
father was Hipponicus (son of Callias) first in wealth of all the
Greeks. The richest dowry went ... with his daughter's hand.
(32) About the same time my father, seeing that the festival
assembly at Olympia was beloved and admired by the whole
world and that in it the Greeks made display of their wealth,
strength of body, and training, and that not only the athletes
were the objects of envy but that also the cities of the victors
became renowned, and believing moreover that while the public
services performed in Athens redound to the prestige, in the
eyes of his fellow-citizens, of the person who renders them,
expenditures in the Olympian Festival, however, enhance the
city's reputation throughout all Greece, (33) reflecting upon
these things, I say, although in natural gifts and in strength of
body he was inferior to none, he disdained the gymnastic contests, for he knew that some of the athletes were of low birth,
inhabitants of petty states, and of mean education, but turned
to the breeding of race-horses, which is possible only for those
most blest by Fortune and not to be pursued by one of low estate, and not only did he surpass his rivals, but also all who
had ever before won the victory. (34) For he entered a larger
number of teams in competition than even the mightiest cities
had done, and they were of such excellence that he came out
first, second, and third. Besides this, his generosity in the
sacrifices and in the other expenses connected with the festival
was so lavish and magnificent that the public funds of all the
others were clearly less than the private means of Alcibiades
alone. And when he brought his mission to an end he had
caused the successes of his predecessors to seem petty in
comparison with his own and those who in his day had been
victors to be no longer objects of emulation, and to future
breeders of racing-studs he left behind no possibility of surpassing him.*

2. Dionysius' Disasters in 388 B.C.

The political importance of winning the favor of the assembled Greeks at Olympia had long been recognized by cities and tyrants. It was not often that one of them met with the humiliations which fell to the lot of the famous tyrant Dionysius of Syracuse when he sought to dazzle the throngs of visitors. However, the remarkable successes of Dicon, a Syracusan, at the festivals in this decade, with his fourteen wreaths for foot-racing, must have restored some prestige to his city   (Pausan VI 3, 11; Diodor. Sic. XV 14).

Diodorus Siculus XIV 109*: When it was about time for the
   Olympic games, Dionysius (tyrant of Syracuse) sent over for
the contest an excessive number of four-horse chariots, far
excelling the others in speed, and tents, as lodgings, which
were interwoven with gold and decked out with expensive,
cleverly embroidered trappings. He also sent the best rhapsodes to make him famous by reciting at the festival poems of
his own composition; for he was utterly mad about poetry. His
brother Thearides was sent along in charge of all this. When
the latter arrived at the festival he attracted much attention,
due to the beauty of the tents and the number of his four horse
chariots. As soon as the rhapsodes undertook to recite the
poems of Dionysius, a crowd gathered quickly because of the
fine voices of the performers and all were amazed. But later,
observing how bad the poems were, they burst out laughing at
Dionysius and felt such contempt for him that some ventured to ·
tear down and plunder his tents. Furthermore, Lysias, the
orator, who was then at Olympia, urged the crowd not to admit to the sacred games the embassy sent by an impious tyrant;
it was at this time that Lysias delivered the speech entitled
"Olympiacus". During the actual race, it was Dionysius' hard
luck that some of his chariots were thrown off the course and
that the others were wrecked by crashing into each other.
With similar hard luck, the ship carrying the embassy was
driven to shore by storms at Tarentum in Italy after setting
sail for Sicily from the games. Therefore it is said that the
sailors, when they had returned safely to Syracuse, spread
throughout the city the report that the poetry was so bad that
not only the rhapsodes were wrecks, but also the chariots and
the ship.

B. Fines Paid by Athletes at Olympia
in the Fourth Century B.C.

Pausanias V, 21*: (2) As you go to the stadium along the road
from the Metroum, there is on the left at the bottom of Mount
Cronius a platform of stone, right by the very mountain, with
steps through it. By the platform have been set up bronze
images of Zeus. These have been made from the fines inflicted
on athletes who have wantonly broken the rules of the contests,
and they are called Zanes (figures of Zeus) by the natives. (3)
The first, six in number, were set up in the ninety-eighth
Olympiad (388 B.C.).* For Eupolus of Thessaly bribed the
boxers who entered the competition, Agenor the Arcadian and
Prytanis of Cyzicus, and with them also Phormio of Halicarnassus, who had won at the preceding Festival. This is said
to have been the first time that an athlete violated the rules of
the games, and the first to be fined by the Eleans were Eupolus
and those who accepted bribes from Eupolus. Two of these
images are the works of Cleon of Sicyon; who made the next
four I do not know. (4) Except the third and the fourth these
images have elegiac inscriptions on them. The first of the inscriptions is intended to make plain that an Olympic victory is
to be won, not by money, but by swiftness of foot and strength
of body. The inscription on the second image declares that
the image stands to the glory of the deity, through the piety of
the Eleans, and to be a terror to law-breaking athletes. The
purport of the inscription on the fifth image is praise of the
Eleans, especially for their fining the boxers; that of the sixth
and last is that the images are a warning to all the Greeks not
to give bribes to obtain an Olympic victory.

(5) Next after Eupolus they say that Callippus of Athens, who
had entered for the pentathlum, bought off his fellow-competi-
tors by bribes, and that this offence occurred at the hundred
and twelfth Festival (332 B.C.). When the fine had been imposed by the Eleans on Callippus and his antagonists, the
Athenians commissioned Hypereides to persuade the Eleans to
remit them the fine. The Eleans refused this favour, and the
Athenians were disdainful enough not to pay the money and to
boycott the Olympic games, until finally the god at Delphi declared that he would deliver no oracle on any matter to the
Athenians before they had paid the Eleans the fine. (6) So
when it was paid, images, also six in number, were made in
honour of Zeus; on them are inscribed elegiac verses not a
whit more elegant than those relating the fine of Eupolus.

C. The Philosophers Examine Greek Athletics

1. Socrates (469-399 B.C.)

In the fourth century B.C. a new type of literature, the Socratic Essay, became the fashion. The authors of these "Memorabilia", which were written in dialogue form, professed to reproduce the teachings of their respected teacher, Socrates, from whom, as is well-known, no written word has come directly. In such an essay, among other items of interest the reply of a certain Epigenes to Socrates, as reported by that old soldier and historian, Xenophon (430-354 B.C.), makes it clear that the word "athlete" had become a term applied to a specially trained group of persons.

Xenophon <u>Memorabilia</u> I 2*: (4) Of the body he (Socrates) was not neglectful, nor did he commend those who were. He did not approve that a person should eat to excess, and then use immoderate exercise, but recommended that he should work off, by a proper degree of exercise, as much as the appetite received with pleasure; for such a habit, he said, was peculiarly conducive to health, and did not prevent attention to the mind.

Xenophon <u>Memorabilia</u> III 12: (1) Noticing that Epigenes, one of his followers, was both very young and weak in body, he said to him. "How very unlike an athlete you are in frame, Epigenes!" "I am not an athlete, Socrates," replied he. "You are not less of an athlete", rejoined Socrates, "than those who are going to contend at the Olympic games. Does the struggle for life with the enemy, which the Athenians will demand of you when circumstances require, seem to you to be a trifling contest? (2) Yet, in the dangers of war, not a few, through weakness of body, either lose their lives, or save them with dishonour .... (5) Nor, because the city does not require warlike exercises publicly, ought we, on that account, to neglect them privately, but rather to practise them the more; for be well assured that neither in any other contest, nor in any affair whatever, will you at all come off the worse because your body is better trained (than that of other men); since the body must bear its part in whatever men do; and in all the services required from the body, it is of the utmost importance to have it in the best possible condition. (6) For even in that in which you think that there is least exercise for the body, namely, thinking, who does not know that many fail greatly from ill-health? and loss of memory, despondency, irritability, and madness, often, from ill-health of body, attack the mind with such force as to drive out all previous knowledge. (7) But to those who have their bodies in good condition, there is great assurance from danger ... and to secure consequences the reverse of what we have stated what would a man in his senses not undergo? (8) It is disgraceful, too, for a person to grow old in self-neglect, before he knows what he would become by rendering himself well-formed and vigorous in body; but this a man who neglects himself can not know; for such advantages are not wont to come spontaneously."

Transportation to Olympia in Socrates' Day

Travellers from Athens to Olympia, so it appears from the following conversation, regularly walked the two hundred and twelve miles. Probably each had a slave attendant along to carry the camping equipment.

Xenophon, Memorabilia III 13: (5) A person being afraid of the journey to Olympia, "Why", said Socrates to him, "do you fear the journey? Do you not walk about at home almost all day? And, if you set out thither, you will walk and dine, walk and sup, and go to rest. Do you not know that if you were to extend (in a straight line) the walks which you take in five or six days, you would easily go from Athens to Olympia? But it will be better for you to start a day too soon than a day too late; for to be obliged to extend your days' journeys beyond a moderate length is disagreeable; but to spend one day more on the road gives great ease --- "

(6) Another saying that he was utterly wearied with a long journey, Socrates asked him whether he carried any burden. "No, by Jupiter", said he, "I did not, except my cloak." "And did you travel alone," said Socrates, "or did an attendant accompany you?" "An attendant was with me". "Was he empty-handed, or did he carry anything?" "He carried, certainly, the bedding and other utensils." "And how did he get over the journey?" "He appeared to me to come off better than myself." "If you, then, had been obliged to carry his burden, how do you imagine that you would have fared?" "Very ill, by Jupiter; or rather, I should not have been able to carry it at all." "And how can you think that it becomes a man trained to exercise to be so much less able to bear fatigue than a slave?"

2. Plato (427-344 B.C.) and Military Gymnastics

Plato, whose ancestry could be traced back six generations to Solon, is an important witness for the history of Greek athletics. For in addition to being a great philosopher and pupil of Socrates he had acquired a practical knowledge of the physical training system which he sought to improve. In his boyhood his prosperous parents are said to have put him under the training of the Argive wrestling teacher, Aristo, and such was his fine bodily condition that, so it is reported, his name originally Aristocles was changed by his teacher to that of Plato (platy -- 'broad-shouldered'). Later, he is said to have competed in wrestling in the Isthmian games. This experience coupled with that gained in his military expeditions (three according to Diog. Laert. III 8) enabled him to speak with authority on the subject of military gymnastics. Plato was far in advance of his own time with his plan of physical training for women: "I assert without fear of contradiction that gymnastics and horsemanship are as suitable to women as to men" (Laws VII 804).

Plato, Republic III 403-404*

After music [to the ancient Greeks "Music" included reading, writing, mathematics, harmony, poetry, drawing, and music in its narrowest sense] comes gymnastic, in which our youth are next to be trained.

Certainly.

Gymnastic as well as music should begin in early years; the training in it should be careful and should continue through life. Now my belief is, --and this is a matter upon which I should like to have your opinion in confirmation of my own, but my own belief is, --not that the good body by any bodily excellence improves the soul, but, on the contrary, that the good soul, by her own excellence, improves the body as far as this may be possible. What do you say?

Yes, I agree.

Then, to the mind when adequately trained, we shall be right in handing over the more particular care of the body; and in order to avoid prolixity we will now only give the general outlines of the subject.

Very good.

That they must abstain from intoxication has been already remarked by us; for of all persons a guardian should be the last to get drunk and not know where in the world he is.

Yes, he said; that a guardian should require another guardian to take care of him is ridiculous indeed.

But next, what shall we say of their food; for the men are in training for the great contest of all -- are they not?

Yes, he said.

And will the habit of body of our ordinary athletes be suited to them?

Why not?

I am afraid, I said, that a habit of body such as they have is but a sleepy sort of thing, and rather perilous to health. Do you not observe that these athletes sleep away their lives, and are liable to most dangerous illnesses if they depart, in ever so slight a degree, from their customary regimen?

Yes, I do.

Then, I said, a finer sort of training will be required for our warrior athletes, who are to be like wakeful dogs, and to see and hear with the utmost keenness; amid the many changes of water and also of food, of summer heat and winter cold, which they will have to endure when on a campaign, they must not be liable to break down in health.

That is my view.

The really excellent gymnastic is twin sister of that simple music which we were just now describing.

Why, I conceive that there is a gymnastic which, like our music, is simple and good; and especially the military gymnastic.

What do you mean?

My meaning may be learned from Homer; he, you know, feeds his heroes at their feasts, when they are campaigning, on soldiers' fare; they have no fish, although they are on the shores of the Hellespont, and they are not allowed boiled meats but only roast, which is the food most convenient for soldiers, requiring only that they should light a fire, and not involving the trouble of carrying about pots and pans.

True.

And I can hardly be mistaken in saying that sweet sauces are nowhere mentioned in Homer. In proscribing them, however, he is not singular; all professional athletes are well aware that a man who is to be in good condition should take nothing of the kind.

Yes, he said; and knowing this, they are quite right in not taking them.

Then you would not approve of Syracusan dinners, and the refinements of Sicilian cookery?

I think not.

Nor, if a man is to be in condition, would you allow him to have a Corinthian girl as his fair friend?

Certainly not.

Neither would you approve of the delicacies, as they are thought, of Athenian confectionery?

Certainly not.

All such feeding and living may be rightly compared by us to melody and song composed in the panharmonic style, and in all the rhythms.

Exactly.

There complexity engendered licence, and here disease; whereas simplicity in music was the parent of temperance in the soul; and simplicity in gymnastic of health in the body.

Plato, Republic III 410-12

And thus our youth, having been educated only in that simple music which, as we said, inspires temperance, will be reluctant to go to law.

Clearly.

And the musician, who, keeping to the same track, is content to practise the simple gymnastic, will have nothing to do with medicine unless in some extreme case.

That I quite believe.

The very exercises and toils which he undergoes are intended to stimulate the spirited element of his nature, and not to increase his strength; he will not, like common athletes, use exercise and regimen to develope his muscles.

Very right, he said.

Neither are the two arts of music and gymnastic really designed, as is often supposed, the one for the training of the soul, the other for the training of the body.

What then is the real object of them?

I believe, I said, that the teachers of both have in view chiefly the improvement of the soul.

How can that be? he asked.

Did you never observe, I said, the effect on the mind itself of exclusive devotion to gymnastic, or the opposite effect of an exclusive devotion to music?

In what way shown? he said.

The one producing a temper of hardness and ferocity, the other of softness and effeminacy, I replied.

Yes, he said, I am quite aware that the mere athlete becomes too much of a savage, and that the mere musician is melted and softened beyond what is good for him.

Yet surely, I said, this ferocity only comes from spirit, which, if rightly educated, would give courage, but, if too much intensified, is liable to become hard and brutal.

That I quite think.

On the other hand the philosopher will have the quality of gentleness. And this also, when too much indulged, will turn to softness, but, if educated rightly, will be gentle and moderate. ...

Exactly.

And so in gymnastics, if a man takes violent exercise and is a great feeder, and the reverse of a great student of music and philosophy, at first the high condition of his body fills him with pride and spirit, and he becomes twice the man that he was.

Certainly,

And what happens? If he do nothing else, and holds no converse with the Muses, does not even that intelligence which may be in him, having no taste of any sort of learning or enquiry or thought or culture, grow feeble and dull and blind, his mind never waking up or receiving nourishment, and his senses not being purged of their mists?

True, he said.

And he ends by becoming a hater of philosophy, uncivilized, never using the weapon of persuasion, -- he is like a wild beast, all violence and fierceness, and knows no other way of dealing; and he lives in all ignorance and evil conditions, and has no sense of propriety and grace.

That is quite true, he said.

And as there are two principles of human nature, one the spirited and the other the philosophical, some God, as I should say, has given mankind two arts answering to them (and only indirectly to the soul and body), in order that these two principles (like the strings of an instrument) may be relaxed or drawn tighter until they are duly harmonized.

That appears to be the intention.

And he who mingles music with gymnastic in the fairest proportions and best attempers them to the soul, may be rightly called the true musician and harmonist in a far higher sense than the tuner of the strings.

You are quite right, Socrates.

Plato, Republic IV 424

---Then to sum up: This is the point to which, above all, the attention of our rulers should be directed, -- that music and gymnastic be preserved in their original form, and no innovation made. They must do their utmost to maintain them intact. And when any one says that mankind most regard
          'The newest song which the singers have,'
they will be afraid that he may be praising not new songs, but a new kind of song; and this ought not to be praised, or conceived to be the meaning of the poet; for any musical innovation is full of danger to the whole State, and ought to be prohibited. ...

(442) And, as we were saying, the united influence of music and gymnastic will bring them into accord, nerving and sustaining the reason with noble words and lessons, and moderating and soothing and civilizing the wildness of passion by harmony and rhythm?

Quite true, he said.

Republic V 452-453:

Then, if women are to have the same duties as men, they must have the same nurture and education?

Yes.

The education which was assigned to the men was music and gymnastic.

Yes.

Then women must be taught music and gymnastic and also the art of war, which they must practise like the men?

That is the inference, I suppose.

I should rather expect, I said, that several of our proposals, if they are carried out, being unusual, may appear ridiculous.

No doubt of it.

Yes, and the most ridiculous thing of all will be the sight of women naked in the palaestra, exercising with the men, especially when they are no longer young; they certainly will not be a vision of beauty, any more than the enthusiastic old men who in spite of wrinkles and ugliness continue to frequent the gymnasia.

Yes, indeed, he said: according to present notions the proposal would be thought ridiculous.

But then, I said, as we have determined to speak our minds, we must not fear the jests of the wits which will be directed against this sort of innovation; how they will talk of women's attainments both in music and gymnastic, and above all about their wearing armour and riding upon horseback!

Very true, he replied.

Yet having begun we must go forward to the rough places of the law; at the same time begging of these gentlemen for once in their life to be serious. Not long ago, as we shall remind them, the Hellenes were of the opinion, which is still generally received among the barbarians, that the sight of a naked man was ridiculous and improper; and when first the Cretans and then the Lacedaemonians introduced the custom, the wits of that day might equally have ridiculed the innovation.

No doubt.

But when experience showed that to let all things be uncovered was far better than to cover them up, and the ludicrous effect to the outward eye vanished before the better principle which reason asserted, then the man was perceived to be a fool who directs the shafts of his ridicule at any other sight but that of folly and vice, or seriously inclines to weigh the beautiful by any other standard but that of the good.

Very true, he replied.

First, then, whether the question is to be put in jest or in earnest, let us come to an understanding about the nature of woman: Is she capable of sharing either wholly or partially in the

actions of men, or not at all? And is the art of war one of those
arts in which she can or can not share? That will be the best way
of commencing the enquiry, and will probably lead to the fairest
conclusion.

That will be much the best way.

Shall we take the other side first and begin by arguing against
ourselves; in this manner the adversary's position will not be undefended.

Why not? he said.

Then let us put a speech into the mouths of our opponents.
They will say: 'Socrates and Glaucon, no adversary need convict
you, for you yourselves, at the first foundation of the State, admitted the principle that everybody was to do the one work suited
to his own nature.' And certainly, if I am not mistaken, such an
admission was made by us. 'And do not the natures of men and
women differ very much indeed?' And we shall reply: Of course
they do. Then we shall be asked, 'Whether the tasks assigned to
men and to women should not be different, and such as are agreeable to their different natures?' Certainly they should. 'But if
so, have you not fallen into a serious inconsistency in saying that
men and women, whose natures are so entirely different, ought to
perform the same actions?' What defence will you make for us,
my good Sir, against any one who offers these objections?

That is not an easy question to answer when asked suddenly;
and I shall and I do beg of you to draw out the case on our side. ...

(454) Why we valiantly and pugnaciously insist upon the verbal
truth, that different natures ought to have different pursuits, but
we never considered at all what was the meaning of sameness or
difference of nature, or why we distinguished them when we assigned different pursuits to different natures and the same to the
same natures.

Why, no, he said, that was never considered by us.

I said: Suppose that by way of illustration we were to ask the
question whether there is not an opposition in nature between bald
men and hairy men; and if this is admitted by us, then, if bald
men are cobblers, we should forbid the hairy men to be cobblers,
and conversely?

That would be a jest, he said.

Yes, I said, a jest; and why? because we never meant when we constructed the State, that the opposition of natures should extend to every difference, but only to those differences which affected the pursuit in which the individual is engaged; we should have argued, for example, that a physician and one who is in mind a physician may be said to have the same nature.

True.

Whereas the physician and the carpenter have different natures?

Certainly.

And if, I said, the male and female sex appear to differ in their fitness for any art or pursuit, we should say that such pursuit or art ought to be assigned to one or the other of them; but if the difference consists only in women bearing and men begetting children, this does not amount to a proof that a woman differs from a man in respect of the sort of education she should receive; and we shall therefore continue to maintain that our guardians and their wives ought to have the same pursuits.

Very true, he said.

(455) Next, we shall ask our opponent how, in reference to any of the pursuits or arts of civic life, the nature of a woman differs from that of a man?

That will be quite fair.

And perhaps he, like yourself, will reply that to give a sufficient answer on the instant is not easy; but after a little reflection there is no difficulty.

Yes, perhaps.

Suppose then that we invite him to accompany us in the argument, and then we may hope to show him that there is nothing peculiar in the constitution of women which would affect them in the administration of the State.

By all means.

Let us say to him: Come now, and we will ask you a question: -- when you spoke of a nature gifted or not gifted in any respect, did you mean that one man will acquire a thing easily, another with difficulty; a little learning will lead the one to discover a great deal; whereas the other, after much study and application, no sooner learns than he forgets; or again, did you mean, that the one has a body which is a good servant to his mind, while the body of the other is a hindrance to him? -- would not these be the sort of differences which distinguish the man gifted by nature from the one who is ungifted?

No one will deny that.

And can you mention any pursuit of mankind in which the male sex has not all these gifts and qualities in a higher degree than the female? Need I waste time in speaking of the art of weaving, and the management of pancakes and preserves, in which womankind does really appear to be great, and in which for her to be beaten by a man is of all things the most absurd?

You are quite right, he replied, in maintaining the general inferiority of the female sex: although many women are in many things superior to many men, yet on the whole what you say is true.

And if so, my friend, I said, there is no special faculty of administration in a state which a woman has because she is a woman, or which a man has by virtue of his sex, but the gifts of nature are alike diffused in both; all the pursuits of men are the pursuits of women also, but in all of them a woman is inferior to a man.

Very true.

Then are we to impose all our enactments on men and none of them on women?

That will never do.

(456) One woman has a gift of healing, another not; one is a musician, and another has no music in her nature?

Very true.

And one woman has a turn for gymnastic and military exercises, and another is unwarlike and hates gymnastics?

Certainly.

And one woman is a philosopher, and another is an enemy of philosophy; one has spirit, and another is without spirit?

That is also true.

Then one woman will have the temper of a guardian, and another not. Was not the selection of the male guardians determined by differences of this sort?

Yes.

Men and women alike possess the qualities which make a guardian; they differ only in their comparative strength or weakness.

Obviously.

And those women who have such qualities are to be selected as the companions and colleagues of men who have similar qualities and whom they resemble in capacity and in character?

Very true.

And ought not the same natures to have the same pursuits?

They ought.

Then, as we were saying before, there is nothing unnatural in assigning music and gymnastic to the wives of the guardians -- to that point we come round again.

Certainly not.

The law which we then enacted was agreeable to nature, and therefore not an impossibility or mere aspiration; and the contrary practice, which prevails at present, is in reality a violation of nature.

That appears to be true.

We had to consider, first, whether our proposals were possible, and secondly whether they were the most beneficial?

Yes.

And the possibility has been acknowledged?

Yes.

The very great benefit has next to be established?

Quite so.

You will admit that the same education which makes a man a good guardian will make a woman a good guardian; for their original nature is the same?

Yes.

I should like to ask you a question.

What is it?

Would you say that all men are equal in excellence, or is one man better than another?

The latter.

And in the commonwealth which we were founding do you conceive the guardians who have been brought up on our model system to be more perfect men, or the cobblers whose education has been cobbling?

What a ridiculous question.

You have answered me, I replied: Well, and may we not further say that our guardians are the best of our citizens?

By far the best.

And will not their wives be the best women?

Yes, by far the best.

And can there be anything better for the interests of the State than that the men and women of a State should be as good as possible?

There can be nothing better.

(457) And this is what the arts of music and gymnastic, when present in such manner as we have described, will accomplish?

Certainly.

Then we have made an enactment not only possible but in the highest degree beneficial to the State?

True.

Then let the wives of our guardians strip, for their virtue will be their robe, and let them share in the toils of war and the defence of their country; only in the distribution of labours the lighter are to be assigned to the women, who are the weaker natures, but in other respects their duties are to be the same. And as for the man who laughs at naked women exercising their bodies from the best of motives, in his laughter he is plucking
'A fruit of unripe wisdom,'
and he himself is ignorant of what he is laughing at, or what he is about; -- for that is, and ever will be, the best of sayings,
'That <u>the</u> <u>useful</u> <u>is</u> <u>the</u> <u>noble</u> <u>and</u> <u>the</u> <u>hurtful</u> <u>is</u> <u>the</u> <u>base</u>.'

3. Aristotle (384-322 B.C.)
and his Sane Comments on Athletics

Aristotle, <u>Politics</u> IV 16*: What is the physical condition of the parents which will be most beneficial to the children they beget is a question we shall have to discuss more particularly

when we come to treat of the supervision of children. ... For a
vigorous habit of body in one who is to lead a political life, for
health and for the procreation of healthy children, what is
wanted is not the bodily condition of an athlete nor on the other
hand a valetudinarian and invalid condition, but one that lies between the two. The right condition then, although it is one of
discipline, is disciplined not by violent exercises nor for one
purpose only like an athlete's, but for all the actions of a liberal
life. Also this condition should be the same for women as for
men.

Politics V   3: As it is evident that the education of the habits
must precede that of the reason and the education of the body
must precede that of the intellect, it clearly follows that we
must surrender our children in the first instance to gymnastic
and the Art of the Trainer, as the latter imparts a certain
character to their physical condition and the former to the
feats they can perform.*

Politics V   4: At the present day the States, which enjoy the
highest repute for care in the education of children, generally
produce in them an athletic condition whereby they mar their
bodily presence and development; while the Lacedaemonians,
although they avoided this mistake, render them brutal by the
exertions required of them in the belief that this is the best
means to produce a valorous disposition. Yet, as we have
several times remarked, valour is neither the only virtue nor
the virtue principally to be kept in view in the superintendence
of children; and, even if it were, the Lacedaemonians are not
successful in devising the means to attain it. For neither in
the animal world generally nor among uncivilized nations do we
find valour associated with the most savage characters, but
rather with such as are gentle, like the lion's. There are
many uncivilized nations who think very little of slaying and
eating their fellow creatures ... yet they are absolutely desti-
tute of valour. Nay if we look at the case of the Lacedaemonians themselves, it is well known that, although they maintained
their superiority to all other peoples so long as they alone were
assiduous in the cheerful endurance of laborious exercises,
they are now surpassed by others in the contests both of the
wrestling-school and of actual war. The fact is that their pre-
eminence was due not to their disciplining their youth in this
severe manner but solely to their giving them a course of
training, while the other nations with whom they had to contend
did not. But it is right that we should base our judgment not

upon their achievements in the past but at the present day; for at present they have competitors in their educational system, whereas in past times they had none. We may conclude then that it is not the brutal element in men but the element of nobleness which should hold the first place ... and that to give up our children overmuch to bodily exercises and leave them uninstructed in the true essentials i.e. in the rudiments of education, is in effect to degrade them to the level of mechanics by rendering them useless in a statesman's hands for any purpose except one and, as our argument shows, not so useful as other people even for this.

The duty then of employing gymnastic and the method of its employment are admitted. Up to the age of puberty gymnastic exercises of a comparatively light kind should be applied with a prohibition of hard diet and compulsory exercises, so that there may be no impediment to the growth. The fact that these may have the effect of injuring growth may be clearly inferred from the circumstance that in the list of Olympian victors it would not be possible to find more than two or three who have been successful in manhood as well as in boyhood; for the effect of their training in youth is that they lose their physical vigour in consequence of the enforced gymnastic exercises they perform. When our youths have devoted three years from the age of puberty to other studies, it is then proper that the succeeding period of life should be occupied with hard exercises and severities of diet. For the intellect and the body should not be subject to severe exertion simultaneously, as the two kinds of exertion naturally produce contrary effects, that of the body being an impediment to the intellect and that of the intellect to the body.

D. Diogenes the Cynic (404-323 B.C.)
Visits the Isthmian Festival

The selection below consists of extracts from two of the eighty extant speeches written by the entertaining sophist, Dio the 'Golden-Mouthed' (40-108 A.D.?) who was forced into the position of travelling lecturer because of his banishment from Rome by Domitian. Because of its central location the Isthmian festival, held biennially, probably in April, was always largely attended and its nearness to Corinth may have accounted for the lower moral tone prevailing there as compared with the Olympic Festival. Diogenes the Cynic, native of Sinope, was notorious for his biting scorn and by Plato was nick-named "The Mad Socrates".

Dio Chrysostomus, Oration VII*: (6) When it was time for the
Isthmian games and everybody was at the Isthmus, Diogenes
went down too ... And he always gave an interview to anyone
who wished to meet him.

(9) It was possible at that time around the temple of Poseidon
to hear many wretched sophists shouting at one another and each
reviling the other and their so-called pupils wrangling with one
another over something, many authors reading aloud from their
stupid works, many poets chanting their poems, with others
complimenting their work, many magicians giving an exhibition
of their magic, many seers interpreting portents, a myriad of
lawyers twisting law suits, and finally no small number of ped-
dlers peddling the wares which each happened to have.

(11) When someone asked Diogenes if he too had come to see
the games, he said, "No, but to compete in them myself." The
man with a laugh asked who his competitors were. ... "Hardships," replied Diogenes, "which are very difficult and uncon-
querable by men stuffed with food and dazed, men who eat all
day and snore all night, but they can be conquered by men who
are slender, without flesh, and with waists more tapering than
wasps. Or do you fancy that these pot-bellied men are of some
use, men who ought rather to be sacrificed, cut up, and served
at a banquet, just as I think sensible people do with the flesh
of whales after they have boiled it in salt and water and melted
off the fat which they then use to grease people who need it
(the way we do with tallow from dolphins back home around the
Pontus). I really believe these athletes have less intelligence
than swine.

Oration VIII: (10) Once when he put the wreath of pine onto himself, the Corinthians sent servants over to order him to take
it off and to do nothing illegal. ... (14) Later, noticing someone leaving the field in the midst of a large crowd and not
walking on the ground, but borne aloft by the crowd, with some
people following and shouting, others jumping for joy, raising
their arms toward heaven, others throwing wreaths and rib-
bons at him, as soon as he could draw near he inquired what
all the uproar about him meant, and what had happened. The
man answered, "I have won in the two hundred yard race for
men, Diogenes." "What is that!" he said. "You have not become wiser, not a bit, because you got ahead of the men who
were running with you ... nor will you live freer from misery."
"No by Zeus", the other retorted, "but I can run faster than
any other Greek." "No doubt", said Diogenes, "but not faster

than hares or deer -- and yet these animals are the most cowardly of all ... . Don't you know ... that speed is a sign of cowardice; the same creatures which are the swiftest are likewise
the most cowardly." (22) After this he noticed two horses tied
to the same place who were fighting and kicking each other while
a large crowd gathered around to watch, until one of the horses,
tired out, broke away and ran off, whereupon Diogenes went up
to the one horse who was left there, put a wreath on his head
and proclaimed him an Isthmian victor, because he had won in
the kicking match (pancratium). Then there arose loud laughter and outcries from all and many marvelled at Diogenes and
made fun of the athletes, and they say that some even went off
without seeing them at all -- that is, those who had poor lodgings
or were without any at all.

VI. GREEK ATHLETICS IN THE HELLENISTIC AGE

(322-146 B.C.)

The conquests of Alexander the Great of Macedon (333-323 B.C.), including, as they did, not only Greece but also large areas of Asia and of Africa, ushered in an era of many profound changes for the Greeks. Numberless groups during the next century were to leave their stagnant home towns to carve out a new life in those progressive centers of trade, commerce, and farming newly founded in Asia and in Egypt. Many other Greeks were to earn their livelihood as professional soldiers in the armies of foreign rulers. The result was that the old city states dwindled in importance, that leagues of cities with broad general interests developed, and that Greece as a whole became more world-conscious.

These many changes in the way of life for the Greeks, however, seem to have been accompanied by only a very few changes in their practice of athletics. From all the papyrus rolls of prose and poetry written in the great literary centers of the Hellenistic world very little remains today; and only a relatively few inscriptions cut in stone have come to light. Even so the testimony from this small corpus of evidence gives clear indications of the general pattern of athletic history for the two centuries after Alexander and demonstrates that its general trends were much the same as those of the two previous centuries.

The four major festivals of Greece, as well as the Panathenaea at Athens, were held as usual and were thronged with visitors from far and near. Under the patronage of wealthy rulers from Macedonia and outside of Greece proper expensive events like the chariot race could still retain their glamour. Small local festivals took on added importance and many new athletic festivals, frankly imitating those in the mother country, were founded in the new settlements abroad.* In the case of the competitors it is hardly possible to determine whether more of them were professional athletes as compared with the previous centuries or not. Most of the athletic news which has trickled down from the third and second centuries does concern the feats of men who evidently made athletics their business. But the amateur, Sosibius, honored by Callimachus and the statesman, Aratus, reported to have won many an athletic victory in his youth, may be representative of a larger group than has been suspected.

The curve of interest in athletics in the Hellenistic Age still
followed closely the curve of prosperity. Cities of Southern Italy
and of Sicily no longer figured in the Victor Lists for they had been
eclipsed by such rich commercial centers as Rhodes* and other
places in the Eastern Mediterranean. So, as will be seen, it was
a ruler from Pergamum or from Alexandria and not from Syracuse
who was seeking the fame of a chariot-race victory at Olympia or
Delphi. Athletic idols from many parts of the Greek world were,
as in previous centuries, holding the audiences at the major games
enthralled by spectacular performances. The name of Philinus of
Cos was on the lips of all in the first quarter of the third century
because of his twenty-four victories in the footraces at Olympia,
Delphi, Nemea and the Isthmus (Pausan. VI 17, 2; Theocrit. VII
120); at the end of the century, a Cleitomachus of Thebes and a
Caprus of Elis were winning acclaim for their boxing feats
(Pausan. V 21, 10; VI 15, 3); while fifty years later, in the second
century, a Leonidas of Rhodes was breaking all records by maintaining his running speed at its prime for four Olympiads, with
twelve awards (Pausan. VI 13, 4).* Finally, in these centuries as
in previous ones there could still be heard grumbling remarks
about the over-eating of athletes and their fixed schedules of exercises. However, as will be seen, these objections were now being
voiced, not by idealistic philosophers, but by the "Military" whose
requirements of training for professional soldiers were of course
far different from those of coaches for prize-winning athletes.

Remains of gymnasia and palaestrae which have been uncovered,
together with their inscriptions, show that the Greeks after Alexander's day housed their organized system of physical training in
carefully designed buildings with well-landscaped surroundings.*
It was in the Hellenistic Age, too, that a new word, periodonikes
(circuit champion), came into general usage to describe athletes
who had won all four major festivals. After 190 B.C. inscriptions
include the word, added as a title of honor.*

A. A List of Victors in the Games at Olympia,
296 B.C.

A papyrus fragment found at Oxyrhynchus, Egypt, contains a
list of the victors in the various events at Olympia in Olympiad
121. A comparison of this with another papyrus fragment (P. Oxy.
222 cited in Chapter IV, above) which gives the events and some
of the winners at Olympia from 480-448 B.C. will reveal how
little the festival had changed in six generations. The only new
additions to the program of events seem to have been a two-horse

chariot race and races with colts. The home towns of the victors
are named in both of the fragments and are significant. In 296
B.C. no victories for the Western Mediterranean area are recorded; in the equestrian events northern Greece has evidently
begun to play an important role.

FGH 257a (Jacoby II b, 1196) = P Oxy XX 2082:

Pythagoras from Magnesia on the Maiandros, the stade
race (200 yds.); this man had two Olympic victories, two Pythian,
five Isthmian, seven Nemean.

Apollonius of Alexandria, the double race (400 yds.)

Pas. cho... (?), a Boeotian, the long race (probably 3 mi.)*

Timarchus from Mantinea, the pentathlon

Amphiares from Laconia, the wrestling

Callippos from Rhodes, the boxing

Nicon from Boeotia the pancratium; this man had two
Olympic victories, two Pythian, four Nemean and four Isthmian

Sosiades of Tralles, the junior wrestling

Antipater from Ephesus, the junior stade race

Myrceus from Arcadia was proclaimed for the junior
wrestling

Pythagoras of Magnesium, the hoplite race twice (400 yds.)

The four-horse chariot of Archidamus of Elis; the horse
(with rider) of Pandion of Thessaly; the two-horse chariot of
Tlasimachus of Ambracia; the four-colt chariot belonging to the
same man.

B. A Boxing Match: Pollux vs. Amycus

From Theocritus (300-260 B.C.?), a pastoral poet who belonged
to the Golden Age of Alexandrian poetry, there comes what has been
described by one writer on Greek Athletics as "incomparably the
best description of a fight which we possess."* In an era when
artificiality marked so much of the writing Theocritus sounds a
refreshingly natural note. Real people who could have been his
early neighbors appear on the pages of his bucolic idylls, poems
which attracted the attention of the Egyptian court and set him on
the road to fame.   A fisherman asleep in a shack dreaming of
catching a solid gold fish (Idyll XXI); a handsome youth, Delphis,

shining with oil, lately come from the "noble labor of the gymnasi-um" and still carrying his Dorian oil flask (Idyll II); a Sicilian shepherd (Idyll IV) starting off, an amateur, to wrestle at Olympia "carrying his spade" for the digging exercises practised there and "driving his twenty sheep" to provide fresh meat during the month of residence: these are among the persons vividly described in the thirty poems.* So the legend of the famous boxing match supposed to have been held in Pre-Troy days, in the course of Jason's ex-pedition in the Argo, received at the hand of Theocritus no color-less, stereotyped treatment. Pollux, demonstrating correct hand, foot, and head work, as taught in the old-time wrestling school, is pitted by the author against a man of the newer school who reckless-ly violates the orthodox rules and relies wholly on massive bulk and brute strength.

A contemporary, Apollonius Rhodius, had recently written a description of the same two-round fight in Book II of his epic poem entitled "Argonautica".* But Theocritus, by his more careful description of the stance and of the style of hitting on the part of the two opponents, leaves the impression that he, for one, secured his facts about boxing from no library book. It is easy to imagine Theocritus in regular attendance at the prize fights of Syracuse, Cos, and Alexandria where he lived at various periods of his life.

Theocritus Idyll XXII (written circa 275 B.C.)

27-135: Now the Argo had escaped the Clashing Rocks and the baneful mouth of snowy Pontus (i. e. the Bosphorus) and had come to the land of the Bebrycians, bearing the dear sons of the gods. There the crowd of heroes converging from both sides descended the one ladder* and left Jason's ship. They stepped off onto a deeply sanded shore of a wind-protected headland and busied them-selves with spreading the bedding materials and manipulating the fire sticks. But Castor of the nimble steeds and ruddy Polydeuces (i. e. Pollux) went off by themselves, the two of them, straying apart from their comrades and marvelling at the many varieties of trees growing wild on the mountain. Beneath a smooth cliff they found an ever-flowing spring, filled to the brim with pure water; the pebbles below flashed like crystal or silver from the

depths. Lofty pines grew nearby, poplars, planetrees, tapering
cypresses, and there were, besides, fragrant flowers -- work dear
to fuzzy bees --as many as burst into bloom over the meadows just
at the close of spring. There a gigantic man was sitting and sun-
ning himself, an awesome sight. His ears were crushed from hard
boxing, his mighty chest and his broad back bulged with flesh of
iron -- he was like a colossal statue of hammered metal. On his
firm arms just below the shoulder the muscles stood out like
rounded stones which a winter's torrent rolls and polishes in great
swirling eddies. Over his back there was slung a lion's skin fastened at his neck by the paws.

[53-79: Pollux courteously makes inquiries, but meets only
with insulting answers. Amycus, the giant, demands that they
settle their differences in an impromptu boxing match. Instead of
any other prize, the winner is to be considered master with full
powers over the defeated one. Bebrycians and Argonauts are summoned to witness the match.]

Now when the pair had strengthened their hands with oxhide
folds and had wound the long thongs* around their fists, they met
in the centre breathing mutual slaughter. At this point there was
quite a struggle between them in their eager haste, to see which
would get the sunlight at his back. By quick wit, Polydeuces, you
slipped past the huge man and the sun's rays struck Amycus full in
the face. Then Amycus, angered in his heart, rushed forward
aiming his fists straight at the mark, but, as he was attacking,
Polydeuces struck him on the tip of his chin. Then, more aroused
than before, the giant battled wildly and bending over toward the
ground bore heavily down upon Polydeuces. The Bebrycians roared
applause, while the heroes on the other side shouted encouraging
words to stalwart Polydeuces, for they feared that somehow the
Tityos-like fighter would press him hard in the narrow place and

vanquish him. But Polydeuces, son of Zeus, shifting his ground
this way and that, and striking now with his right, now with his left,
gashed the son of Poseidon and checked his attack in spite of Amycus' great strength. The giant came to a standstill drunken with
blows, and spat out red blood while all the heroes cheered in unison
when they saw the grievous gashes around his mouth and jaws; as
his face swelled his eyes became narrower and narrower. Then
Polydeuces continued to bewilder him by making feints from all
directions, but when he saw him utterly helpless, he drove his fist
against his brow square above the nose and laid bare his forehead
to the bone. So, thus struck down, Amycus lay stretched on his
back upon the abundant leaves.

Then, when he stood upright, the battle grew bitter; deadly
blows from the firm thongs they dealt each other. But the leader
of the Bebrycians kept thrusting his hands at his opponent's chest
and just below his neck while the invincible Polydeuces with dis-
figuring blows kept battering Amycus' face all over. The giant's
flesh subsided as he sweated and from a huge man he was fast becoming a small one whereas Pollux displayed ever stouter limbs
and a healthier color as the toil increased.

How then did the son of Zeus bring down the glutton? Tell me,
goddess, for you know; and I, reporting to others will utter whatever you wish in the style which suits your heart's fancy.

Well, then, Amycus, yearning for a master stroke, seized the
left hand of Polydeuces in his own left hand and leaned sidewise in
the lunge forward; then he sought to attack his opponent with his
broad fist brought up from his right flank. Had he hit him, he
would have knocked out the Spartan prince. But Polydeuces ducked
out from under and at the same time with his stout (i. e. right)

hand smote Amycus beneath the left temple with a blow coming
straight from his shoulder; from the gaping temple blood spouted
forth. Next with his left hand (i. e. now freed) he planted a punch
on the giant's mouth; the close-set teeth rattled loose. With blows
that thudded ever sharper and sharper, he battered the man's face
until the cheeks were crushed in. Then Amycus lay flat upon the
ground, and dazed, he raised up both his hands renouncing the combat, for he was near to death. But, O Boxer Polydeuces, though
you were his master, you did nothing brutal to him: just a mighty
oath you had him swear, invoking his father Poseidon from the
deep, that never again would he, wittingly, insult strangers.

C. The Victories of Sosibius

A papyrus fragment now in the British Museum (P Oxy 1783),
purchased in 1920 at Oxyrhynchus, Egypt, and containing parts of
a victory ode for a Sosibius of Alexandria, is of special interest to
students of the history of Greek athletics. The author was Callimachus (circa 310-240 B.C.) known to be the writer of some
800 books.   Before the ten badly broken columns of this papyrus
roll had been laboriously reassembled by papyrologists there had
been only two very brief notices, both coming from writers who
lived more than four hundred years later than Callimachus, which
indicated that this Alexandrian scholar had interested himself in
athletics: Harpocration (s. v. Aktia) mentioned "On Athletic Contests" by Callimachus; Athenaeus in his miscellany "Doctors for
Dinner" (IV 144e) referred to this very poem which has now come
to light.

This athletic ode, if thoughtfully analyzed -- not an easy task
because of its obscure style and missing lines -- adds several details to the picture of athletics in the Hellenistic Age. It shows a
young man of superior family still eagerly seeking renown at the
great games of Greece, quite in the tradition of earlier centuries.
Sosibius had begun his prize winning, it seems, with a victory in
the double foot race at games instituted by Ptolemy I. This was
followed, as the poem states, by a victory in wrestling at the
Panathenaic Games* in Athens. Sosibius, grown older and richer,
like the wealthy aristocrats of earlier centuries, coveted a victory
wreath in chariot racing at the major festivals in Greece. So --
and this is the real subject of the poem -- he entered his chariot

at the Nemean and the Isthmian games. Generous donations to two
temples and a victory ode written by an outstanding poet followed
as a consequence of his two victories.

With the Alexandrian fondness for dramatic discourse abruptly
introduced, the poet has Father Nile voice his pleasure at the victory, has Sosibius tell of his victory in Athens and of his gifts to
the Graces in the Argive Heraeum. Callimachus, himself, describes in the first person an offering by Sosibius which he had seen
at the Pelusium mouth of the Nile. We do not know how many other
Epinikia were written for athletic victors in the Hellenistic Age.
This one which survives gives the impression that Greek athletic
practices were continuing their age old way in spite of changes in
the political picture.

Callimachus, Fragment 384 (Pfeiffer)* (circa 275 B.C.):

And ... let us pour out a libation of song -- to one for whom
the parsley-bearing chariot has lately departed from Ephyra
(i.e. Corinth); whose horse from Asbysta (town near Cyrene,
Africa) still keeps the creaking of the axle ringing in its ears.
As though it had happened today this word spoken for a sweet
message darts around my lips:

"O Divinity (Poseidon), you by whom the sons of Sisyphus
of old (i.e. Corinthians) do swear, you who are enshrined at
either end of a wave-girdled narrows, holding the sacred
Isthmus at the tip where Pelops' land stops (at the one end
Cromnites*, at the other end Lechaeus) there where a decision
as to feet, hand, or swift horse is the most straightforward and
where true justice outruns gold -- gold which as a fair snare for
men [was devised by Phoenix?]
.... 4 lines missing ....
in order that someone dwelling on the Cinyphas River (i.e. far
to the west) may learn that Sosibius* and Alexander's city were
twice-wreathed, close by either boy*, one of whom was the
brother of Learchus, and the other, the boy who was nursed by
a mother from Myrina (i.e. Lesbos) and that the Nile bringing
its exceedingly fruitful annual flood may speak as follows:

"Lovely gifts my nursling paid me .... for not yet had anyone brought to the city a prize ... of these tomb festivals and
I, a mighty river, I, whose source no mortal man knows, became for this one man more mild so that women's white ankles
forded me without difficulty and a child crossed on foot with
knees dry.*
..... 8 lines missing .....

(Sosibius seems to be the next speaker) and at Athens there were placed throughout a sacred building, vases, -- no token of ornament but of wrestling -- when with no fear of grown men we gave to the chorus leading the revel to Glauce's (i. e. Athena's) temple the occasion of sweetly calling out Archilochus' hymn of victory*; and O Ptolemy, son of Lagus,* before your eyes I chose to start my prize-winning career with the double-race
... 13 lines missing ...
the stranger hitting the mark in both (i. e. Isthmian and Nemean Games); no longer shall we leave the daughters of Euronyme standing lightly clad in the Heraeum.* Thus in harmony with what I tell some man shall sing a song.

(Callimachus seems to be the next speaker) The sacred offering above I heard about from others but the following which he (i. e. Sosibius) set up as a memorial at the lowest mouth of the Nile (i. e. Pelusium) I myself saw when I was a sojourner by the Sea of Casius: "From Cyprus a Sidonian bark brought me here" (probably some phrase like "I read on the memorial" is to be supplied)
.... about 13 lines missing ....
And the man for whose victories we sing is a man who feels friendship for people, not forgetful of the small folk, which is a thing you could see but seldom in a rich man unless his intelligence surpasses his good fortune. Neither let me praise him as much as he deserves nor let me pass him by -- I fear the people's tongue in either case ....
... about 13 lines missing.

D. The Victory of Attalus of Pergamum at Olympia
(circa 265 B.C.)

An inscription discovered in 1885 on portions of a large monument base near the temple of Athena in Pergamum (Asia Minor) is important as it gives clear proof that in the Hellenistic Age the prestige of a victory wreath in the chariot race at Olympia was still eagerly sought by wealthy entrants from all over the Greek world. Indeed, under the influence of the horse-loving Macedonians the events with horses seem to have increased in importance at Olympia. New races with chariots drawn by pairs of colts and a race between single colts with riders were introduced shortly after the time of this inscription (Pausan. V 8, 2).

The Attalus here mentioned as the winner in the chariot race with four colts was the father of Attalus I (241-197 B.C.) and a nephew of Philetaerus.*

<u>Inscriptions from Pergamum</u> No. 10 (Fränkel)*: Many chariots
   came from Libya, many from Argos, many from rich Thessaly,
   and with them was counted also that of Attalus. A barrier was
   stretched, holding them all back together by a braided rope.
   The barrier*, removed with a loud sound, let out the swift
   colts, and they swept over the course at full stretch, running
   scattered. The chariot of Attalus like a whirlwind stirred the
   dust under the horses' hoofs, always in the lead. The other
   teams were still striving with panting breath when he was written on the hearts of the myriads of Greeks then present as
   spectators. The glorious fame paid to the Olympia wreath came
   to Philetaerus and the houses of Pergamum.*

E. Cleitomachus of Thebes, Orator and Boxer at Olympia
(between 216-204 B.C.)

An anecdote related by Polybius (203-121 B.C.?) about a famous boxer of the previous generation sheds light on the popularity
of boxing, the psychology of audiences, and the athletic activities
of ambitious foreign monarchs in the Hellenistic Age.

Pausanias* (VI 15, 3) recites the remarkable record of this
Cleitomachus of Thebes who seems to have been a true successor
of Theagenes of Thasos (see Chap. IV): at the Isthmus, on the
same day, a victory in the men's wrestling-match, a victory over
all competitors in the boxing-match, and in the pancratium; at
Delphi, three victories in the pancratium; at Olympia in 216 B.C.,
the first after Theagenes to be proclaimed winner in both boxing
and pancratium.

Polybius XXVII 9*

When after the Macedonian victory the news of the cavalry en-

gagement was spread abroad in Greece, the attachment of the

people to Perseus, which had been for the most part concealed,

burst forth like fire. The state of their feelings was, I think,

more or less as follows. The phenomenon was very like what hap-

pens in boxing contests at the games. For there, when a humble

and much inferior combatant is matched against a celebrated and

seemingly invincible athlete, the sympathy of the crowd is at once

given to the inferior man. They cheer him on, and back him up

enthusiastically; and if he manages to touch his opponent's face, and gets in a blow that leaves any mark, there is at once again the greatest excitement among them all. They sometimes even try to make fun of the other man, not out of any dislike for him or disapproval but from a curious sort of sympathy and a natural instinct to favor the weaker. If, however, one calls their attention at the right time to their error, they very soon change their minds and correct it. This was what Cleitomachus did, as is told. He was considered to be a quite invincible boxer, and his fame had spread over the whole world, when Ptolemy*, ambitious to destroy his reputation, trained with the greatest care and sent off the boxer Aristonicus, a man who seemed to have a remarkable natural gift for this sport. Upon this Aristonicus arriving in Greece and challenging Cleitomachus at Olympia, the crowd, it seems, at once took the part of the former and cheered him on, delighted to see that someone, once in a way at least, ventured to fit himself against Cleitomachus. And when, as the fight continued, he appeared to be his adversary's match, and once or twice landed a telling blow, there was great clapping of hands, and the crowd became delirious with excitement, cheering on Aristonicus. At this time they say that Cleitomachus, after withdrawing for a few moments to recover his breath, turned to the crowd and asked them what they meant by cheering on Aristonicus and backing him up all they could. Did they think he himself was not fighting fairly, or were they not aware that Cleitomachus was now fighting for the glory of Greece and Aristonicus for that of King Ptolemy? Would they prefer to see an Egyptian conquer the Greeks and win the Olympian crown, or to hear a Theban and Boeotian proclaimed by the herald as victor in the men's boxing-match? When Cleitomachus had spoken thus, they say there was such a change in the sentiment of the crowd that now all was reversed, and Aristonicus was beaten rather by the crowd than by Cleitomachus.

F. Attitude of Military Leaders toward Athletics

Beginning with the great Theban general, Epaminondas (420-362 B.C.), there had been heard disapproving words from military leaders on the subject of the professional training given to athletes. Epaminondas rejected the gymnastic exercises that aimed at strength, as rendering one unfit for military service, and would practise only those developing agility. He warned his fellow Thebans that if they wanted the sovereignty of Greece they must make more use of the camp and less of the wrestling school. He refused to accept in his army any of the heavy-weights from the athletic schools (Nepos, Epam. 2.4; 5.4; Plutarch Reg. et Imper. Apophth. 3 D). However, Aratus of Sicyon, elected general of the Achaean League in 245 B.C. at the age of twenty six, appears to have been a notable exception. He is reported to have been a winner in pentathlon matches (Plutarch Aratus 3) and in the chariot race at Olympia (Pausan. VI 12, 3). But Philopoemen (252-183 B.C.), his popular successor in the League, being of a more soldierly temperament than Aratus, chose to pattern himself after Epaminondas. His biographer clearly states this general's attitude toward athletics.

Plutarch, Philopoemen III 2*: He was strongly inclined to the life of a soldier even from his childhood, and he studied and practised all that belonged to it, taking great delight in the managing of horses, and handling of weapons. Because he was naturally fitted to excel in wrestling, some of his friends and tutors recommended his attention to athletic exercises. But he would first be satisfied whether it would not interfere with his becoming a good soldier. They told him, as was the truth, that the one life was directly opposite to the other; the requisite state of body, the ways of living, and the exercises all different: the professional athlete sleeping much, and feeding plentifully, punctually regular in his set times of exercise and rest, and apt to spoil all by every little excess, or breach of his usual method; whereas the soldier ought to train himself in every variety of change and irregularity, and, above all, to bring himself to endure hunger and loss of sleep without difficulty. Philopoemen, hearing this, not only laid by all thoughts of wrestling and contemned it then, but when he came to be general, discouraged it by all marks of reproach and dishonour he could imagine, as a thing which made men, otherwise excellently fit for war, to be utterly useless and unable to fight on necessary occasions.

G. Building Plans for an Athletics Plant
in the Third Century B. C.

As early as the time of Solon, the term gymnasium was applied to selected sites where youths were trained in gymnastic exercises (Aeschin. in Timarch. 138). Athens, it is well known, had three such gymnasium centres located on the outskirts of the city and named Academy, Lyceum, and Cynosarges. Such gymnasia in their very earliest days may have been little more than shaded courses (dromoi) convenient to some running water where athletes could exercise and bathe. When gymnastic training was developed into a regular institution, subject to well-formulated rules, a slightly more elaborate athletics plant became necessary. A simple building, called palaestra, seems to have been added on to the exercise grounds "gymnasium". This afforded space for an undressing room, for the various steps in the care of the body, for storage of clothes and athletic implements as well as for areas equipped for exercises used in training boxers and wrestlers. Herodotus (VI 126) mentions that the wealthy Cleisthenes of Sicyon of the early sixth century provided a "dromos and palaestra" for the suitors (see Chap. III). Vase paintings, beginning with the end of the sixth century, picture the activities in such a building. A confusion of terms began very early in the ancient writers, the part, palaestra, being often used to express the whole, gymnasium (e.g. Ps. Xenophon, Constit. of Athens II 10).

An architectural type of gymnasium comprising in its parts a well-planned unit was not, however, any sudden improvisation; several centuries were required before it was completely evolved. By the middle of the fifth century, the anonymous author of the treatise on the constitution of Athens, quite evidently an old oligarch, was grumbling that baths, rooms for undressing, gymnasia, formerly the prerogative of the wealthy, had come into common use for the poor. Before another century had elapsed, Plato in the settings of various dialogues (Lysis 3; Euthyd. 20; Theaet. 2, 144c; Phaedr. 227a) was casually mentioning some essential parts of a palaestra-gymnasium: the room for undressing; the roofed track, the open air track, the court; in his Laws (VI 3) he discussed the care of the landscaped grounds. Lycurgus, the statesman and orator of the late fourth century, the man who is credited with having raised the architectural level of public buildings at Athens to that of her long famous religious structures, is accredited as one of the first to have erected a gymnasium building (Pausan. I 29, 16) which could take its place with the other notable monuments of Attic architecture.*

Only a few traces are left of the early, informal palaestra-gymnasium. But remains of building foundations and colonnades dating from the Hellenistic Age, just after Lycurgus, have been uncovered in many places in the Greek world. In addition, there is very fortunately written evidence from the pen of a famous architect. For Vitruvius in a text book "On Architecture," written in Italy just before 27 B.C., explains the approved construction of a building and grounds which he calls "palaestra, Greek-style." The account provides a statement of terminology and principles which make it, in spite of its many omitted details, even today a priceless guide to the ruins of gymnasia at Olympia, Epidauros, Delos, and Athens.

Vitruvius, On Architecture V 11*

Although the building of a palaestra is not customary in Italy, I have decided to explain it (since its style of construction has been preserved) and to point out what was its plan according to the Greeks.

For a palaestra, colonnades should be constructed to form either a square or a rectangle and of such a size as to provide a walk around them two stades in length (1200 ft.). "Diaulos" is the Greek word for that distance. Three of these porticoes should be built of single depth; the fourth which faces south should be double so that rain drops can not reach the inner section when storms are accompanied by gales. In the three single porticoes spacious halls (exedrae) should be built with seats on which philosophers, rhetoricians, and other folk who enjoy intellectual pursuits may sit and carry on discussions. However in the double portico the divisions should be arranged as follows: in the centre an area for youth activities (ephebeum): a very large hall with seats, a third longer than it is wide. To the right (of the ephebeum) the punching bag area (coryceum); next beyond that, the area for applying powders (conisterium); opening off from the conisterium, at the corner of the portico, there should be located the place for cold bathing

which the Greeks call "loutron"; (returning) to the left of the ephebeum, the oil store-room (elaeothesium); next to the elaeothesium,
the cooling room (frigidarium) with a passageway leading into a
room adjoining the furnace (propnigeum) which should be located
in the corner of the portico. Next, on the inside, in the frigidarium
section, there should be located the vaulted sweating room, twice
as long as wide, which should have in one corner the domed
sweating chamber (Laconicum) of the same style as has been described above (Chap. X); in the corner opposite the Laconicum, a
place for hot bathing.

In the palaestra, colonnades should be built and divided off just
as I have described above.

On the outside, three porticoes should be laid out; one, as you
go out of the palaestra; two at the right and left (respectively)
equipped with a running course one stade long. Of these, the one
which faces north should be built double and extremely wide; each
of the other two, single, designed in such a way that they have
path-like borders in the sections which are next to the walls and in
those which are next to the columns. These borders are to be not
less than ten feet wide. The part between them is to be hollowed
out so that the step down from the borders to the level centre is one
and one half feet. The level centre should be at least twelve feet
wide. Thus persons, fully dressed, will not be crowded off by
those who are oiled and exercising. This kind of a portico is called "Xystos" by the Greeks and their athletes exercise in such in-
door tracks in winter time.

Open air promenades should be laid out next to the Xystos and
the double portico --the Greeks call such promenades, paradromides, but we (i.e. Romans) call them "Xysta". Athletes, when

the weather is fair in winter time, leave the Xystos and take their exercise in the paradromides. The promenades (or Xysta) should be so laid out that there are groves of plane trees between two porticoes and, among the trees, there should be constructed paths for walking and also some stopping places there paved with Signine (a type of concrete).*

Behind the Xystos there should be a stadium so designed that crowds in a wide space can view athletic contests.

This brings to a conclusion my description of buildings in a city and their proper arrangment.

156

VII. FROM THE FALL OF CORINTH TO THE AGE OF HADRIAN

(146 B.C.--A.D. 118)

A. Introduction

In 146, as a consequence of the capture of Corinth by the Roman Mummius, Greece fell under the control of the Roman state, a nation which had had no tradition of athletic festivals organized in the Greek manner. In fact, the ordinary citizens of Rome are said to have looked with actual disfavor at that time on the foreign system of physical training as practised by the Greeks.* Even so, such was the vigor of the Greek athletic spirit that this second loss of independence in government brought of itself no immediate change in Greek athletic pursuits. The evidence shows that the major festivals in Greece continued to be well-attended, with as many or perhaps more minor athletic festivals being celebrated than before; while in the Hellenized cities of more prosperous Asia the many newer festivals attracted competitors from far and near.

Much of this stability of Greek athletics was due to the sympathetic attitude and support of the Roman generals and magistrates. They seem early to have realized the political importance of the old athletic-religious festivals and perhaps to have acquired a taste for witnessing their athletic events. It was at the well-attended Isthmian Games of 196 B.C. that Flamininus had read his dramatic proclamation that the Romans were pronouncing Greece free to live under her own customs and laws, no longer subject to Macedonia (Appian <u>Rom</u>. <u>Hist</u>. IX 4). Mummius, fifty years later, though he had helped destroy that freedom for the Greeks, nevertheless went directly to the Olympic festival where his important votive offerings* were accepted by the impartial administrators of Olympia. The brutal Sulla (80 B.C.), in his unfortunate enthusiasm for Greek athletics, is reported to have transferred to Rome all of the athletic events (save the foot races)* of the 175th Olympic Festival (Appian <u>Civil</u> <u>Wars</u> I 99). Mark Antony's courteous letter, quoted below, shows his willingness as triumvir to cooperate with the Athletics Guild of Ephesus.

But in spite of this generally sympathetic attitude of Roman officials toward the Greek athletic system, the Greek people's capacity for athletics must have been in some measure adversely affected by the wars of the period. The levies and assessments weakened the older group financially, while military service consumed the strength and, in many cases, the lives of able young men.

Various accounts in the ancient writers testify to conditions in
Greece during the years just before and after the Corinth disaster
(Polyb. XXXVI 17; Livy XXXVIII 1-12; 30-35; Strabo VIII 4, 11;
IX 3, 8; Appian **Mithrid. Wars** chap. V ff; Plut. Sulla 12-27). No
doubt through sheer necessity more than one gymnasium site was
reduced to a ploughed field such as the one described by Dio Chrysostomus (Orat. VII 39), fictitiously placed in Euboea (A.D. 82-96)
but probably to be seen anywhere in Greece. Long before Pausanias' day in the last half of the second century after Christ, much of
the Greek countryside had become depopulated and many a town
sagged in ruins.*

Whether in the midst of this general economic decline the rank
and file of the Greek populace could still actively support the formal athletic getherings or participate in them in any numbers as
amateurs, or whether they were compelled to leave the field open
more and more to touring professionals from outside cannot be
exactly determined.* But with the numerous minor festivals mentioned in inscriptions, to say nothing of the major ones, new and
old, there was clearly need for many more competitors than the
few professionals whose names happen to be preserved because
they were spectacular victors. It is probably a safe conjecture
that the young folk of Greece, wars or no wars, did really support
their athletic games by personal participation. Contrary to what
has often been asserted, amateurs probably did not entirely dis-
appear from the athletics scene. Inscriptions from this era testify to the importance of gymnasia and to the courses of physical
training pursued by the general public in the various towns of
Greece. For example, one from the first century after Christ
(IG VII 1777) cites a gymnasium class of fifty-five adults at Thes-
piae in Boeotia, among them an artist, a tanner, and a man in public service.*

Not only did the spirit of Greek athletics remain alive in Greece
after the Roman conquest but it proved strong enough to invade Italy once more and this time to capture to some degree the interest
of the Roman public. Unlike Southern Italy and Sicily, Latium,
half-way up the western coast of the peninsula, had not become the
home of Greek colonies in the seventh and sixth centuries before
Christ. Indeed, in spite of its friendly attitude toward those
Greeks in Italy and its trade with them, this district with its city
of Rome seems to have clung to its old habits and mode of life.
It was not affected by the Hellenization of its southern neighbors.*
As has been seen in Chapters III and IV above, the people of Magna
Graecia as far north as Cumae felt an enthusiasm for athletic fes-
tivals in those early days which rivalled that of the homeland. But

in Rome the young folk down to the second century before Christ
and later received only an informal training in a type of sports
best suited to develop soldiers.* For their recreational gatherings
the Romans favored showy spectacles of chariot-racing and gladiatorial combats* and it was only after a considerable span of years
that any large segment of the population was won over to the Greek
idea of recreational athletics. In fact it seems to have required
considerable prodding from the high levels of administration before
the people could accept the imported athletic exhibits as even di-
verting entertainment unless well buttressed by other attractions;
and there is no evidence that Roman citizens themselves were as a
rule interested to enter them as competitors.

To Marcus Fulvius is given the credit of having introduced into
Rome in 186 B.C. the innovation of Greek athletic contests. His
general program of events was followed at least to the days of Livy
(59 B.C.--A.D. 27). That historian reports (XXXIX 22): "For
ten days, then, in a magnificent style Marcus Fulvius held the
games which he had vowed at the time of the war in Aetolia. Many
actors came over from Greece to honor him. Also a contest of
athletes was then, for the first time, put on as a show for the Romans; a hunt of lions and panthers was given, and the games, in
respect to their number and kind, were celebrated almost as in
these days." Suetonius' account of the games provided by Julius
Caesar in 45 B.C. (Caesar 39) shows the wide difference still ex-
isting, a century and a half later, between the traditional Greek
games and the new Roman notions of them: three days of athletic
contests were supplemented by many days of other sports, such as
combats with wild beasts, a naval battle, comedies, and exhibition
riding by the young folk.*

When the peaceful days of the Golden Age of Augustus at last
arrived, a new, more prosperous era began for Greek athletic history, both in Greece and in Italy, and continued far beyond the
first century. Perhaps because his student days at Apollonia had
given him a first-hand acquaintance with Greek ways, athletics,
Greek style, became one of Augustus' special interests (Suetonius
Octav. 45).* In a summary which Augustus made of his life-time
achievements he mentions as worthy of note: "Twice in my own
name I provided athletic games for the public with athletes summoned from everywhere; and the third time in the name of my
grandson" (Monumentum Ancyranum XXII).

Two major festivals and possibly more, frankly imitating Olympia and competing with it, were instituted by Augustus: one at the
new Nicopolis in Northwestern Greece and one at Naples. At

Olympia the equestrian events apparently recovered some of their
old glamour under imperial patronage. An inscription at Olympia
(Ol. Ins. 220) records that Tiberius (stepson and successor of Augustus) won a chariot race there in person probably in the last decade of the first century B.C.

The poet Vergil, though no devotee of athletic sports himself
(Horace Sat. V 49), followed the Homeric tradition and the taste of
his patron, Augustus. In his epic which was written to glorify the
origins of the Rome of Augustus, he devoted one full book to an account of athletic games. But a comparison of the athletic events
described in the Aeneid (Bk. V) with those in the Iliad (Chap. I a-
bove) will reveal that Vergil's games are contemporary Italian athletic contests. They are surprisingly like the new ActianGames at
Nicopolis.*

Emperors succeeding Augustus continued to sponsor Greek athletic games. For example, Domitian in A.D. 86 founded the Capitoline Games at Rome, destined to be popular for centuries. But
it is clear from the evidence that Greek athletics were never ad-
sorbed into the Roman way of life; they were the excuse for gathering at spectacles where people could watch professionals compete. When at last palaestras became common in Italy--Vitruvius
had begun his discussion of them (Chap. VI above) with the remark
that they were unusual in the Italy of his day (A.D. 14)--they were
used more by persons practising a type of health culture than as
training centers for competitive games.

B. Menodorus of Athens
(circa 150-103 B.C.)

Broken portions of an inscribed monument erected to an Athenian wrestler and pancratiast, Menodorus, have been found at Athens
and interpreted in the light of a better preserved companion monument at Delos (see Dow in Hesperia 4 [1935] 81-9). The text of the
elaborate inscriptions on both monuments, together with the realistically carved victory wreaths awarded at each festival, consti-
tutes a very important athletic document for a period not otherwise
illuminated by much primary evidence. This type of monument
with pictorial wreaths appears to have been a novelty introduced at
this time and to have remained popular throughout the second century B.C.

Menodorus, listed as a son of Gaius, but otherwise unknown,
was a "circuit champion" and his athletic triumphs in pancratium
and wrestling were won at no fewer than eighteen festivals listed
on the Athens monument. All of these, save one, were on the

mainland of Greece. On the Delos monument thirty-six wreaths
were listed for this same athlete.

C.   The Olympic Victors of 72-69 B.C.

Photius, composing in the ninth century after Christ a reader's
digest of two hundred and eighty books in his library (Bibliotheca)
has preserved a list of the Olympic victors of the 177th Olympiad.
Since this was only the second Olympiad after the scandalous trans-
fer of the Olympic Games to Rome by Sulla in 80 B.C., the festival
perhaps had not fully recovered from that blow to its prestige.

A comparison of this list with the two victor lists previously cited (Chaps. IV and VI) will show certain changes. On this occasion
the games seem to have been little more than a series of junior
contests, with a showy professional athlete or two in the senior
contests. The equestrian events add up to nothing more than a
local horse fair with Elean owners competing against each other.
Inscriptions found at Olympia (Ol. Ins. 191-210) and dating from the
first century B.C. confirm the evidence from Photius' list that
local Eleans in that epoch won the chariot races.

The one Roman, as is is to be expected, competed in the long distance race; for foot-racing is known to have been one of the few
athletic sports enthusiastically practised by the Romans. Since
two victors are mentioned for this same event, it is to be inferred
that no decision was reached and that the wreath was disposed of
according to the regulation to be quoted below in the account of the
Naples-Isolympia Games.

Photius Bibl. 97:*

I read as far as the 177th Olympiad (i.e. in Phlegon's
Olympic Victor List) in which Hypsicles of Sicyon was triple
victor: stade, diaulos, hoplite race.

Hypsicles of Sicyon, long race;

Gaius of Rome, long race;

Aristonumidas of Cos, pentathlon;

Isidorus of Alexandria, wrestling--Unthrown, Circuit-
champion;

Atyanas, son of Hippocrates of Adramyttium, junior boxing;

Sphodrias of Sicyon, pancratium;

Sosigenes, Asian, junior foot race (stade);

Apollophanes of Cyparissia, junior wrestling;

Soterichus of Elis, junior boxing;

Calas of Elis, junior pancratium;

Hecatomnus of Miletus, hoplite race; this man was wreathed three times at the same games: stade, double stade, hoplite races;

The horses of Aristolochus of Elis, the four-horse chariot race;

The horse of Hegemon of Elis, the horse-with-rider race;

The colts of the same man, the four-colt chariot race;

The colts of Cletias of Elis, the two-colt chariot race;

The colt of Callippus of Elis, the colt-with-rider race.

D. Mark Antony and the Athletics Guild at Ephesus

A letter written by Mark Antony, probably in 41 B.C.,* was, curiously enough, found copied on the back of a second century medical papyrus coming from Egypt. This document contains one of the earliest references to world-wide athletic victors organized into a synodos (corporation). Inscriptions quoted below will indicate how powerful these organizations became in the later centuries with their ex-athlete officials able to win for their members citizenships, free maintenance, club rooms, exemptions and large pensions. It was, no doubt, the pressure exerted by these clubs of professional athletes which was largely responsible for the dwindling importance of amateurs at the athletic festivals.

Letter of Mark Antony:* Marcus Antonius, Imperator, one of the Triumvirs for establishing the republic, to the Greek Commonalty of Asia *--Greetings.

The petition previously presented to me in Ephesus by my friend and gymnastics trainer, Marcus Antonius Artemidorus, acting in conjunction with Charopinus of Ephesus, eponymous priest of the world-wide guild of Hieronikai-Stephanitae* (i.e. winners in the sacred games and wearers of the wreath) that I write you immediately in regard to the other benefits and honors about which they asked me, to wit, exemptions from military service, public duties, billeting of troops, a truce during the festival (i.e. Ephesian), guarantee of personal safety, privilege of the purple--(this petition) I do cheerfully grant because of my friendship with Artemidorus and because I wish to oblige their priest with a view to the glorification and magnification of the guild.

And now when Artemidorus petitioned me again to ask that they might erect a bronze tablet and inscribe upon it the aforesaid privileges, I consented to the setting up of the tablet as requested, choosing to support Artemidorus in every way. You now have a confirmation in writing of these grants.

E. The Augustan Games at Naples

An inscription set up in Olympia, probably during the first century after Christ, advertised the famous Naples games. These Olympics of the West had been established by Augustus in A.D. 2* and their full title was an imposing one: The Italica-Romaia-Sebasta-Isolympia Games. But in inscriptions it was frequently shortened to "The Sebasta" or "Augustalia." "Isolympia," the last word of the full title, seems to have signified "equal to Olympia in type of contest and rules" rather than "equal in importance to Olympia." This is evident from another inscription where the same iso-prefix is applied to Pythian and Nemean games in such a way that its meaning is unmistakable (Dittenberger Syllog. Ins. Gr.³ 402.9): "the musical contest like the Pythian (IsoPythian); the athletic and horse racing events like the Nemean (IsoNemean) in age limits and in awards." So the few rules and regulations which can with some degree of certainty be read on the seven fragments remaining of this long inscription are as important for the history of the games at Olympia as they are for those at Naples. The age limits, remuneration, procedure in case of a tie, and rules governing the double registration are all spelled out clearly, as nowhere else in the sources for Greek athletics.

Olympia Inscription 56:   (2-3) To those taking part in the Italic-Roman-Augustan-Isolympic contest and festival: Greetings. ...

(11-27) Let no one younger than the seventeenth year take part in the Italic-Isolympic games; and from seventeen to twenty years of age let them take part in the junior athletic events, after that in the senior ones. ... An allowance should be provided for athletes for thirty days before the festival, so as to give all who are undergoing training a drachma for each day, beginning thirty days before the festival, but from the fifteenth day, two drachmas and a half for junior entrants and three drachmas for senior entrants.* Moreover, honors, according to Caesar's orders, for the boys a wreath of (--?) for the men, a wreath of wheat. ... In the case of contests where there are no competitors or in case of a tie let the supervisors of the games dedicate the wreaths in the gymnasium at Naples and let there be inscribed on them for what contest each was dedicated.

An athlete who wishes to register for training in the "Italica" should present himself in Naples no later than thirty days before the festival and should register with the supervisors of the games his father's name, his home country, and in what contest he chooses to try for a decision. Let the athletes also go to the gymnasium. ... Each of the athletes must be registered according to his official name, either in his father's name or in some other way established by law;* if not, let him be fined by the supervisors (-?-) drachmas; if he does not pay the fine, let him be flogged. If anyone arrives later than the appointed time let him announce to the supervisors the reason for his tardiness. Valid excuses are illness, pirates, shipwreck. ... Let anyone who wishes inform against him ... and if he is convicted let him be barred from the contest by the supervisors.*

F. Three Sister Athletes (A. D. 41-47)

A monument base found at Delphi yields an inscription of great interest since it is one of the few pieces of evidence, perhaps the only one, offering proof that women at times entered the major festivals of Greece as contestants. A father had set up the monument, with the approval of the officers at Delphi, for his three daughters who had won in races at Delphi, at Nemea, at the Isthmus, and at minor festivals. The years when the girls competed have been estimated to be from A.D. 41-47, during the reign of the Emperor Claudius.*

How active a role women played in Greek athletic contests has so far not been clearly determined. For some districts of Greece and for certain contests that role may have been more important than has been suspected.*

Syllog. Inscrip. Gr.[3] 802*: Hermesianax, son of Dionysius, of Tralles Caesarea, but also a citizen of both Athens and Delphi, makes this dedication to Pythian Apollo for his daughters who likewise obtained the same citizenships:

Tryphosa, who won at the Pythian games when they were directed by Antigonus and when they were directed by Cleomachidas, and at the next Isthmian games directed by Juventius Proclus, the one-lap race (200 yds.) coming in first among the girls;

Hedea, who won the chariot race in armor at the Isthmian games when they were directed by Cornelius Pulcher, and the one-lap race at the Nemean games directed by Antigonus and again at the Sicyonian games directed by Menoetas ...;

and Dionysia, who won the one-lap race at the Isthmian
games directed by Antigonus, and again at the Asclepieia in holy
Epidaurus under the direction of Nicoteles.

G. Roman Dislike of Greek Athletics

The emperor Nero's notorious tour of Greece (A.D. 66-68) must
have done little for the cause of Greek athletics at Rome (Suet.
Nero 23-26, 53; Dio Cass. LXII 63, 8-10). Time-honored dates of
festivals in Greece were changed to suit the convenience of Nero; a
musical competition and a chariot race with ten horses guided by
Nero himself were added to the conservative program of Olympia.
Nero, as competitor, was everywhere awarded a wreath of victory,
be it a musical or an agonistic contest. The report is that officials
were well paid for such a breach of rules. Finally, Nero as "circuit champion" re-entered Rome in a chariot driven by white horses and surrounded by 1808 wreaths of victory and heralded by a
Neronian version of the old chant of victory (see Chap. IV). This
was surely a sight which still further lowered the reputation of
Greek athletics among the thinking Roman public.

In the writings of the first century after Christ, there are many
expressions of dislike toward the whole system of Greek athletics.
Such remarks, however, also indicate, quite unintentionally, that
the practice of a Greek style of athletic training was becoming a-
larmingly popular.

Seneca, a Spanish-Roman, in the bitter days following his retirement as tutor to Nero (A.D. 62-65) wrote (Epist. 89, 18-19):

I do not include wrestling and the whole course of study
compounded of mud and oil in my Liberal Arts curriculum;
otherwise I should have to include perfumers, cooks, and the
others who cater to our senses. For what is there 'liberal'
about the students of these subjects who are ravenous takers of
emetics, whose bodies are fat while their minds are emaciated
and torpid? Or do we really think that this sort of training is
'liberal' for our young folk who used to be taught by our forefathers to hurl a javelin, standing erect, to cast a stake with a
twirl, to guide a horse, to handle weapons?

The young poet, Lucan, a relative of Seneca, probably expressed his own views when, in his epic on the Civil Wars, he had
Julius Caesar assert (Pharsalia VII 279): "You will meet an army
enlisted from the Greek gymnasia, listless because of their palaestra course and hardly able to bear arms."

The elder Pliny, a northern Italian, author of an encyclopedia which he wrote during the reign of Nero's successor, Vespasian, sarcastically comments (Nat. Hist. XXXV 13):

> The very fine sand from the Nile does not differ much really from the dust of Puteoli--not that it is left in position as a bed for the seas or as a barrier on which waves may break but it is used to take the military spirit out of our bodies in the exercises of the palaestra! ... and I will say no more on this subject or on the subject of earth used in wrestling ointments by use of which our young folk while developing their physical strength are losing their mental vigor.

The younger Pliny twenty-five years later was even more explicit (Epist. IV 22):

> I was present as an adviser at a hearing held by our excellent emperor (Trajan). Athletic games used to be held in Vienne (southern Gaul) as a result of someone's bequest. Trebonius Rufinus, a remarkable man and friend of mine, had had the games stopped and in fact abolished during his office as Duumvir. Charges were brought that he lacked authority to do this. He pleaded his own case eloquently and ably. ... When opinions were asked, Junius Mauricus, the most straightforward and blunt of all men, made the statement that athletic games should not be restored for the people of Vienne and added: "I wish they could be done away with at Rome." It was voted to abolish the games which had tainted the character of the Viennenses as ours have done to all of us.

Plutarch (A.D. 46-120), a Boeotian Greek, who was living in Rome for some years during this same period, gives what he considers as the reason underlying the Romans' prejudice against Greek physical training (Roman Questions 40):

> There are many other regulations for the general public expounded by the priest; one of which is the rule forbidding one to massage himself with oil when outdoors. For Romans looked with a very suspicious eye on the practice of an oil rub on dry skin (i.e. not in connection with bathing) and they are of the opinion that the gymnasium and the palaestra are more to blame than anything else for the slavishness and effeminacy of the Greeks; and that it was these which produced restless idleness in the cities, wrong use of leisure, immorality, and besides, the ruin of young men's physique with their naps, strolls, rhythmic exercises, and exact diets. Under this sort of regime the youth had, without realizing it, lapsed from the practise of arms and loved to be termed limber, athletic, handsome

persons rather than good hoplites and horsemen. To avoid such
changes in personality is difficult for those who strip off their
clothes out of doors. Persons who massage with oil indoors and
for therapeutic reasons, fall into no such errors.*

H. The Boxer Melancomas

In an age when the weaknesses of professional athletes were
often emphasized by authors and artists, Dio Chrysostomus (A. D.
40-112?) wrote a sketch of the professional boxer Melancomas,
who was said to have been a favorite of the Emperor Titus. In all
the literature of the intervening six hundred years since the odes of
Pindar no other such wholesome picture of an all-victorious athlete
has been found.

This essay is of great interest in the history of boxing. It clearly shows the complete change from the old days when foot work and
flashing fists gained a victory (see Theocritus, Chap. VI), to the
current practice of depending upon a stiff defence with the arms
which were encased in heavy wrappings and held out rigid for an
incredibly long time. The goal was to wear out the opponent without an exchange of blows.

At the time of Dio's visit the Olympic festival seems to have
been attracting crowds of visitors to witness its genuine athletic
performances. Apparently it had recovered entirely from the
shock of Nero's visit twenty years earlier--Pausanias records
(X 36, 9) that the officials expunged that Olympiad from the records.

Dio, Discourse 28*

We walked directly up from the harbor to see the athletes as if
we had made the whole trip on purpose to view the games. When
we reached the gymnasium we noticed some men running on the
course outside and there was a din from people cheering them on
while others were going through different kinds of exercises. We
didn't think it best to direct our attention to these but we kept
walking along to where we should see the largest crowd. At last
we noticed an extra large number standing near Hercules Hall with
persons continually joining the crowd while others kept going away
because they couldn't see. At first we tried to get a view by peer-
ing over the heads of others and we did just make out the head and

upstretched hands of the man who was taking his exercise. Then
little by little we wedged our way nearer. He proved to be a
young man, very tall and handsome, and his body appeared, as
one would expect, still taller and more handsome because of the
exercises. These he was performing brilliantly and with spirit so
that he seemed more like a person competing for a prize. When
he stopped exercising and the crowd withdrew we observed him
more intently. He was just like a carefully wrought statue; his
color was like tempered bronze.

After he had gone off I inquired of one of the bystanders, an old
man, who he was. And the man with a sad expression replied:
"Why this is Iatrocles, Melancomas' opponent, the only man who
deigned not to yield to Melancomas, at least until forced to do so.
But he could never accomplish anything of any consequence. He
was always defeated even though the match lasted sometimes for a
whole day. But lately he was discouraged so that at that last bout
at Naples Melancomas won a decision over this man quicker than
over anyone else. But now just see how much he thinks of himself
and in what a crowd he is taking his exercises. For my part I
really believe that he feels happy because of that poor fellow; and
it is not unreasonable that he does, for not only will he win this
wreath here but he knows that all the others are his too."

"What," I said, "is Melancomas dead?" For I knew him by
name though I had never seen him. "Yes, quite recently," he replied, "in fact his funeral was only three days ago."

"In what respect," I inquired, "did Melancomas differ from
this man, and the others--was it in size or in spirit?" "That
man," said he, "my good sir, excelled not only his opponents but
all men in courage and in size and more than that in beauty, too.

And if he had remained a private citizen and done nothing at all he
would have been widely acclaimed because of his looks, for he
attracted the eyes of all wherever he went, even of those who didn't
know who he was. Even so he didn't array himself in fine clothes
or try in any other way to be conspicuous but rather he tried to escape notice. However, when he removed his clothes nobody would
look at anyone else no matter how many boys or men were exercising. And though beauty usually brings laxness even to those who
possess it in moderation, such was his type that he was unusually
self-controlled. He put no great value on beauty but yet he took
care to preserve it even in such a dangerous profession as his.
While he was competing in boxing he was as free from marks as
anyone in the foot races; and yet he had been trained so hard and
was so superior to bodily exertion that he was able to hold his
hands extended in the air for two whole days continuously and no
one could see him letting them down or resting as people usually
do. He forced his opponents to give up first, not only before he
was struck himself, but before he struck them. For he did not
consider dealing blows and receiving wounds a mark of manliness
but rather a method characteristic of persons not possessing endurance and willing to get off easy. But holding out for a long
time, and not being overpowered by the weight of one's hands, and
not being short of breath, and not being overcome by heat, all this
he thought to be proof of a real man." "And he was right," I said,
interrupting ... "And besides," he continued, "he is the first man,
at least whom I know about, to be undefeated from the time when he
began to compete at the Pythian games, for he has carried off very
many and very important wreaths against opponents neither insig-
nificant nor few. And before he was a grown man he had even ex-
ceeded the record of his very famous father, that well-known

Melancomas from Caria who, in addition to winning other contests, was victorious at Olympia. For his father was not undefeated. In spite of being such a person, the fellow died miserably after having gone through every bit of the hard work of athletics but not yet having experienced any of the pleasures of life. He was so ambitious that even when he lay dying he inquired of his boyhood friend, Athenodorus the pancratiast, how many days of the games were left." And as he said this the old man started to cry. "Well," I interposed, "your grief is excusable because he was so near to you." "No, by the gods," he replied, "he was not connected with me at all; he wasn't a member of my family and I never trained him for I train one of the sons of the pancratiasts. But he was such a man that everybody who knew of him mourns for him." "Well, then, you mustn't call him miserable," I replied, "on the contrary, he was unusually fortunate and blessed. ... In my opinion the gods loved him exceedingly and especially by his death honored him so that he would experience no hardship." ... But as I was continuing he interrupted, "What you say is very comforting and I should certainly like to listen to you longer but it is time for me to give my boy his exercises and I am leaving."*

I. Scandals at Olympia

Although there are hints in the authors that at other festivals, particularly at the Isthmian (Dio Chrysost. Orat. 66, 5; Philostr. 45, see Chap. IX below), there were serious lapses in conduct which went unpunished, writers are unanimous in praising the managing directors of the Olympia Festival for their earnest attempt at all times to enforce their rules.

Pausanias mentions some outstanding cases of athletes who erred during the period under discussion in this chapter and the punishment meted out to them by the officials.

1. A Purchase of Victory (12 B.C.)

Pausan. V 21:* (16) It is a wonder in any case if a man has so little respect for the god of Olympia as to take or give a bribe

in the contests; it is an even greater wonder that one of the Eleans themselves has fallen so low. But it is said that the Elean
Damonicus did so fall at the hundred and ninety-second Festival
(12 B.C.) They say that collusion occured between Polyctor the
son of Damonicus and Sosander of Smyrna, of the same name as
his father; these were competitors for the wrestling prize of
wild-olive. Damonicus, it is alleged, being exceedingly ambitious that his son should win, bribed the father of Sosander.
(17)When the transaction became known, the umpires imposed a
fine, but instead of imposing it on the sons they directed their
anger against the fathers, for that they were the real sinners.
From this fine images were made.

2. A Coward Athlete (A.D. 25)

Pausan. V 21: (18) They say that a pancratiast of Alexandria, by
name Sarapion, at the two hundred and first Festival (A.D. 25)
was so afraid of his antagonists that on the day before the pancratium was to be called on he ran away. This is the only occasion on record where any man, not to say a man of Egypt, was
fined for cowardice.

3. The Late Apollonius (A.D. 93)

Pausan. V 21: (12)Afterwards others were fined by the Eleans, among
whom was an Alexandrian boxer at the two hundred and eighteenth Festival (A.D. 93). The name of the man fined was Apollonius. ... This man was the first Egyptian to be convicted by
the Eleans of a misdemeanor. It was not for giving or taking a
bribe that he was condemned, but for the following outrageous
conduct in connection with the games. (13)He did not arrive by
the prescribed time, and the Eleans, if they followed their rule*
had no option but to exclude him from the games. For his excuse, that he had been kept back among the Cyclades Islands by
contrary winds, was proved to be an untruth by Heracleides,
himself an Alexandrian by birth. He showed that Apollonius
was late because he had been picking up some money at the
Ionian games. (14)In these circumstances the Eleans shut out
from the games Apollonius with any other boxer who came after
the prescribed time, and let the crown go to Heracleides without a contest. Whereupon Apollonius put on his gloves for a
fight, rushed at Heracleides, and began to pummel him, though
he had already put the wild-olive on his head and had taken
refuge with the umpires. For this light-headed folly he was to
pay dearly (what amount Pausanias does not state).

J. Titus Flavius Archibius, Victor Incomparable*
(from A.D. 92)

An inscription, found in Naples, but composed by the Athletic Guild of Alexandrians, lists the alleged athletic victories of one of their high officers. Incidentally, it furnishes a roster of the principal athletic festivals of the late first century after Christ, and, by the order in which they are cited, gives some idea of their relative importance. Perhaps it was because of the support of this powerful athletics club that Titus Flavius as a youth had been able to tour the ancient world and collect first prizes at all the important wrestling and pancratium matches.

Inscriptions to be quoted in the next chapter will throw more light on the activities of these far-flung athletic corporations, already shown by Mark Antony's letter to have been well organized one hundred and fifty years before Archibius' day.*

I G XIV 747: To Fair Fortune. The loyal, patriotic, reverent, itinerant guild of Alexandrians hereby honors Titus Flavius Kyr--Archibius ... high priest for life of the Entire Portico, Athlete Incomparable, who won the senior pancratium at Olympia in the 220th and 221st Olympiad (A.D. 101 and 105). In Rome at the third celebration of the great Capitoline games (A.D. 94) held every four years, he won the wreath in the pancratium for beardless youths and at their fourth celebration (A.D. 98) won the senior pancratium and at their fifth (A.D. 102) won the senior pancratium and in their sixth (A.D. 106) likewise won the wreath in the senior pancratium--being the first of mankind to do so; at the Heraclean victory-games in ... held by the Emperor Nerva-Trajan-Caesar-Augustus-Germanicus-Dacicus he won the wreath in the senior pancratium; at the Pythian games he won the pancratium for beardless youths and in the next Pythiad the senior wrestling and pancratium and in the one following that he won the senior pancratium--being the first of mankind to do so; at the Nemean he won the junior pancratium (A.D. 92?) and three times successively the senior pancratium--the first of mankind to do so; at the Isthmian the senior pancratium; at the Actian games he won the wrestling for beardless youths, pancratium and ... at the next celebration the senior pancratium--the first of mankind to do so; at Naples the pancratium for beardless youths and twice in the next successive festivals the senior pancratium; ... wrestling for beardless youth, pancratium and twice in succession senior wrestling, pancratium ... senior pancratium--the first of mankind to do so; in the Balbilleia Games at Ephesus the senior

wrestling, boxing, pancratium--the first of mankind to do so,
and at the sacred four year festival at Antioch he won the
junior pancratium (where age limits are the same as in the
Actian games) and four years later the wrestling and boxing for
beardless youths and at the next the senior pancratium and at
the next likewise, the senior pancratium--the first of mankind
to do so; at the League of Asia Games in Smyrna the wrestling
and pancratium for beardless youths and at the sacred four year
games at Alexandria the pancratium for beardless youths (where
age limits are the same as in the Actian games), and after one
four year cycle the senior pancratium and at the next, likewise
the senior pancratium and at the next, the senior wrestling,
pancratium--the first of mankind to do so; he also has victories
at the Shield of Argos* and at very many other four year games
in wrestling and pancratium contests: junior, beardless, senior.

K.   Trajan and Some Athletic Problems of Bithynia

Pliny the Younger had expressed himself as less than enthusiastic over Greek athletics in the case of the suspended games at
Vienne. So when he was sent to northern Asia Minor in A.D. 111
as Imperial legate with the express commission to unsnarl the
tangled affairs of Bithynia, it is not surprising to find in his detailed reports to his emperor sympathetic recommendations about
aqueducts (Letter 90) but none about athletics.

Pliny's correspondence shows to what extent the businesslike
administration of Trajan interested itself in the welfare of professional athletes. It is not clear whether the payments (obsonia)
granted to victors in contests which carried the honor of a triumphal homecoming were made in cash or were in the form of "food
orders." At any rate they seem to have been a form of pension on
which the athletes set great store. The letters also indicate how
vocal professional athletes, through their guild spokesmen, had
become at the beginning of the second century after Christ.

Letters of Pliny, Book X

39. To the Emperor Trajan:...
    The citizens of Nicaea (in Bithynia) lost a gymnasium by fire
before my arrival and have begun to rebuild it with more and larger sections than it used to have and they have already spent quite
a sum which had been appropriated but there is a risk that the
building will be less than serviceable. The structure is poorly
planned and not compact. Besides, an architect (I do have to admit that he is a rival of the one who began the building) claims that

the walls, though twenty-two feet thick, cannot support the weight placed on them because their centre is stuffed with rubble and they are not even faced with brick work.

40. The Emperor Trajan to Pliny:...

The poor Greeks have a weakness for gymnasiums, so perhaps the citizens of Nicaea have attacked its construction too enthusiastically. But they will have to be satisfied with a gymnasium which is just large enough to suit their needs.

118. To the Emperor Trajan:...

The athletes, Sir, think that those rewards which you fixed for the games called "Iselastic" (i.e. games assuring a triumphal homecoming) should be paid starting with that day on which they receive the wreath of victory; they claim that the day when they are returned in triumph to their home town is not as important as the day when they won the victory by reason of which such a triumphal return is made possible. But I sign the payment "For Triumphal Return" so that I seriously doubt that the day of the victory should be considered rather than the day of the so-called "iselastic" entrance.*

Also the athletes are requesting maintenance payments (obsonia) for that contest which you have now made an "iselastic" one though their victory occurred before you made the change. Their argument is that if their payments are stopped for those victories won in games which used to be "iselastic" and which are no longer so, then it is fair that in the case of the newly-included "iselastic" games payments should be made them for victories won in them prior to their being listed. On this point I am more than doubtful whether there should be any retroactive reckoning or whether they should be given something which wasn't owed them at the time they did their winning. Therefore, please be so kind as to direct my deliberation, that is, to give me your own interpretation of your benefactions.

119. The Emperor Trajan to Pliny:...

The "Iselasticum," in my opinion, is due for the first time when some one makes an "iselastic" entrance into his home town. The maintenance allowances for those contests which at my pleasure became "iselastic" are not retroactive if such contests were not "iselastic" before. That the athletes have stopped receiving grants for their former victories in those games which I decided to take off the "iselastic" list is a point of no consequence. Though the status of the contests was changed no request was made for a refund of what they had previously received!

VIII. THE RENAISSANCE IN THE SECOND CENTURY

A. Introduction

The second century after Christ was a period of renaissance for
Greek athletics. Italy, the Greek mainland, Greek settlements in
Asia Minor and in Africa--all experienced a general revival of interest in athletic training, competitions, and athletic studies. Under the leadership of their Emperor Hadrian, an avowed admirer
of Greece and all things Greek, the Romans began to forget the
prejudices so freely expressed against the Greeks in the first century; and following the fashion set by their travel-minded emperor,
they visited Greece as tourists in ever-increasing numbers.

The four major festivals of Greece seem to have regained their
old brilliance with throngs of visitors present. Lucian, in the
middle of the century, pictures the scene at Olympia in his essay
"The Death of Peregrinus." He remarks (35) that he had attended
four Olympic festivals but found the fourth one the best of all.
Private donors, in this era, paid for many building projects in
Greece which added to the comfort of spectators at the games.
The most famous of such millionaire philanthropists was Herodes
Atticus. The list of his benefactions to his homeland included a re-
building of the stadia at Delphi and at Athens with a view to seating
the audience more comfortably and, greatest boon of all, an aque-
duct at Olympia. This brought pure water from springs high up in
the Alpheius valley to the parched crowds in the sultry heat of
August.* Lucian (Peregrinus 19) refers to the prevalence of fevers
when the old inefficient method of providing water was in use.

Under the Romans, whose thoroughness in organization and
whose respect for old customs is well attested, the administration
of Olympia was smoothly run under the usual Olympic Council
assisted by a corps of officials, whose total number was about
equal to those of earlier days. Inscriptions which contained the
names of officials, from the highest to the lowest, were regularly
inscribed--most thriftily--on fallen roof-tiles and those which
chance has preserved (Ol. Ins. 59-141) indicate that such records
were kept from 36 B.C. to A.D. 265. That the same time-
honored rules were still scrupulously observed may be inferred
from an inscription found on a statue base at Olympia which is
thought to belong to the early second century after Christ (Ol. Ins.
54). According to this a Tiberius Claudius Rufus of Smyrna had
sojourned at Olympia in a seemly fashion for the number of days
prescribed for residence before the contests and had "conscien-
tiously performed the training exercises under the eyes of the

Hellanodicae in accordance with the traditional custom of the games" (lines 5-10).

For those who would learn of the historical development of Greek athletics from its beginnings, the second century is an important one. Many of the learned men of that period, especially those whose origin was Asia Minor, followed the general trend towards antiquarianism and devoted time to a study of Greek athletics in the past. To mention only three, Phlegon, as we have seen (Chap. II), compiled a list of the Olympic victors from 776 B.C.; Lucian wrote a lively sketch of athletics in the days of Solon (Chap. III); Pausanias, who has been repeatedly quoted in chapters before this one, visited the sites of the four festivals to study their historical monuments and archives. Since these men and the other scholars who have also been cited had access to sources not now available, the surviving corpus of their writings, even though much of it is to be classed as secondary evidence, is a precious legacy preserving much information about earlier athletic practices. And of course these second century writers published a considerable amount on the problems of the athletics system of their own day.

The source material to be quoted below will mention definitely great numbers of athletic festivals, Greek style, held in every part of the Roman empire, and the many honors accorded the victors. But not so definite is its information about the nationality of contestants or the class of society to which they belonged. There are, however, sound reasons for believing that the athletic competitors in this era were still predominantly Greeks and of about the same class of society as athletes had always been ever since professionalism began to flourish in the fifth century B.C. The outstanding athletes whose names are known appear to have been the descendants of those Greeks who had left the mainland at the close of the fourth century B.C. (see Chap. VI) to take up residence in Asia Minor or Egypt. There is hardly a reference to a victor of Roman origin and very few from the Greek mainland are mentioned.

There is no mention of amateurs unless it be Galen's casual remark in the "Exhortation" about "cobblers, carpenters, builders" serving as opponents to arrogant professional athletes. But, as was true for the previous centuries, the athletes who happen to be mentioned in the source material which has come down to us represent only a tiny segment of the whole number of individuals who contested in the various festivals. A careful tabulation of the athletes who are now known by reason of recent archaeological findings might yield more precise information as to their provenience and social class.

In Hermopolis, Egypt, the home city of three of the star athletes to be mentioned in this chapter, there have been found papyri which contain fragments from the records of municipal administration.* There seems to be no reason why the picture they present may not safely be taken as being typical of life in the other cities shared by Greek colonists throughout the Greco-Roman world. In these Hermopolis papyri we find retired athletes who are city administrators, who are praised as civic benefactors, and are, besides, high officers in world-wide guilds. They are elected to membership in the Museum at Alexandria, travel widely, and on census lists proudly add "apog." (apo gymnasiou) to their names to indicate that they belong to the group who have had the advantage of an education in the Greek gymnasium.* Asclepiades, subject of the pompous inscription to be cited below, is revealed to have been, in his days of retirement, president of the local senate and a very respected leader in his community. Part of his report is preserved wherein he notifies the Senate of the run-down conditions of certain arable fields where he had been sent with two fellow senators on a personal tour of observation (C P Herm 7 col. 2).

These wealthy honored athlete citizens of Hermopolis who were important enough to receive cordial, approving letters from Roman emperors in answer to their requests about athletic benefits are a far different group from the athletes pictured by Galen in his often quoted denunciation of athletes and athletics. The good doctor surely could not have seriously meant that all professional athletes were men with "minds quenched in mire, unable to do accurate thinking, witless like dumb beasts." It is a significant indication of the true state of affairs that Galen admittedly addressed this exhortation not to regard athletics as a worthwhile vocation to a group of young men (probably in his native Asia Minor) who could, if they chose, reach success in medicine or in any one of the fine arts. Galen's worry evidently was that such talented young men would be tempted to follow the popular trend toward athletics and its quick returns.*

It seems probable that, under the Roman empire, Greek young folk of good families looked with increasing favor on a life-time career in athletics. All the more so since they had been shut out from many other possibilities of livelihood after the Romans assumed the responsibilities of defense and of the government of their fatherland. In such a profession their youth could be spent in a glorious whirl of highly remunerative performances. Dio Chrysostomus (Discourse LXVI 11) in the century before had alluded to a payment of five talents made to secure the services of athletes who had been victors at Olympia. Pliny's account of the "iselasticum" maintenance allowance has been cited (Chap. VII). In this era, when athletes reached retirement age they no longer needed to fear as Euripides' athletes (Chap. IV) did, that they would be cast away like "old cloaks." Athletic guilds could make room for many of them among all the major and minor officials needed for the management of their world-wide organizations. Besides, their own home cities were compelled to pay them assured pensions, accompanied by full exemptions to them and to their sons from burdensome public services.*

B. Galen on Gymnastic Exercises

Galen (A.D. 130-200), born in Pergamum, spent many years of his life studying medicine in Asia Minor and practising it in Alexandria and Rome. On more than one occasion he touched upon athletic matters in his hundreds of essays on medicine, philosophy, rhetoric, and grammar. A discussion of gymnastic exercises is to be found in his long Greek work on "Health" (better known by its Latin title "De Sanitate Tuenda"). These exercises, some of them the very same ones used informally by athletes like Milo in the sixth century B.C. (see Chapter III above), are presumably the ones in vogue in Galen's own day. They provide a glimpse of what went on behind the scenes in the way of training before a professional athlete like Melancomas or Archibius stepped forth to receive the acclaim of a festival audience.

As Gardiner aptly observes (GASF 509): "When we come to Galen, we seem to pass from the free and open atmosphere of the playing-field and country into the artificial air of the town gymnasium. The simple exercises of the earlier period ... have given place to a scientific system of physical training based on the teaching of generations of gymnastai. ... There is little in our modern systems of physical education which we will not find anticipated in Greek medical writings."

Maintenance of Health Bk. II*

8   (1) Wrestling, the pancratium, boxing, and running I term types of gymnastic exercises ... and in addition (2) the following: pitylisma, ecplethrisma, shadow-boxing, sparring, jumping, throwing the discus and the javelin, and exercising the body by the use of a punching bag, or a ball (small or large), or jumping weights ... .

9   (10) Now it is time to turn our consideration to the individual features of the several exercises, making clear from the first that also in these there are several differences. ... There are some exercises which exercise one vigorously, violently, or the opposite. (11) Now by "vigorous" exercise, I mean one performed with strength but without speed; and by "violent," one combining strength with speed. The word used may be either "strength" or "force"-- it makes no difference.

(12) Accordingly, digging is a vigorous and strong exercise, and likewise reining four horses at once is sufficiently vigorous but neither demands a quick motion. (13) In the same way, picking up any kind of heavy load and either standing still with it or walking forward a little--this and walking uphill belong to the vigorous sort of exercises. (14) In these exercises the members that move first, lift and support all the other parts of the body as though they were a load. And again, in this category belongs the exercise of climbing a rope hand over foot the way they train the boys to do in the palaestra for the purpose of making them vigorous. (15) Similarly, whoever takes hold of a rope or some high beam and hangs from it as long as he can is practising a strong and heavy exercise, but not a rapid one. (16) And so is the person who stretches out his arms with fists closed, straight in front of himself or up in the air, and holds them motionless as long as he can. A person who goes up to somebody and challenges that person to pull down both his arms, yet does not allow him to do so is, in a still better way, strengthening his muscles and sinews, since it is for these parts that all such exercises are especially adapted. And still more is he developing them if he clasps something heavy with the fingers of each hand (such as the jumping weights of the palaestra) and (17) holds his hands steady, stretched either straight forward or

up in the air. Then if he should challenge someone to pull his
hands down or even bend them by force, meantime keeping himself
motionless and rigid--bracing himself not only in his arms, but in
his legs and back--he will be getting no scant exercise for strengthening his limbs. ...

(19) These exercises, then, afford one a chance to display his
great strength and at the same time to secure practice. It also
invigorates and strengthens parts of the body if a person grasps
another around the waist with the hands and fingers interlocked
and then orders the man who is held to break loose; or else he may
himself be seized in that manner by another and try to get loose.
(20) Another exercise of similar type is as follows: a person
comes up beside some one who is bending forward, throws his
arms about his hips, and picks him up like a load, at the same
time swinging him upward and around; and it is still more of an
exercise if he bends over and straightens up while still holding the
man! (21) This is precisely the way for anyone to strengthen his
whole back. Similarly, persons strengthen themselves by thrusting chest against chest, each trying hard to push his opponent
backwards; or by hanging from someone's neck and trying to pull
him down.

(22) But such exercises can be taken without a palaestra or
deep dust in any well-trodden place by persons standing erect;
however, wrestling exercises which persons practice against each
other to develop strength require either deep dust or the palaestra.
(23) These are as follows: one man winds both his legs around
either one of his opponent's legs, then grapples hand to hand, trying to get a strong thrust against his opponent's neck with one
hand (whichever one is on the side of the leg-hold) and with the
other, resisting his opponent's free arm. (24) It might just be

possible also to get a hold about the top of his opponent's head and
force him to bend backwards. Such wrestling exercises develop
strength for each partner, as is also the case when one encircles a
leg of his opponent with his own or drives both of his legs against
both of his opponents. ...

(25) There are a thousand and one other such strengthening
exercises in the palaestra, in all of which the gymnastics trainer
(paidotribes) has both experience and practice; he is a different
person, of course, from the coach (gymnastes), just as the cook
is different from the doctor-- (26) a fact which seems again to be
coming into our consideration.* This has already been discussed
in that book which we entitled "Thrasybulus" and shall be mentioned
here only enough to suit the present discussion. First, let us go
clear through the different types of exercises. We have, then,
finished discussing the strengthening exercises.

10 (1) It is now time to pass on to the exercises which develop
speed apart from strength and force. These are running, shadow-
boxing, sparring, the exercise with the punching bag, and that with
the small ball, when it is carried on by players standing apart and
running to and fro. (2) Somewhat of this nature are ecplethrisma
and pitylisma. Ecplethrisma consists of running repeatedly, back
and forth the length of a plethron (about 100 ft.) without swerving,
but cutting a little off the length of each lap until finally one cuts
it down to a single step. Pitylisma consists of standing on tiptoe,
stretching one's arms upwards, and then moving them quickly,
bringing one forward and the other back. (3) Persons usually
practise this while standing near a wall, so that in case they lose
their balance they may right themselves easily by catching at the
wall. In this way those who are doing the exercise forget about

possible falls, and the exercise becomes safer.

(4) Quick motions, but yet not violent, are those executed in the
palaestra by rolling quickly on the ground, either with others or
alone. (5) It is possible to perform a quick exercise while standing erect, too, if persons crowd together in a group and each man
quickly changes places with his neighbor. (6) It is also possible to
practise a quick exercise with the legs alone by standing erect and
repeatedly jumping up with a backward kick,* or sometimes bringing forward each leg in turn. (7) And with the arms, too, it is
possible to practice a quick exercise of similar style, without holding jumping weights, if you shake them up and down with palms
open or closed, as you prefer, and increase their rate of speed.
Such are the quick exercises and they are classified as I have indicated.

(8) And now we come to the violent exercises. These, as has
been stated, combine strength and speed. Whatever exercises
have been classified as "strong" may all be used as violent exercises by accelerating their speed. (9) Not the least violent are
such exercises as digging, hurling the discus, and jumping continuously without intervals of rest. (10) Likewise, hurling any of
the heavy weapons without pausing and moving about quickly while
clad in heavy armor are both to be classed as violent exercises.
Of course, even those who are taking some exercise of this violent sort rest for a short time.

11 (1) All these, then, are varieties of exercises, and they
have the differences just enumerated. Besides, they vary in that
one exercises especially the hips or the hands or the legs, another
the whole back or only the chest or the lungs. (2) Walking and
running are exercises especially for the legs; sparring and shadow-

boxing for the hands; bending down and straightening up continuously are exercises for the hips, so is picking up some weight from
the ground, or supporting something in the hands for a long time.
(3) Some place jumping weights in front of them about six feet
apart, then stand between them, bend over and pick them up; with
the right hand they raise the weight on the left; with the left hand,
that on the right.   Then they replace each weight in its original
position, and repeat the performance many times in succession,
keeping their feet fixed in one position.   (4) This motion affords
greater exercise for the transverse sections of the back; the motion mentioned just above exercises the parts which run lengthwise.
Deep breathing in and out, audibly, is an exercise especially
adapted to the chest and lungs.

C.   Ancient Games of Ball

Ball-playing in its various forms was a type of athletic exercise
always popular with old and young in both ancient Greece and Rome.
Homer mentions the exhibition of ball tossing given by the dancing
Phaeacians (Odyss. VIII 370) and again Princess Nausicaa's ball
game on the seashore with her attendants, while waiting for the
clothes to dry (Odyss. VI 100).   Apollonius Rhodius in the 3rd
century B.C., imitating Homer, includes a similar mention of
ball playing in his "Argonautica" (IV 948 ff).   It is a curious fact,
however, that in the writers of the two great centuries of Greece,
the fifth and fourth B.C., no passages survive which explain any
kind of ball game and its paraphernalia.   But thanks to research-
minded scholars of the later Roman Empire we have numerous
bits of information which, when pieced together, provide considerable material for a picture of ancient ball games; and thanks to an
amazing archaeological find in 1922 we can actually see two Greek
ball games as carved by a sixth century B.C. Greek sculptor.*

The many statements, some of them obscure, made by ancient
lexicographers on the subject of ball games have been discussed
in various reference books.*   The longest and most illuminating
pieces of written evidence, all three from the end of the second
and the beginning of the third centuries after Christ, are quoted
here.

1. Pollux on Ball-Playing

Pollux, native of Naucratis, Egypt, was at one period of his
life a school teacher in Athens, at another, like Galen, an official
on the staff of the Emperor Commodus. In the dictionary of technical terms which he compiled he included the names and defini-
tions of the various types of ball games.

<u>Onomasticon</u> IX : (104) The various games of ball were called by
the names Episkyros, Phaininda, Aporrhaxis, and Urania.
Episkyros is also called Ephebike (young men's ball) and also
Epikoinos (crowd ball). It is played in this way: two opposing
sides, equal in number, draw a line between them with a stone
chip which they call <u>skyros</u>. Depositing the ball on this, each
side then draws on both sides a line behind the centre boundary;
the side which gets hold of the ball first hurls it over the heads
of the other side, whose business it is to intercept the ball in
motion and to throw it to the opposite side, until the one side
pushes the other beyond the back line.*

(105) Phaininda is so named either from Phainidos, its
originator, or from <u>phenakizein</u> (to cheat), because the player
gestures toward one person but throws the ball at another, thus
deceiving the one expecting it. The game with the small ball
which is called Harpastum from Harpazein (to seize) might very
likely resemble Phaeninda and someone might call the above the
"Game with the Soft Ball."

Apporrhaxis (bounce ball): one must strike the ball smart-
ly down to the ground, then meet its bounce and strike it back
with the hand; the number of bounces is counted.

(106) Urania (sky ball): the player bending backwards
tosses the ball up toward the sky; each of the other players
tries to leap up ahead of the rest and to seize it before it falls
to the ground, just as Homer seems to indicate was done among
the Phaeacians.

When they threw the ball against a wall, however, the
number of bounces back was counted. And the person who was
defeated was called "donkey" and had to do whatever was dic-
tated. The person winning was called "king" and did the dic-
tating.

2. Athenaeus on Ball-Playing

Athenaeus, also from Naucratis, in his encyclopaedic miscellany "Deipnosophistae" included remarks on ball playing which

amplify the data furnished by his fellow townsman and contemporary,
Pollux. His citations from writers of the fourth century B.C. hint
at what a large corpus of "ball game" literature has been lost.

Sophists at Dinner I*:   (14) The folliculus, as it was called (it was
   apparently a kind of ball), was invented by Atticus of Naples,
   trainer of Pompey the Great, as an aid in physical exercise.
   The ball-game now called harpastum was formerly called
   phaininda, which is the kind I like best of all.

   Great are the exertion and fatigue attendant upon contests
of ball-playing, and violent twisting and turning of the neck.
Hence Antiphanes (fl. 388 B.C.): "Damn me, what a pain I've
got in my neck!" He describes the game of phaininda thus:
(15) "He seized the ball and passed it with a laugh to one, while
the other player he dodged; from one he pushed it out of the way,
while he raised another player to his feet amid resounding shouts
of 'out of bounds,' 'too far,' 'right beside him,' 'over his head,'
'on the ground,' 'up in the air,' 'too short,' 'pass it back in the
scrimmage.'" The game was called phaeninda either from the
players shooting the ball or because, according to Juba the
Mauretanian (1st century B.C.), its inventor was the trainer
Phainestius. So Antiphanes: "You went to play phaeninda in
the gymnasium of Phainestius." Ball players also paid attention to graceful movement. Damoxenus (4th century B.C.), at
any rate, says: "A youngster, perhaps sixteen or seventeen
years old, was once playing ball. He came from Cos; that
island, it is plain, produces gods. Whenever he cast his eye
upon us seated there, as he caught or threw the ball, we shouted
together, 'what rhythm! what modesty of manner, what skill!'"

   Even Ctesibius, the philosopher of Chalcis, liked to play
ball and many of King Antigonus's friends would strip for a
game with him. Timocrates the Laconian wrote a treatise on
ball-playing.

   (19) Aristonicus of Carystus, Alexander's ball-player, was
made citizen by the Athenians because of his skill, and a statue
was erected to him.

   (20) Sophocles also played ball with great skill when he
produced the Nausicaa.

3. Galen on Ball-Playing

   The following essay by the learned Galen, though written from
a medical standpoint to emphasize the physical and mental benefits to be derived from the game with the small ball, contains in

addition much illuminating comment on other athletic exercises.

Exercise with the Small Ball*

(1) How beneficial to one's health gymnastic exercises are,
Epigenes, and how they should point the way to diet have been
satisfactorily discussed by the most eminent philosophers and
physicians of olden times*; but how much superior to other exercises are those with the small ball has never yet been adequately
set forth by former writers. I am justified then in sending you my
conclusions on it, both for criticism by you--you do have an experience in this game far above average--and for a circulation, advantageous to me, among your acquaintances.

Now I maintain that the best gymnastic exercises of all are
those which not only exercise the body but also bring delight to
the mind. The men who devised hunting with hounds and the other
kinds of hunting were philosophers and were accurately acquainted
with man's nature because they mixed into the toil of it, pleasure,
delight, rivalry. But in the game with the small ball there are
other special advantages which I shall now set forth.

(2) First, its convenience. At any rate, if you would call to
mind how much equipment and how much leisure is needed for all
phases of the chase but especially for hunting with dogs, you
would clearly understand that it is impossible for anyone taking
part in the government or working at the trades to participate in
such sports. ... But ball playing alone is so democratic that not
even the poorest person lacks equipment for it, for it takes no
nets, no weapons, no horses, no hunting dogs, but just a ball and
a small one* at that. So little does it interfere with a man's pursuits that it does not compel him to slight a single one of them for
its sake. And what could be more convenient than the sport which

admits persons of every station and of every walk in life?

That it is also the most satisfactory, all-around exercise you could best ascertain by looking into the nature and possibilities of every other exercise. You will find that one is violent, another mild, another exercises the lower more than the upper part of the body, or some special part, such as the hips, head, arms, or chest. But of the other exercises there is none that keeps in motion all parts of the body equally and that can be increased to a very violent one then toned down again to the mildest one; but exercise with the small ball is the only one to accomplish this. ... Whenever the players stand on opposite sides and work hard to prevent the man in the middle from snatching the ball away, then it becomes a very important and violent exercise requiring a mixture of numerous neck-holds and wrestling grips. The result is that the head and the neck are exercised by the neck-holds, while the sides, chest, and abdomen are exercised by the encircling clinches, the shoving, the bracing, and the other wrestling holds. In this manner of playing, too, the hips and the legs are put to a severe strain; for of course there is need of a firm footing in such exertion. The combination of running forwards and jumping sideways is no slight exercise for the legs--rather, if the truth be told, it is the only exercise that calls into play properly all the leg muscles. For as persons move forward, one set of tendons and muscles functions, as they dodge back another set functions more actively, and similarly even another set as they leap sideways. But whoever moves the legs in only one kind of motion, as is the case with runners, causes them to be unevenly and irregularly developed.

(3) Just as this exercise is a good one for the legs, so it is also an especially good one for the arms, since the players are

accustomed to catch the ball in all sorts of positions. The arms, too, will have the various muscles strained in varying degrees, at different times, due to the variety of catching positions.

That playing with the small ball trains the eye is readily understood, if you remember that a man will surely fail to catch the ball unless he accurately observes in advance where its weight will carry it. Besides, he sharpens his judgment by planning how not to let the ball slip and how to hinder his opponent. ... Mental exertion, alone, makes a person thin; but if it is combined with some physical exercise and rivalry ending in pleasure, it very greatly assists the body to health and the mind to intelligence. This is no unimportant advantage of an exercise, if it can help both the body and the mind toward the perfection innate in each.

It is not hard to see that ball-playing can train men in the two most important activities which the supreme laws of state obligate its generals to undertake ... to attack at the right moment ... and to guard accumulated plunder. Now, really, is there any other exercise so suited to training one either to guard his gains, or to retrieve his losses, or to foresee the plans of the enemy? I should be amazed if anybody could mention one. Most exercises have the very opposite effect, making people lazy, sleepy and dull. Even those who work at wrestling tend to become corpulent rather than intelligent; at any rate, many have grown so fat that they have a hard time of it to breathe. Such persons would be of no account as generals of a war or as administrators of imperial and civil affairs--a person would trust any mission to pigs sooner than to them.

Perhaps you may suppose that I am in favor of running and other weight-reducing exercises. Such is not the case. Lack of moderation I everywhere condemn, and I maintain that every art should practise moderation; whatever lacks moderation is not good. Therefore I do not approve of running, for it wears a man down thin and furnishes no training in bravery. Victory in battle comes not to the fleet of foot, but to those who are able to prevail in a hand-to-hand encounter; and therefore the Spartans did not become the most powerful people because of running fast but by boldly standing their ground. And if you would look at it from the standpoint of health, exercise is unhealthful exactly to the extent that it develops the parts of the body unequally. In running, some portions of the body are necessarily overtaxed, while others are absolutely idle. Neither of these conditions is beneficial but both nourish the seeds of disease and weaken one's strength.

(4) I heartily commend, then, any exercise which can provide physical health, harmonious development of the limbs, and mental excellence--and all of these are furnished one by the exercise with the small ball. It can benefit the mind in every way, and it trains evenly all parts of the body, thus contributing in the highest degree to health and thus effecting a symmetry in the physical condition-- for it causes no immoderate corpulence and no excessive thinness. Furthermore, it is adapted to actions requiring strength and is suitable to those which demand speed. Thus ball-playing, in its most strenuous form, is in no particular inferior to any other sport.

Let us consider it, on the other hand, in its mildest form. There are times when we need that type, either because of our age which is either not yet equal to severe exertion, or no longer so, or because we wish to relax from work or recuperate from an illness. Here too, it seems to me, this sport has a great advantage over any other; for there is no other that is so mild if you

wish to practise it mildly. The person who desires moderate, not
excessive exercise should move forward quietly at times and then
again remain in his place, without exerting himself very much,
and afterwards should enjoy a soft rub-down with oil and a hot bath.
This exercise is the gentlest of them all, so that it is very helpful
for a person needing rest, decidedly effective in restoring impaired
strength, and very beneficial for old and young alike.

Whatever exercises are more arduous than what I have just described, yet milder than the excessively strenuous kind, are practised by the use of the small ball. A person should know this if he
wishes to take part in the game correctly in every way. For if
ever because of some necessary work, as often happens to all of
us, you should overtax either the lower or the upper part of the
body, or merely the hands or the feet, you have the opportunity in
this game of resting the members previously wearied. The parts
which have previously remained altogether idle can then be
brought to a condition of exercise equal to that of the parts formerly exercised. Throwing the ball vigorously from a suitable distance, which requires little or no exertion on the part of the legs,
allows rest for the lower parts of the body but exercises the upper
parts rather strenuously. If a person quickly runs over a considerable area and throws occasionally, from a great distance, he
exercises the lower parts of the body more strenuously. But
quickness and speed in the game, without heavy exertion, serve
more to develop the lungs; vigorous action in tackling, throwing,
and catching, without speed to be sure, serves more to stretch
and to strengthen the body. If the vigorous action is at the same
time speedy, this will greatly exercise both the body and the
breathing, and will be the most violent of all exercises. How
much it is proper to strain or to relax in individual cases, can

not be put in writing--there is no telling the amount for each person; but in actual experience--the final authority for everything--one can discover and teach the correct amount. For the correct kind of exercise is not beneficial if it is spoiled by the amount used. This should be the concern of the gymnastics trainer (paidotribes) who is to be in charge of the exercises.

(5) And now let me bring this discussion to a conclusion. In stating the advantages of this exercise, I do not want to omit the one that it is free from the dangers which most other sports encounter. Sprints have killed many a man before now, by causing him to burst an important blood-vessel. Likewise, a loud shouting, violently sustained without a pause, has been the cause of very serious ills to many. Horseback riding of a strenuous sort has ruptured parts in the region of the kidneys, and has often brought injuries to the chest or sometimes to the spermatic passages, to say nothing of stumbling done by horses, because of which riders have oftentimes been pitched from their seat and instantly killed. So, too, jumping has injured many, and discus throwing, and bending exercises. What need is there even to mention the men from the wrestling school? They are all maimed no less than the Prayers of Homer, as that poet puts it: "Lame and wrinkled and eyes askance" (Iliad IX, 503). In this condition you can see the men from the wrestling school lame, wrenched, bruised, or altogether disabled in some part. If indeed, besides the advantages already mentioned, there is present in exercises with the small ball this advantage that they are free from danger, then from the standpoint of benefit derived, they must be the best exercises of all ever devised.

D. Galen on Athletics as a Profession

This is an attack on professional athletics, written in the last quarter of the second century by an outstanding member of the medical profession. However, it is very doubtful whether it should be taken as anything more than an exaggerated, sarcastic account of current tendencies in athletics.

For seven centuries, as has been seen, athletes and their practices had been under violent attack by men who owed their fame to professions other than athletics--by Xenophanes, the philosopher; by Euripides, the dramatist; by military leaders and others. It was now no longer an outcry against trends toward professionalism, for professionalism had come to stay.

The quarrel was about different methods of training and had been one of long-standing between professors of medicine and of athletics. It seems to have originated after Herodicus (Plato Republic III, 406) had added "Health Science" to the repertoire of an athletics trainer. Physicians had felt that coaches were therein treading on medical toes; they therefore countered with a new subject named "Hygiene" to be taught to athletes by a medically-accredited "Hygienist."*

Galen should be forgiven for the rabid tone of this essay for it was no doubt the out-pouring of a heart embittered by the exalted position of athletes at the courts of Marcus Aurelius and of Commodus where he served. As a competent doctor he must also have been irritated by the medical brashness of athletic coaches who imposed on their students unnatural rules for living.

What kind of answer coaches made to such charges from the doctors will be clearly seen in the selection to be quoted from Philostratus.

Exhortation to the Arts*

(9) Come now, young men, as many of you as have heard my words, enthusiastically set about the learning of an art, so that no swindler or impostor may ever mislead you and teach you a useless or degrading trade; you know, of course, that those pursuits which do not have the betterment of life as their ultimate aim are not arts. I am quite sure that you do realize about most pursuits, such as tumbling and whirling in a circle without becom-

ing dizzy, like the performances of Myrmecidas the Athenian and
of Callicrates the Spartan, that they are not arts at all.   But only
of athletics am I mistrustful, for I fear that this pursuit may trick
some young man into preferring it to some art--promising as it
does, physical strength, assuring glory with the crowd, and the
honor of daily grants of money from the public treasury exactly
like war heroes.   Therefore we had better investigate this occupation in advance; a person is easily deceived in what he has not previously investigated.

(11) Now all the blessings in nature can be divided into mental,
physical, and worldly, and no other variety can be thought of besides these.   That athletes have never shared in even a dream of
mental blessings is clear to anyone.   Why, in the first place, they
don't even know whether they have a mind, so far do they fall short
of understanding reason itself.   Always accumulating a quantity of
flesh and blood, they keep their minds quenched in mire, unable to
do any accurate thinking and witless like dumb beasts.

Perhaps then they would claim that athletes attain some of the
physical blessings.   I wonder, will they lay claim to the most
prized one--health?   But you could not find any other people in a
more dangerous physical condition, that is if we are to believe
Hippocrates when he said: "The perfect condition which these
fellows strive for is dangerous."   And indeed the following: "To
keep well avoid too much food, too little toil," is one of Hippocrates' apt statements which everyone likes.   But athletes practise
the reverse of this, overexerting, overstuffing, acting like fren-
zied Corybantes, and wholly disregarding the words of that man of
old.   For Hippocrates suggested as a health program: "Work,
food, drink, sleep, love--all in moderation."   Yet athletes toil

at their exercises every day beyond what is seemly and they cram
in their food by force, often prolonging their meal until midnight.

Corresponding to their other practices, their sleep is immoderate, too. For when people who lead normal lives are coming home
from work, hungry, then these athletes are just getting up from
sleep. Hence their mode of life resembles that of swine, but with
this exception, that swine do not overexercise or force themselves
to eat, whereas athletes do have just such experiences, and at
times their backs are torn by the laurel.

Now the ancient Hippocrates, in addition to what I quoted before,
also says this: "Excessive and sudden filling or emptying or warm-
ing or chilling or otherwise stirring the body is dangerous," and he
adds, "Any excess is hostile to nature." But athletes give no ear
to these utterances nor to the others which they transgress, though
he stated them clearly, but their practices are all directly the
opposite of his health doctrines. And for this reason I should say
that their regimen is a practice for illness not for health. This,
I think, was Hippocrates' belief when he said: "A permanently
healthy state is better than the unnatural condition of athletes."
By what he said not only did he plainly show that their mode of
life is contrary to nature but he did not call their condition (diathesis), a permanent state (hexis), thereby taking away from them
even the designating word by which all the ancients designate persons who are really well. For "hexis" means a lasting "diathesis"
and one hard to alter, whereas the perfect condition of athletes is
dangerous and subject to change. Because of being perfect it has
no room for further improvement, and because of being unable to
remain the __me, or even stationary, it has left only the down
grade. Such is their physical condition while competing, but

when they have retired it surely is much worse. Some die shortly, some live longer but do not reach old age.

Just as walls once shaken by siege engines readily collapse at some chance disaster, unable to resist an earthquake or any other shock a little serious, so athletes' bodies, unsound and weak from blows received in practice, are liable to injury at any chance incident. Eyes that have often been gouged are filled with rheum because they have no more power of resistance. Teeth repeatedly battered lose their hold in time and readily fall out. Joints that have been wrenched become weak in the face of any force from outside and every kind of break or fracture is easily started. From the standpoint of bodily health, then, it is evident that no other class is more miserable than the athletes. So one might reasonably assert that athletes were so named very aptly, the word athlete being derived from athlios (miserable), or else miserable persons (athlioi) deriving their name from the athlete, or else both in common, as it were, from one source are named from the word athliotes (misery).*

(12) But since we have now considered the greatest of physical blessings, namely health, let us pass to the rest. As for beauty, the facts of the case are that not only is natural beauty not improved a bit for athletes but that, actually, many with well-proportioned limbs are totally changed by the coaches, who take them in hand, overfatten them, and gorge them with flesh and blood. Even the faces of some the coaches render absolutely misshapen and ugly, especially of those who have practised the pancratium or boxing. When they have finally broken or twisted some of their limbs, or gouged out their eyes, then, I suppose, and then especially, the beauty resulting from athletics is clearly evident! This

is the good fortune their beauty meets with while they are well, but when they stop exercising their physical faculties go to ruin, and their limbs, all twisted as I said, are responsible for all kinds of deformity.

(13) But perhaps they will make no claim to any of the benefits mentioned, but will lay claim to strength. Yes, indeed, I am positive that they will assert that they are the strongest of all men. But, by the gods, what sort of strength will be theirs, and useful for what? For agricultural labors? No doubt they can very successfully dig or harvest or plow or do some other kind of farm work! But perhaps they have strength for warfare.* Summon again, I beg you, a Euripides who will hymn them thus: "Do men fight foes with discus held in hand?" (See Chap. IV above.) Or is it rather in regard to cold and heat that they are strong, rivalling Hercules himself, so that they, too, summer and winter alike go clad in a single skin, always without shoes, and sleeping on the ground under the open sky? Why, in all these respects they are weaker than newborn babes.

In what else, then, will they exhibit strength? Or for what cause will they be arrogant? Surely not, I suppose, merely because they are able to throw down, in a palaestra or stadium, such men as cobblers, carpenters, or builders.

But, by Zeus, that famous Milo from Crotona did once pick up one of the sacrificed bulls on his shoulders, and he carried it through the stadium. What surpassing witlessness not to realize even this much that a short while before, when the bull was alive, the animal's mind held up its own body and with much less exertion than Milo put forth; in fact the bull could even run as he held himself upright. Yet the bull's mind wasn't worth anything--just about like Milo's! ... [the rest of the story has been told in Chapter III above].

That athletic training is useless in the real business of life, I am quite sure has become clear. Furthermore, that athletes are not worth much even in the exercises which they practise, you would understand if I should tell you that well known fable which one of the not uninspired poets compiled and put into verse. It runs as follows: If Zeus willed that all living creatures should dwell in conditions of harmony and equality, so that the herald at Olympia would summon not only men to compete, but would allow all the animals, too, to come into the stadium, not one man, I think, would receive the crown. "For in the long distance race," to quote the poet, "the horse will be the best; in the stade race the hare will carry off the honors; in the diaulos the deer will be a champion. Of human beings not a one would count in the foot races. O nimble trained experts, O 'athlioi' (miserable) men!"

Nor would any of the descendants of Hercules* appear stronger than an elephant or a lion. "I think," continues the poet, "the bull will be awarded the wreath in boxing, and the ass, if he wishes, will bear away the prize in the kicking match. And in an elaborate history it will be recorded that an ass won the pancratium against full-grown men. 'Twas the twenty-first Olympiad, when victory came to Brayer!"*

This fable very pleasantly shows that athletic strength does not result from training devised by man. And yet if athletes are not superior to animals even in strength, what one of the other blessings would they attain?

(14) Then, too, if someone should claim that physical pleasure is the benefit derived, I should reply that athletes have no share

in this either while competing, or when retired, if, during the
time of their training they are involved in toil and troubles, and not
only exercise but even eat under compulsion; and if, when they
have arrived at the time to retire, they find themselves disabled in
nearly every part of their bodies.

Perhaps, then, it is because of collecting larger sums of money
than anyone else that athletes put on airs. And yet you can see for
yourselves that all of them are in debt, not only during that period
when they are competing, but also when they have quit training.
You could never find one solitary athlete wealthier than any rich
man's business agent picked at random. Nor is this getting rich
out of one's business the main consideration either; the important
thing is to master an art which will, as it were, swim out to safety
with you if you get shipwrecked.*

Therefore, if you are thinking, any of you, of preparing to make
money safely and honestly, you must train yourselves in a profession which can continue throughout life.

In the first class there are included medicine, oratory, music,
geometry, arithmetic, logic, astronomy, grammar, and law. Add
to these, if you wish, the plastic arts and drawing; for even if
these are executed by the hands, however, work in them does not
require the strength of youth.

One of these arts, then, a young man should take up and practise, unless his mind is utterly brutish; and preferably the best
art among them, which is, as we claim, medicine. This will be
proved next.

E. The Athletic Career of Asclepiades
(from A.D. 181 to 196)

An inscription found in Rome, written at the end of the second
century, provides eloquent testimony of what changes had taken

place in athletic competitors and competitions in the course of seven centuries.

At the beginning of the fifth century B. C. it was a Simonides, Bacchylides, Pindar, or some noted sculptor who recorded the brilliant athletic performances of sons of prominent citizens at festivals held chiefly on the mainland of Greece.   And in those days a simple statement of what, where, when was deemed sufficient. In 472 B.C. for example, Callias, a famous pancratiast, was content to have inscribed on the pedestal of his statue at Olympia along with the name of the sculptor, merely "Callias, an Athenian, son of Didymias--the pancratium" (Ol. Ins. 146). Yet from another source we know that his career included thirteen victories at the four major festivals and at the Panathenaea (I G I 419; Pausan. V 9, 3).   But our Asclepiades, acting as his own press agent, boasted of his victories the world over.   His words imply that it was a common occurrence for athletes of his day to win as the result of some deal or subterfuge.

One hundred years had passed since Archibius listed his victories at the various festivals (see Chap. VII); none of the games had been discontinued, it will be seen, but throughout the length and breadth of the Roman Empire they were still attracting athletes of note.

I G XIV 1102:* Of Marcus Aurelius Demetrius who is high-priest of the whole athletic meet, president for life of the athletic guild (i. e. Heracles), supervisor of the imperial baths, citizen of Alexandria, citizen of Hermopolis, pancratiast, circuit champion, wrestler extraordinary, I am the son: Marcus Aurelius Asclepiades, also called Hermodorus, eldest of the temple-wardens of the great Sarapis, high-priest of the whole athletic meet, president for life of the athletic guild, and supervisor of the imperial baths; citizen of Alexandria, Hermopolis, and Puteoli, senator of Naples, Elis, and Athens, and citizen and senator of many other cities; pancratiast, circuit-champion, the unvanquished, the unshakable, the unchallenged, winner in all the contests that I ever entered; neither challenging, nor finding any one who dared to offer a challenge to me, nor did I divide the wreath in a tie, nor decline, protest, or skip a contest, nor hold a contest according to royal favor nor get a victory in any newly-introduced festival; but in all the meets that I ever entered I won the wreath in the actual ring, and I was approved in all their preliminary trials.

I competed in three countries, Italy, Greece, and Asia; and I won the pancratium in all the following festivals: the

Olympia at Pisa in the 240th Olympiad (A.D. 181); the Pythia at
Delphi; the Isthmia twice; the Nemea twice (the second time by
withdrawal of my opponents); the games called the Shield of
Hera at Argos; the Capitolia in Rome twice (the second time by
withdrawal of my opponents after the first draw); the Eusebea at
Puteoli twice (the second time by the withdrawal of my opponents
after the second draw); the Sebasta at Naples twice (the second
time by the withdrawal of my opponents after the second draw);
the Actia at Nicopolis twice (the second time by the withdrawal
of my opponents); five festivals at Athens: Panathenaea, Olympia, Panhellenia, Hadriania twice; five festivals at Smyrna:
the Asiatic League twice (the second time by the withdrawal of
my opponents), likewise at Smyrna the Olympia and Hadriania
Olympia: at Pergamum the Augustea three times (the second
time by the withdrawal of my opponents from the outset, the
third time by their withdrawal after the first draw); at Ephesus
three times, in the Hadriania, Olympia, and Barbillea (by the
withdrawal of my opponents after the first draw); at Epidaurus
the Asclepiea; at Rhodes the Halea; at Sardis the Chrysanthina;
and numerous meets for cash prizes, including the Euryclea*
in Sparta, the Mantinia, and others.

Altogether I competed for six years, and retired from athletics at the age of twenty-five because of the dangers and jeal-
ousies that came my way. After I had been retired for some
time,* under compulsion I competed in my native city of Alexandria and won the pancratium in the sixth Olympiad (A.D. 196)
of the local Olympics.*

F. Some Correspondence of the Heracles Athletics Guild

An organization of athletes who had won the wreath at sacred
contests and who were worshippers of Heracles rose to great
prominence in Rome in the first century after Christ. They seem
to have had their headquarters in Sardis, originally, and their
membership quite certainly included the elite of the athletic world.
The two following letters explain how they secured new executive
buildings in Rome.

1. Letter from the Emperor Hadrian, A.D. 134

IG XIV 1054 b:*

Good luck! The Emperor Caesar Trajan Hadrian Augustus,
son of the deified Trajan Parthicus, grandson of the deified
Nerva, pontifex maximus, holding the tribunician power the
eighteenth time, consul the third time, father of his country,
to the xystic* guild of the athletes; the sacred and garlanded

victors who keep the cult of Heracles, greeting.

I shall order given to you the site which you desire and a building for keeping your society's records; and if you think necessary the doing over of the documents, that is for you to decide.

Given through your representative Ulpius Domesticus. Farewell.

Rome, May 5.

2. Letter from the Emperor Antoninus Pius, A.D. 143

IG XIV 1055 b:

Good luck! The Emperor Caesar Titus Aelius Hadrian Antoninus Augustus, son of the deified Hadrian, grandson of the deified Trajan Parthicus, descendant of the deified Nerva, pontifex maximus, holding the tribunician power the sixth time, imperator the second time, consul the third time, father of his country, to the xystic guild of the athletes, the sacred and garlanded victors who keep the cult of Heracles, greetings.

I have ordered a site assigned to you where you will put your cult objects and your records, near the baths erected by my deified grandfather, just in the spot where you gather for the Capitoline games.

Farewell. Given through your representative Ulpius Domesticus, the manager of my baths. Written from Rome, May 16, in the consulship of Torquatus and Herodes.

3. A Certificate of Membership (A.D. 194)

On a papyrus roll from Egypt there has come to light a notice sent round to members by the ex-athlete officers in charge of the Heracles Athletics Guild. The extracts from this important document which are quoted below give information about the details of business routine in such a guild. They also indicate the high esteem in which such organizations of professional athletes were held by those at the top of Rome's society.

The simple fact, told in ten lines, that Herminus, also known as Moron, a boxer from Hermopolis, had paid the required registration fee and was therefore a fellow member, is expanded into a document of eighty-two lines. Of these, thirty-two are used to include two thank-you letters written, one hundred and fifty years previously, to the club by the Emperor Claudius; a letter is also

included from the Emperor Vespasian assuring them that their
special privileges would be continued. The receipt itself is followed
by thirty-one lines which list officers of the club, with their full
names, citizenship, and athletic victories the world over. To all
this there was at some time prefixed at the top of the papyrus roll
a short abstract of its contents; there was joined to the main text
at the end another receipt, duly countersigned, which credits Herminus, acting as priest in the League of Asia Games, with having
paid a fee of fifty denarii.

The family of Herminus-Moros, it seems, had been an important one at Hermopolis for three generations, in the "gymnasium"
set. The facts are reported in the fragments of a census report
filed by Herminus at the census office (P Lond 935). Two of the
high officers who signed this membership certificate were retired
athletes of some fifty to sixty years of age--well-known through
information of their activities contained in inscriptions: Demetrius,
father of Asclepiades (see Asclepiades ins. above) and Demostratus Damas of Sardis (see note at end of "Asclepiades"). Both were
contemporaries of Galen and like him, popular in court circles.
In no way do they resemble those short-lived or broken down retired athletes pictured on Galen's pages (esp. Exhortation 11 above).

P Lond III 1178:

Lines 2-3: The sacred Hadrian-Antoninus-Septimius
itinerant xystic guild to members of the same guild--Greetings.

Lines 8-15: Tiberius Claudius Caesar Augustus Germani-
cus Sarmaticus, pontifex maximus, holding the tribunician
power the sixth time, consul-elect the fourth time, imperator
the twelfth time, father of his country, to the itinerant xystic
guild, Greetings.

I was happy to receive the gold wreath which you sent me
on the occasion of my victory over the Britons (i. e. A.D. 43),
furnishing proof as it does of your good-will toward me.

Given through your representatives Tiberius Claudius Her-
mas, Tiberius Claudius Cyrus, Dion son of Mikkalus of Antioch.
Farewell.

[Lines 16-30 contain Claudius' letter which thanked the club for
cooperating in games held in his honor (A.D. 47) by his friends
the King of Commagene and the King of Pontus.]

Lines 32-40: The Imperator Caesar Vespasian Augustus
to the sacred itinerant xystic guild of worshippers of Heracles,
Greetings.

Since I am aware of the sound reputation of you athletes and of your liking for honors I, too, propose to continue all the privileges which Claudius granted you upon request.   Farewell.

Lines 41-51: Know ye that Herminus also called Morus (moron), a boxer from Hermopolis, aged *-- is a fellow-member and that he has paid in full the complete registration fee required by law, one hundred denarii. I have put this in writing for your information. Farewell.

Done at Naples at the 49th celebration of the great four-year Sebasta-Italica-Romaia Games, in the second consulships of Lucius Septimus Severus Pertinax Augustus and of Clodius Septimius Albinus Caesar, 10 days before the Kalends of October (i.e. Sept. 22, A.D. 194); the following men being high priests of the Portico Complete, presidents for life and managers of the imperial bath: Marcus Aurelius Demostratus etc., etc. --(followed by names and honors of other officers).

IX. GREEK ATHLETICS IN THE LATER ROMAN EMPIRE

A. Introduction

What was the course of Greek athletics in the confusing days of the later Roman empire? Did the route lead steadily downward with a continued lowering of ethical standards, with a grosser and grosser type of athlete trained to satisfy a public whose taste had been debased by Roman gladiatorial combats? Some writers on the history of Greek athletics are of the opinion that such was the case. But the evidence found in a pair of essays by Galen and Philostratus and in the crude pictures on a mosaic floor does not seem to furnish a solid foundation for such sweeping conclusions. Especially since all three pieces of evidence are to be dated within the first generation of this two-century period and the two essays were written by men with a strong bias. It seems more reasonable to postpone a definite answer to these questions until someone has gathered all of the pertinent references to athletics from the large extant corpus of Christian and pagan literature written in the third and fourth centuries and studied them with reference to the information contained in the papyri, inscriptions, and works of art. Here only a bare sketch of the probabilities may be offered, supported by a few of the better-known passages from the ancient writers.

The third and fourth centuries were years of kaleidoscopic changes for the Roman world. Emperors of diverse social backgrounds succeeded one another, often in dizzying succession; the empire was divided East and West and the seat of government was transferred from one city to another until it finally came to rest in the new Constantinople; a generation could pass without a citizen of Rome who stayed at home setting eyes on his emperor.* Enemies from the north and east constantly threatened the empire so that armies were hurried from one harassed outpost to another. In the field of religion, too, all was conflict and change. The vigorously growing Christian Church, after many disheartening setbacks, was to emerge triumphant before the end of this period and exult in the dismantling of the old pagan temples and shrines.

But in the realm of athletics, conditions appear to have been stationary since writers mention no new and startling changes. Throughout the two centuries a wide variety of writers allude to the usual Greek athletic festivals, to professional athletes from Asia Minor and Africa, and to the special grants and honors accorded them. One is left with the general impression that athletic events moved along much as they had in the second century. Of course it is reasonable to suppose that the general economic, social, and moral conditions of the period cast their shadows on both athletes and spectators. Whether there was a falling off in attendance and in popularity for the original Olympia festival at Elis is not certain but is indicated since the records of officials suddenly cease in 265 (Chap. VIII, Intro.). Some of the other numerous "Olympia" festivals with their more lenient rules may have begun to eclipse the parent one.* In the third century, at any rate, victor athletes felt it necessary for clearness to specify the address of the renowned festival: Olympia-in-Pisa (Asclepiades, Chap. VIII E above; C P Herm 73, 2).

The type of intensive training to which a prospective athlete was subjected is described in detail by the third-century writer, Philostratus. Candid, full length portraits laid in tile mosaics as the decoration for a floor in Caracalla's Baths show what the students and their trainers looked like to a Roman craftsman.* The exaggerated corpulence and muscular build-up of the students leave their heads grotesquely small by comparison; their facial expressions are not improved by the glare of the sun in the open palaestra (indicated by the shadows); and they are obviously foreigners from the East.* Perhaps the artist's imagination, rather than the whole system of Greek athletics in the third century, should be blamed a little for the unattractiveness of these undergraduates in a School of Athletes. The portraits of alumni, busts only, used as another part of this floor design and the full-length figures of serious, bearded trainers, wrapped in cloaks, leave an impression of persons who are less dull-witted. This tallies better with information about important professional athletes to be found in inscriptions and papyri. At Tusculum a mosaic pavement was found, probably from the same century as the one in Caracalla's Baths. In this a series of robust, but more symmetrically developed athletes are pictured hard at practise for various events. But here again their appearance may be due to the artist who perhaps used copies of Greek statues as his models.*

Dio Cassius (155-240), a native of athletics-minded Bithynia, stopped his account of the festival career of the Emperor Elagabalus to enter on the historical record a bit of recent athletics gossip:

> Sardanapalus (i.e. Elagabalus) conducted games ... in which an Aurelius Helix covered himself with glory; he towered so far above his opponents that he had the desire to compete at Olympia in wrestling and in the pancratium on the same day--

he actually did win both of them at the Capitoline Games. But the officials at Elis begrudged him the honor for fear that he might become the "eighth Successor of Heracles"* as the saying goes. So they left out the summons for wrestlers to proceed to the stadium, although on the bulletin board this contest had been announced in writing. In Rome he did win both, a feat which no one else had achieved there (Rom. Hist. LXXX 10).

In the third century probably many a Christian bishop like Cyprian of Carthage (248) fulminated against the wickedness and folly of Greek athletic games and preached that: "True Christians must shun with eyes and ears those vapid, dangerous, tasteless performances"(De Spectaculis 8). Yet athletics was so much a part of the life about them that the Church fathers let fall many a metaphor implying a full knowledge on their part of athletics training and an appreciation of it.*

In 267 we find a Roman emperor, Gallienus, stating clearly that special exemptions should be granted even a descendant of famous athletes. In answer to the request of Ploution, an exathlete and at the time of the correspondence, the sponsor of Aelius Asclepiades of Hermopolis, he sent a gracious reply with such remarks as:

Why is it not fitting for the descendant of illustrious athletes to gain a request easily? So let Aelius Asclepiades, also called Neilus, be excused from all military services, public offices, liturgies that he may enjoy my generosity due to the athletic successes in his family line (C P Herm 119 verso 3).

One hundred years later the learned Emperor Julian, who dedicated his short reign as Augustus (361-3) to the restoration of various phases of the pagan religion, wrote an earnest plea to Corinth to release Argos, her poor neighbor, from paying a burdensome tax. Her Nemean festival, he remarked, should have made her exempt. If the letter (Epist. Juliani 35) is an authentic one, as seems probable, it provides interesting information about the continuity of the old athletic festivals on the mainland of Greece. Three festivals at Argos besides the Olympia and Delphi festival are mentioned in it as still keeping to their old athletics program; only Corinth,it seems, had succumbed to the un-Greek attraction of wild beast hunts in an amphitheatre and was spending the tax money wrung from Argos on the purchase of bears and panthers!

In Daphne, a suburb of Antioch, the famous Olympia athletics festival* seems to have suffered no eclipse in the fourth century

in spite of the strong forces of Christians in that city and their re-
lentless attacks on pagan temples. Libanius, it is true, leaves a
sketch for the years 332 to 383 of what he calls the "deterioration
in the games" in his home town of Antioch and this has been quoted
by some to prove the total collapse of athletics in the fourth century. But a careful evaluation of his charges set forth in his essay,
"On the Enlargement of the Plethron" (Orat. X), will show that what
he calls "deterioration" is merely "a wider public interest." In
his opinion the preliminary try-outs of athletes in the Testing Hall
(Plethron) had become too popular. He complains that they were
attended by throngs who were not well-groomed and not well-bred
enough to maintain a dignified silence during any phenomenal
wrestling hold--screaming in both Greek and Latin and even indulging in a whistle at times! The hours had had to be changed to suit
the convenience of the working classes, and the various uncles of
Libanius, acting as supervisors, had thought it best, twice, to
double the seating capacity of the hall--and still the place was too
small for those who wished to attend. All this convinced the sophist Libanius that the Antioch Olympia festival was slipping!*

A recommendation (cited in the Theodosian Code*) made by the
Emperors Valens, Gratian, Valentinian to the proconsul of Africa
and dated March 10, 376, gives evidence of the attitude of fourth
century emperors East and West toward athletic games: "We do
not begrudge, nay we encourage pursuits which please a people and
keep them happy; and so athletic contests shall be restored ..."
(15, 7, 3). Two athlete statue bases found in the gardens of St.
Peter-in-Chains, in Rome, bear inscriptions which still further
corroborate the impression that there was official sanction and
public approval of Greek athletic shows all through the fourth century. One of the statues was dedicated to Philumenos, a pancratiast from Lydia, by the same trio of emperors as above. Because
he had won in every pancratium contest, East and West, the emperors state that they deem him worthy of eternal fame and so have
set up his statue in the Guild Hall of Athletes in Rome. The inscription ends with the significant statement that not only the
Guild members were pleased at this mark of distinction for Philumenos but that all of the Roman people and the Senate heartily
approved of this dedication (CIL VI 10154 = Dessau 5164). The
second of the two statue bases of a still later date carries an inscription honoring "Joannes, a wrestler from Smyrna, Unthrown"
and was dedicated by the Emperors Valentinianus, Theodosius,
and Arcadius (384-392), who state that "Joannes deserves to be
conspicuous among all, hence this statue is set up"(CIL VI 10153 =
Dessau 5156).

The last Olympic victor of whom we happen to have record was an Armenian prince named Varaztad who won the boxing match in 385. As in the case of the strong men of the sixth century B. C. (Chap. III G above), his feats became legendary and he was acclaimed "by even the athletes at the Olympian Games" according to the fifth century Armenian historian, Moses of Chorene.* Also like some of those contestants, nine centuries earlier, he returned from the stadia to serve his country in public office. For the historian reports that Theodosius the Great, in 390, appointed him King of Armenia and that he reigned for four years.

The closing days of the famous Olympic festival are shrouded in almost as much obscurity as the days of its beginnings. A tradition is reported by two later writers that the final observance fell in the days of an Emperor Theodosius. Georgius Cedrenus, an historian of the eleventh century, places the end of the Olympic Games in the time of Theodosius the Great (392-5): "At this time the Olympic festival ceased which had been celebrated every four years. This festival began at the time when Manasses was King of the Jews and was maintained until the reign of Theodosius the Great."* A scholiast of about the same era as Cedrenus, in the course of a learned note explaining a passage of Lucian, put the closing years of the Olympic Games at a later date, in the time of Theodosius II (408-50). The scholiast's conventional story of the early origins of Olympia, similar to the accounts in Chapter II above, concludes with the statement: "The games lasted until the time of the younger Theodosius who was the son of Arcadius. When the temple of Zeus was burned the Elean festival and the Olympic games ceased" (Schol. ad Lucian. Rhet. praec. 9). Both of these statements, unadorned by details as they are, sound a bit like general conclusions arrived at in the absence of direct evidence. Perhaps no official mention of games after Theodosius was to be found in the sources. From this meager evidence, are we to believe, as some writers assert, that the Olympia festival, or any of the others, abruptly ended? We know that pagan literature survived for many years even after a sweeping edict of 408 which ordered all pagan temples and images destroyed. It seems more reasonable to conclude that both at Olympia and elsewhere in Greece athletic festivals very gradually declined in importance, not because of the stroke of a pen wielded by an emperor hostile to the idea of athletics--the records reveal no such individual-- but because of the inexorable march of events: barbarian invasions, economic decline, plagues, famines, and even earthquakes.

As late as the sixth century, we still hear of the athletic games at Antioch. Further, the revised Code of Justinian in 528 still carried on its pages an old law ascribed to Alexander Severus (about 227) which specified the conditions of exemption from costly services for a victor in the sacred festivals. Since the Emperor Justinian explained in his preface to this revision of the Code that its purpose was to present a new resumé of previous legislation in which outmoded, unnecessary laws were either to be revised or omitted altogether, it looks as though the learned committee of jurists in charge of revision had felt that this law was still needed. Victor athletes touring the festivals, their rewards, the problem of corruption were, then, problems still present one hundred years after Theodosius.

Cod. Justin. X 53: Concerning Athletes. Athletes are by custom excused from civil obligations if they give proof of themselves: that they have competed all of their life; that they have won no fewer than three wreaths at a sacred festival--at least one of them in Rome or in Ancient Greece; that they have won the wreath fairly without bribing or buying off their opponents.*

Probably the most remarkable feature of the athletics system of the Greeks was its vitality, a vitality which enabled it to weather centuries of changes in the social, political, and religious life of the world about it.   Tradition reports that someone named Heracles organized the first formal athletic games on the banks of the Alpheius in the thirteenth century B.C. From that dim, distant day until at least the end of the fourth century of the Christian era, Olympia, her daughter festivals, and all the distant cousins of those festivals exerted a powerful, unifying influence on ancient life. True, as early as the sixth century B.C., thoughtful critics had pronounced a verdict that Greek athletics was gravely ill; all through the centuries which followed, one and another of the thinking public had confirmed that diagnosis, making note of additional serious symptoms with their probable causes. But still the patient survived, active and popular, eventually reaching a merry old age. In fact, long after the foot hills of Mt. Parnassus, the slopes of Mt. Cronos, and the vale of Nemea ceased to reecho with the cheers of spectators, rooting for their favorite athletes, there could still be heard from behind the curtain which had fallen on the Roman empire the muffled cheers of enthusiastic spectators at athletic contests in far off Asia Minor.

B. Request for an Athlete's Pension
(A.D. 267)

Among the papyri fragments found at Hermopolis, Egypt, there are several formal applications made by athlete victors for the

payment of a maintenance grant legally due them. These requests
make use of the same formula and, as it appears, were filed in
triplicate. A fellow-citizen, often an ex-athlete, usually made the
application in behalf of the victor.

The drain on city treasuries must have been a serious one for
the papyri show that in the one year of 266-7 the public treasury of
Hermopolis paid for rewards to professional athletes more than
seven talents (Méautis, Hermopoule-la-Grande, 155). A strange
feature of these generous grants was that the victor entitled to
them could sell his maintenance rights to non-victor individuals.
A papyrus fragment of about 212 records a business transaction
whereby Turbon, victor twice in a boxing contest, sold his maintenance rights for one thousand drachmas to a senator of Antinoopolis who purchased them for his two sons to use (P Lond III,
1164 i, p. 165).

Corpus Papyr. Hermop. 54:* To the right excellent senate of Her-
    mopolis the Great, a city of ancient origin, first in religion and
    splendor,* from Aurelius Leucadius of Hermopolis, victor in the
    the sacred games, pancratiast, through his duly appointed spon-
    sor, Aurelius Appian, also called Demetrius, of Hermopolis:
    from the maintenance grant fund I hereby request to be sent to
    me from the city treasury because of the sacred iselastic games
    which I won and the wreath which I received: one talent, 2640
    drachmas--reckoned at the rate of 180 drachmas a month from
    the month of Phamenoth, tenth year (i. e. of the reign of Gallie-
    nus), to the thirtieth day of Mecheir, fourteenth year, total of
    forty eight months,* and for the victory I won first and for which
    I received a wreath in the sacred, iselastic, world-wide games
    in the city of Sidon, now a colony--games which have rules
    exactly like Olympia and carry the distinction of the purple--
    one talent, 450 drachmas--at the rate of 180 drachmas a month
    from the sixth day of Phamenoth, eleventh year, to Mecheir
    inclusive of the fourteenth year, a total of thirty five months
    and twenty five days. The total of my claim is two talents,
    three thousand and ninety drachmas of silver (2 tal. 3090 dr. of
    silver) with due respect to all the rights inherent in the city and
    in the senate. Dated, 14th year of the Emperor ... Gallienus
    ... month of Phamenoth.

C. A Wrestling Match from a Third-Century Novel

In a third-century novel, "Aethiopica," there is an account of
a wrestling match between a trained Greek athlete and a brute
giant. The author, Heliodorus of Phoenicia, appears to have been

as close an observer of wrestling contests as Theocritus, some five hundred years earlier, had been of boxing. The hero, Theagenes, was a little breathless from having just subdued a crazed bull; he was worried over the fact that he was to be sacrificed to the Sun God in a few moments, but true Greek that he was, he remembered to wrestle in form.*

Aethiopica X:*

(31) And when he had drawn near the gathering, Hydaspes looked at Theagenes and said to him in Greek:

"Stranger, you must compete with this man. The people so order."

"Let their will be done," answered Theagenes, "but what kind of a contest is it to be?"

"Wrestling," replied Hydaspes.

"Why not a contest with sword and armor?" he countered, "so that by achieving or suffering something worth while I may satisfy Chariclea. So far she has managed to preserve silence about our relations or else, as it seems, has absolutely rejected me."

"What you mean by bringing in the name of Chariclea," said Hydaspes, "you may perhaps know; but at any rate you must wrestle and not play the gladiator with a sword. It is not lawful to see blood spilt before the time of the sacrifice."

Then Theagenes, realizing that Hydaspes was worried lest his victim, Theagenes, be killed before the sacrifice, said:

"You do well to save me for the gods, who will, in fact, take care of me."

And with that he picked up a handful of dust and sprinkled it over his shoulders and arms, which were still wet with perspiration from his struggle with the bull; then shaking off what dust did not cling to him, he thrust out his hands with palms open, braced his feet firmly, flattened back his knees, arched his shoulders and back, and advanced his neck a little; drawing in his whole body, he stood aquiver for the wrestling holds. The Ethiopian laughed disdainfully as he surveyed him, and with gestures of derision he seemed to belittle his opponent. All at once he made a rush and clamped his arm like a cross bar around Theagenes' neck. Hearing the murmur of applause at this blow the giant swelled with pride and laughed dully. Theagenes, however, as one accustomed from youth up to gymnastic exercises with their oil massage, and thoroughly versed in Hermes' technique of gymnastics, decided to yield at first and test his opponent's power, not joining in close conflict with a bulk so prodigious and so savagely stirred, but by experience outwitting his rude strength. At once, accordingly, though a little shaken by the assault, he pretended to be hurt more than he was; and exposed the other side of his neck to attack. As the Ethiopian lunged a second time, Theagenes gave way and pretended that he was nearly thrown down on his face.

(32) Noticing this, and feeling encouraged, the Ethiopian unguardedly now was rushing for the third time, and with arm extended again was intending to throw his opponent. But Theagenes, stooped as he was, all at once ducked and escaped the giant's downward shove; then with his right hand Theagenes pinned his opponent's left arm and drew him forward; he was already staggering toward the ground because he had thrust his arm against empty air. Next, Theagenes, reaching up under the Ethiopian's armpits, encircled his back and with difficulty clasped his arms around his opponent's fat belly. Then Theagenes dislodged the man's feet by applying his heel violently, in quick succession against both of his opponent's ankle joints. He forced him to sink down on his knees, bestrode him, and with his feet forced down the giant's legs from below by the groin. The wrists by which the Ethiopian was support-

ing his chest off the ground he knocked out from under him. Finally, Theagenes brought his arms into a tight hold around the giant's
temples, pushed against his back and shoulders, forcing him to lie
prone upon the ground.

D.   Philostratus, Handbook for the Athletics Coach

Many manuals on the subject of Physical Training were current
in antiquity, but only one and that one a late compilation of the
third century, has survived. Even this manual but narrowly escaped oblivion, for the one imperfect manuscript of it was not discovered until 1844 near Constantinople. Its discoverer, Minoides
Mynas, after inaccurately editing it, selfishly withheld the manuscript from eager scholars. By a mere accident it was brought to
light at a sale of manuscripts in 1898. The author was a sophist
named Philostratus, probably the second of the three literary men
who bore that name. His reference in Chapter 46 to Helix, the
famous athlete who was the subject of Dio Cassius' anecdote, cited
above, gives the only clue to the date of this composition. This
would place it at sometime after the first quarter of the third century.

In the description of the "tetrad" system in vogue in his own
day, Philostratus is of course to be considered a reliable witness;
his idea that coaches should be, as it were, psychiatrists with considerable medical knowledge about anatomy and the laws of heredi-
ty probably reflects the newer tendencies of his day. But in the
account of the history of the games--the theory about the gradual
introduction of the various contests and the elaborate explanation
of the origin of each--Philostratus is no better and no worse than
his sources. Much that was pure fiction about the early days had
crept into records, even into those of Elis, in the thousand years
since the foot-race won by Coroebus had been listed as the first
entry of an Olympic Victor List.

Philostratus' clear definition of terms and description of athletic events make his manual a useful commentary for the whole of
this book.

On Gymnastics*

(1) I consider gymnastics a science, and one inferior to none of
the arts, so much so that monographs have been composed on the
subject for the benefit of those who may wish to take training.
Now the old system of gymnastics produced athletes like Milo,

Hipposthenes, Pulydamas, and Promachus, and Glaucus the son of
Demylus, and the men even before their time; Peleus, for instance,
and Theseus, and even Hercules. The system in the time of our
fathers saw men of less ability but still outstanding and noteworthy.
But the style of gymnastics now prevailing has caused such a change
in the condition of athletes that people in general feel disgust for
the persons who devote themselves to that pursuit.

(2) I propose now to explain the causes for this decadence and to
set down what I know about the subject, for the benefit of the coach
as well as for the student, and to speak in defence of Nature who
is being maligned just because the present athletes are far inferior
to those of the olden days; certainly the lions which Nature raises
now are not of any meaner variety and the physical appearance of
dogs, horses, and bulls is the same; as for her trees, the vines
are of the same quality, and the fig trees' gifts, and she has made
no changes in gold, silver, and stones, but just as she originally
planned them, she still produces them all of the same standard as
those of former times. But in the case of athletes, whatever good
qualities they once had, it was not Nature who was rushed from
the course: she still produces high-spirited, well-built, quick-
witted beings, for that is Nature's province--but the lack of sound
physical training and strenuous exercise have robbed Nature of
her own power. And how this has come about I shall explain later.
First, however, let us inquire into the origins of running, boxing,
wrestling, and such sports, and see how and when each began. In
every case, the records of Elis will be cited, for information on
such subjects should be given very accurately.

(3) Taking the contests as a whole, the light exercises are as follows: the one-stade (i.e., 600 ft.) race, the long-distance race,
the race in armor, and the two-stade race; the heavier exercises
are the pancratium, wrestling, and boxing. The pentathlon was a
combination of both heavy and light exercises; for wrestling and
discus-throwing are heavy, while javelin-throwing, jumping, and
running are light exercises. Before the time of Jason and Peleus,
the jump won a wreath by itself, and the discus separately, and a
javelin was enough for a victory in those days when the Argo was
afloat (i.e., one generation before the Trojan War). Telamon
was then the champion in discus-throwing, Lynceus in hurling the
javelin, and the sons of Boreas in running and jumping, in which
Peleus was second, but he stood supreme in wrestling. When
they were holding contests in Lemnos, they say that Jason to
please Peleus united the five exercises into one contest, and that
Peleus in this way obtained the victory and won also the reputation

of being the best soldier of his day, partly because of the valor
which he showed in battles but partly, too, because of his training
in the pentathlon, which resembles a battle in that a javelin is also
thrown in this contest.

(4) The origin of the long distance race was as follows: couriers
from Arcadia used to go back and forth in Greece with news about
war, and they were charged not to ride horseback but by their own
efforts to make the run. Running as many stades in one brief day
as are included in the long-distance race trained them as couriers
and afforded practice for war.

(5) The one-stade race was invented thus: when the people of Elis
were making the appointed sacrifice the offering was laid upon the
altar but fire was not for the moment applied to it. Runners were
lined up a stade away from the altar and a priest, torch in hand,
took his stand in front of it as umpire; the one who ran to the altar
first lighted the fire, and departed as an Olympic victor.

(6) When the people of Elis had sacrificed, then the ambassadors
of the Greeks, whoever happened to be there, were expected to
offer a sacrifice. That their approach might not be made without
ceremony, runners ran a stade away from the altar as though to
invite the Greeks, and back to the same place as though to announce
that "Hellas would be glad to come." So much then concerning the
origin of the two-stade race.

(7) Hoplite races are of high antiquity, especially the one at Nemea,
which is called the "armor race" as well as the "Horse race," and
is held in honor of Tydeus and his comrades, the famous seven.
The race in armor at Olympia was included, as the people of Elis
maintain, for the following reasons: Elis was engaged in a war
with the people of Dyme, a war so truceless that not even the Olympian games brought an armistice. When Elis was winning on the
day of the games, one of their hoplites is said to have run from the
battle into the contest field, bringing the good news of the victory.
The foregoing explanation is a credible one but I have heard the
same story about the Delphians, at the time when they were war-
ring against some of the cities of Phocis, and about the Argives,
when they were worn by continual warfare against the Lacedaemonians, and about the Corinthians, both when they were fighting in
the Peloponnesus itself and beyond the borders of the Isthmus.
But I have a different opinion about the hoplite race, for I agree
that it was devised originally because of war, but that it took its
place among the other contests to show that war was starting a-
gain, for the shield indicates that the armistice has ceased and
that arms are needed.. If you listen to the herald carefully, you

will see that before the whole throng he is proclaiming that the
games, the dispensers of prizes, are ceasing, and that the trumpet is sounding the war god's cry, summoning young men to arms.
This herald's cry also bids them take the oil and carry it away,
not for the purpose of anointing someone but as a sign that the a-
nointing has now ceased.

(8) The hoplite race at Plataea in Boeotia was considered the best
on account of the length of the run as well as on account of the armor which reached to the feet and protected the athlete as if he
were fighting, and because it was introduced on the occasion of a
brilliant deed, the struggle with the Persians, and because the
Greeks devised it against the barbarians, and especially, because
of the law in operation regarding contestants, a law which Plataea
passed long ago. A man once crowned by them as victor, should
he compete the second time, must furnish guarantors for his person: for such a man was sentenced to death, if he were defeated.

(9) Boxing was an invention of the Lacedaemonians, and was once
adopted by the barbarian Bebrycians, and Polydeuces was best at
it, wherefore the poets sang of him in this pursuit (see Chap. VI
B). The ancient Lacedaemonians started to box for the following
reason: they had no helmet and they did not think fighting beneath
one appropriate to their country's standards, but a shield served
the purpose of a helmet to the person who knew how to handle it.
Therefore, that they might ward off the blows from their faces,
and, if struck, they might endure the blows, they practiced boxing
and thus hardened their faces. As time went on, however, they
gave up boxing and the pancratium as well, deeming it dishonorable
to engage in the sort of contests which give an excuse for slander-
ers to accuse Sparta of having no spirit, if one man in the sport
should acknowledge defeat.

(10) The old style of boxing match used the following kind of an
outfit:* The four fingers were thrust into a band and they projec-
ted out so far as to form a fist when clenched, and they were held
together by a strap which ran down the forearm as a support. But
nowadays the style has changed; they tan the hides of very fat oxen
and make a sharp boxer's strap, one which will protrude from the
hand, while the thumb does not work with the fingers in striking,
so that the whole hand does not deal the blow. This is to avoid
giving serious injuries and for that reason pigskin straps are
ruled out of the contests because they consider that blows from
them are painful and hard to heal.

(11) That wrestling and the pancratium were devised for use in
war is shown, first, by the exploit at Marathon, which was fought

through in such a way by the Athenians as to appear nearly like
wrestling, and, secondly, by the affair at Thermopylae, when the
Lacedaemonians, after their swords and spears were broken,
worked havoc with their bare hands. Of all the sports the pancratium is prized the highest even though it is composed of uncompleted wrestling and uncompleted boxing--that is, it is the favorite
with all others except with the officials at Elis who rank wrestling
as a test of strength and a "grievous" contest, to use a poetic expression. This is not only because of the intricacy of the holds in
which the body must be lithe and agile, but also because three performances are given by the same contestants, that number of falls
being necessary. Though thinking it a shocking thing to give a
wreath of victory in the pancratium and boxing match without the
dust of an actual contest, they make an exception of wrestling.
Their regulation allows such a victory to be granted to curved and
distressful wrestling. Now it is clear to me why the law prescribes
this. For, although it is a trying ordeal to take part in the contests
at Olympia, it seems to be harder still to train for them. As for
the light exercises--the entrant in the long distance race will practice running eight or ten stades and the entrant in the pentathlon
will practise some one or other of the light exercises, the contestants in the other three races will practise the two-stade run or the
one-stade, or both. But there is nothing hard about any of this;
for the style of light exercises is the same whether men at Elis are
giving the training or others. But the athlete in the heavier exercises is trained by men at Elis, in the season of the year when the
sun at its hottest bakes the mud in the vale of Arcadia, and he has
to endure dust hotter than the sand of Ethiopia, and he must patiently bear up from noon on. And the most exhausting of these
exercises which are so strenuous is wrestling; for the boxer only
when the hour of contest comes will deal or receive injurious blows
and kick against someone's shins, but in training he will practise
only shadow-boxing; the entrant in the pancratium in the actual
contest will employ every form used in the pancratium but in training will employ now one, now another mode; whereas wrestling is
the same in the preliminary contest as it is in the real one; for
practice wrestling as well as the actual match gives proof of a
man's knowledge and of his ability, and wrestling is rightly called
curved, for it is so--even the upright kind. Wherefore the men at
Elis award the wreath to the one who is the best trained and solely
on those grounds.

[Chapters 12-13 contain a chronicle of the dates when each contest
was supposed to have been introduced at Olympia and a list of the
first victors in each.*]

(14) What now must one understand by the term gymnastics? How
else can it be regarded than as a science composed of the work of
the medical school and of the elementary wrestling school--more
complete than the latter and only a portion of the former? I shall
show how much of each it contains. How many different kinds of
wrestling holds there are, the paidotribai (i.e., wrestling school
teachers) will show, laying down the principles of the opportune
moment, the attack, the extent of practice, and the rules for defending oneself or for breaking through another's defence; and the
gymnastes (athletics coach), too, will instruct in these subjects an
athlete who is not yet acquainted with them. But there comes a
time when it is necessary to practice wrestling or the pancratium,
how to get out of range when the adversary obtains an advantage,
or how to parry a thrust, none of which a gymnastes would understand, unless he were well versed in the paidotribes' lore. Up to
this point the two professions are identical. But to purify the
humors, to get rid of excessive secretions, to soften the rigid
type, and to fatten or to alter in some particular, or to warm up
some portion of a person's frame, this all belongs to the science
of the gymnastes. The paidotribes either will not understand how
to do these things or if he should have some idea of them he will
probably use his knowledge with injurious effect on the boys, and
so harm the free coursing of their pure blood. By so much, then,
is the study of gymnastics more complete than that of the art outlined above (i.e., the paidotribes' art) and in addition it is related
to medical science in the following way; ailments such as those we
call catarrh, dropsy, consumption, and epilepsy physicians check
by irrigations, or by drinks of something, or by application of
poultices, but the science of gymnastics checks such complaints
by diet and massage. Yet if anyone suffers a fracture, a wound,
a dimming of the eyesight, or a dislocation of some joint, he should
refer it to a physician. Gymnastics is not concerned with this sort
of disability.

(15) From the above I think that I have shown how much gymnastics
is related to those two departments of knowledge (i.e., the paidotribes' art and medical science) and besides I think I see the following differences: A single individual does not master the whole
of medical science, but one man is a specialist in wounds, another
in fevers, another in eye troubles, and another may successfully
treat consumptives. Yet, since it is an important work to practice only a small part of the whole science, physicians are right
in claiming that they have a working knowledge of the whole subject. But nobody would proclaim all gymnastics as his field. For
the expert in foot racing will not understand the fine points of

wrestling or of competing in the pancratium; while the coach of the heavier exercises will be unfamiliar with the rest of the subject.

(16) The sphere of this science then is settled, but its origin is to be found in man's natural capacity to wrestle, to box, and to run upright. For there would be none of such activities unless this capacity were present to cause them. And just as iron and bronze provide the origin of the smith's art, and land and everything pertaining to land provide the origin of farming, and the fact that there is a sea, of seamanship, so let us consider that the science of gymnastics is born in a man and grows right along with him. The story goes that gymnastics did not exist before the time of Prometheus, but that he was the first to devise exercises for himself, which Hermes in turn used in training others, and marvelled at Prometheus for the invention, and that the wrestling school of Hermes was the first one; finally that, as to the men supposed to have been fashioned by Prometheus, they were men who practiced in the mud and who believed that they had been made by Prometheus because his sytem of gymnastics had made their bodies capable and well-knit.

(17) At the Pythian and at the Isthmian games and wherever else in the world there are games, the coach wraps himself in a cloak when he anoints the athlete, and no one will take it off from him without his consent, but at the Olympic games he does his directing unclad. This, in the opinion of some, is because the men of Elis wish to try out the coach at that season of the year to see whether he can endure exertion and heat; but according to the account at Elis, it is because of Pherenice, a woman of Rhodes, who was a daughter of the boxer Diagoras, and so masculine in appearance that at first the men of Elis thought her a man. At any rate she wrapped herself in a cloak at Olympia and trained her own son, Peisidorus. He was a boxer, too, right handy in that sport, and not a whit inferior to his grandfather. When they discovered the deception, they hesitated to put Pherenice to death out of regard for Diagoras and his children--for all the members of Pherenice's household were Olympic victors (see above Chap. IV B 2)--but a regulation was put in writing that the coach thereafter was to disrobe and was not to be accepted unquestioned.

(18) The coach there (i.e., at Olympia) has a strigil, too, perhaps for this reason: the athlete at Olympia must needs cover himself with dust from the wrestling ground and be sunburned; now in order that his physical condition may not be harmed by these circumstances, the strigil will serve to remind the athlete of oil and tell him to apply it so ungrudgingly that he may be scraped clean after

being rubbed with it. There is a story that a coach killed an athlete at Olympia with a sharpened strigil because he did not exert
himself to win. And I accept the story, for it is better for it to be
believed than not. So let the strigil serve as a sword to be used on
good-for-nothing athletes, and let the coach at the Olympic games
wield some authority higher than the Olympic judges.

(19) The Lacedaemonians used to insist that coaches know all about
military tactics, as they considered the contests a preliminary
training for war. This is to be expected from a country where
even the dance, the most carefree of pastimes in time of peace,
was correlated closely with things military; for the Lacedaemonians danced in such a way as though about to dodge a missile or to
hurl one, or to leap from the ground, and to handle a shield skill-
fully.

(20) Instances where coaches have spurred the athletes on to victory by admonishing, rebuking, threatening, or by subtly tricking
them, are many and too numerous to account, yet let me tell the
more significant ones.

[In Chapters 20-24, Philostratus rehearses the well-known
stories of Glaucus being told by a coach to "hit with the plough-
stroke"; of Arrichion, when about to give up, being reminded
"What a wonderful epitaph! 'He never failed at Olympia!'"; of
Promachus' victory inspired by an alleged message from his
girl which actually had been dreamed up by his coach; of Man-
drogenes spurred on by a letter sent to his mother by the coach
with the message: "If you should hear that your son is dead,
believe it: but if you should hear that your son is defeated,
don't believe it"; of Optatus who had a coach willing to go bond
for him.]

(25) Since a stream of such examples comes pouring out, and I am
confusing recent stories with ancient ones, let us turn rather to
the coach himself to see what sort of man is going to supervise
the athlete and what training he must have. The coach should not
be garrulous nor, on the other hand, untrained in speech, so that
the effectiveness of the training should not be lessened by talka-
tiveness nor the exercise appear too boorish from being performed
without correct speech. He should also be thoroughly grounded in
the subject of Physiognomy. I insist upon this for the following
reason: an Olympic judge or Pythian president of the games examines a junior athlete on such points as: whether he has a tribe and
native country, whether a father and family, whether he is free-
born or illegitimate, and in addition to all, whether he is young
and not beyond the age limit for boys. But whether he is self-

controlled or not, a hard drinker or an epicure, whether he is bold
or cowardly--the laws make no mention about such matters even if
it were possible to ascertain the facts. But a coach must understand these things thoroughly, as he is a sort of judge of the athlete's
nature. So let the coach be familiar with all marks of character in
the eyes by which are revealed the sluggish type, the high-strung
type, the indifferent type, the type of scant endurance, and the in-
temperate type. The characteristics of dark-eyed people are of
one kind, but of a different kind are those of persons with bright-
blue eyes or with gray-blue ones or with bloodshot eyes. Still different are the characteristics of those with eyes yellowish, spotted,
protruding, or sunken. By stars Nature has indicated the seasons,
but characters she has indicated by eyes. Again, as in sculpture,
the characteristics of parts of the body should be carefully noted
as follows, to see whether the ankle corresponds to the wrist,
whether the lower arm matches the lower part of the leg and the
upper arm, the thigh, and whether the hip corresponds to the
shoulders; the back should be compared with the belly and the
breast should project in a way similar to the buttocks, while the
head, the crowning feature of the whole, should be in proper proportion with all these other parts.

(26) At the close of these remarks, we should not get the impression that the topic of exercises is coming next, but the person to
take the exercises is to strip now and submit to an examination as
to his natural qualifications, that is, what they are, and of what
use. It does not seem reasonable, does it, that there is such consideration of dogs and of horses, on the part of men interested in
the chase and in horsemanship, that they do not use the same ones
for every purpose, nor even for every kind of hunting, but that they
use some dogs for one purpose, some for another, and some horses are trained to assist in hunting, others in battles, races or
drawing chariots, and not only this, but each one is employed according as he is best adapted to some side or trace of the chariot,
whereas in the case of men, with no examination, they are entered
in Olympic or Pythian games as contestants for the herald's announcement of victories such as a Hercules coveted. Accordingly,
I urge the coach to direct his attention toward the comparison of
parts of the body which I mentioned, but before the comparison
even, to study the characteristics of the body's humors.

(27) And yet there is something which takes precedence over this
which seemed important even to Lycurgus, the Spartan. For in
his efforts to furnish athlete-soldiers for Lacedaemon he decreed:
"The girls shall receive training in gymnastics and be allowed to

run in public contests." His purpose, of course, was to insure
them healthy childhood and the bearing of better offspring conse-
quent on improving their physique. Besides, when the girl came
to preside over her husband's house, she would not be afraid to
carry water or to grind grain, because she would be accustomed to
exercise from girlhood. And, then again, if she should be mated
to some fellow student who had taken gymnastics with her, she
would bear better children, tall, strong, and sound. And Lacedaemon became as great as she was in war, because marriages were
arranged on this basis.

(28) Now since it is best to begin with a man's birth, the coach
should proceed first, to investigate the parentage of the boy athlete,
that is, to see if the parents were married when young, both of
good stock, and free from diseases such as settle upon the nervous
system, the region of the eyes, and visit the ears, or internal organs. ... Young parents, if both are without blemish at the time
of the marriage, bestow strength upon the athlete, pure blood,
powerful frame and untainted humors as well as normal size, and
I would still further claim that they bestow also a wholesome
beauty.

(29) I have shown what kind of children good stock and youthful
parentage will produce; what is produced by parents more advanced
in years can be detected in the following way: the skin of such
persons is soft, the collar bones shaped like ladles, and the veins
are prominent as in people who have worked hard, their hips are
poorly built, and the muscular system is weak. As they take their
exercises there are plainer indications. For sluggish and raw-
blooded by reason of their cold nature, they perspire more from
the flat surfaces than from the convex and concave parts of the
body, and they derive no color from exertion unless we should
pump the perspiration from them, nor are they able to do any lifting but require pauses for rest. And they are exhausted by their
efforts out of proportion to their achievements. I consider this
type unsuitable for any contests--for virility is not their strong
point--but especially so for the pancratium and boxing, since with
tender skin such as theirs, they are susceptible to bruises and
wounds. These should, nevertheless, receive some training but
should be flattered by the coach since they need flattery in their
work and drill. In cases where only one parent seems to have
been past his prime, the failings will be similar, but less noticea-
ble.

(30) The condition of the blood will give proof of diseased constitu-
tions; it must needs appear turbid in that case and saturated with

bile. Such blood, even if it is once given a touch of life by the
coach, will change back and become turbid again; for poor origin
and difficulties go hand in hand. A protruding pharynx should give
some clue, and shoulder blades like wings, and a neck long and too
sunken at the point where the collar bones come together. And,
then, too, those whose chest is too narrow or unduly expansive
show a striking tendency to disease. For the former must have
their internal organs crowded together and cannot breathe nor bear
up well under the exercises and are continually tormented by poor
digestion; while the latter have organs that are heavy and loose,
their breathing is sluggish, they are slow in their attack and their
food will be less well assimilated because more of it will pass to
the intestine than to the nourishment of the body. So much for the
parentage of the contestants; now I must set forth the qualifications
required for entrants in each of the contests.

(31) The contestant in the pentathlon should be heavy rather than
light, and light rather than heavy, slender, of good build, tall, and
of muscle not excessive, but not light either. He should have legs
long, rather than in proportion to his body, and hips that are flexible and limber on account of bending backward in throwing the
spear and the discus, as well as on account of the jump. He will
jump with less jolting and will break nothing in his body, if he
gains a firm footing, letting his hips down gradually. His hands
should be long and his fingers also, for he will hurl the discus far
better if the discus rim is sped upwards from the hollow of his
hand because of the length of his fingers; and he will hurl the javelin with less trouble if his fingers do not barely reach the strap,
as will be the case if they are short.

(32) The best candidate for the long distance race should have a
powerful neck and shoulders just as for the pentathlon, but he
should have light, slender legs just like runners in the one-stade
race. For the latter by the aid of their hands stir their legs into
the quick run just as though their hands were wings. The runners
in the long distance race do this near the goal but the rest of the
time they move almost as if they were walking, holding up their
hands in front of them, wherefore they need stronger shoulders.

(33) No one any longer makes any distinction between the contestants for the hoplite, stade, and two-stade races, since Leonidas
of Rhodes (from 164 B.C.) won the three of them for four Olympiads; still we should distinguish between those entering for just one
of these and those who do so for all of them. The entrant in the
hoplite race should be furnished with a long waist, well-developed
shoulder, and a knee tilted upwards in order that, with these parts

holding it up, the shield may be carried easily. Of the runners in
the one-stade race (least strenuous of the sports), those of symmetrical build are very good, but better than these are those who are
not too tall but yet a bit too tall for their proportion; excessive
height lacks firmness, just like plants which have shot up high.
They should be solidly built, for the fundamental thing in running
well is to stand well. Their proportions should be as follows: the
legs should balance with the shoulders; the chest should be smaller
than normal and should contain sound inner organs; the knee must
be limber, the shank straight, hands above average in size; the
muscles should be only medium, for oversize muscles are fetters
to speed. Candidates for the two-stade race should be stronger
than those for the one stade, but lighter than those in the hoplite
race. Those who contest in all three of the races should be assembled from the best and should possess a combination of all the
qualifications which are needed in each single race. Do not consider that this is impossible for there have been runners such as
these even in our day.

(34) The boxer should have a long hand, strong forearm, and upper
arm not weak, powerful shoulders, and a long neck. As for the
wrists, thick ones deal heavier blows, whereas those less thick
are flexible and strike with ease. Well-built hips should support
him, for the forward thrust of the hands throws the body out of
balance unless it is held steady by firm hips. Thick calves, in my
opinion, are not adapted to any of the contests and least of all to
boxing; chiefly because they are especially slow in footwork against
their opponent's legs and are easily caught off guard by the opponent's footwork. The boxer should have straight shins of propor-
tionate size, while the thighs should be well-separated and set
wide apart. For the figure of the boxer is better adapted for attack
if the thighs do not come together. The best kind of a belly is one
which recedes, for such men are nimble and have good wind.
Still, a boxer derives some advantage from a belly, for it wards
off blows from the face when it projects into the path of the opponent's thrust.

(35) Let us pass to those aspiring to wrestle. The regulation
wrestler should be tall rather than in proportion, but built like
those in proportion, with neither a long neck, nor yet one set down
on the shoulders. The latter type of neck is not ill-adapted but
looks rather deformed than athletic, and to anyone who is familiar
with the two kinds of statues of Hercules, ever so much more pleas-
ing and godlike are the high-born types and those without short
necks. Well, then, the neck should stand up straight as in a
handsome horse that is conscious of its own worth, and the throat

should extend down to each collar bone. The shoulder blades
should be drawn together, and the tips of the shoulders erect, thus
lending to the wrestler size, nobility of aspect, force and superiority in wrestling. For such shoulders, even when the neck is bent
and twisted in wrestling, are splendid guards, giving the head the
support of the arms. A well-marked arm is an advantage in wrestling. By well-marked, I mean one of the following kind: broad
veins begin from the neck and throat, one on each side, and travelling across the shoulder run down to both hands, being prominent
both in the upper arm and forearm. Those in whom the veins are
on the surface and plainer to see than usual derive no strength
from them and such veins are unpleasant to look at, just like vari-
cose veins. But in those in whom they lie deep and swell but
slightly, they reveal a delicate, characteristic spirit about the
arms and give the arm of a person advancing in years a more
youthful appearance; while in those who are still young, such arms
tell that they are impetuous and very promising in wrestling. It
is better to have a chest which is prominent and curved outward,
for the organs rest in it as though in a firm well-shaped room and
they are excellent ones, strong, sound, showing spirit at the proper
time. But a chest is comely which is moderately prominent, hard,
all around, and marked with lines; for such a chest is strong and
flexible, and, though not so well adapted to wrestling, it is more
adapted to it than the other kinds. In my opinion, persons with
hollow, sunken chests should neither strip nor take exercises, for
they suffer from stomach trouble, and they have unsound organs,
and are short-winded. The belly should be drawn back in its lowest part--for this is a useless burden to the wrestler--and it
should be carried upon groins that are not hollow but well-rounded,
for such groins in every move which wrestling presents are adapted to press together, and being pressed together, will cause pain
to the opponent rather than suffer pain. A back is comely if it is
straight, but the slightly curved one is more suited to gymnastics
since it is more naturally adapted to the position in the ring--bent
over and leaning forward; but the back should not be marked by a
hollow spine for this will be lacking in marrow--and the vertebrae
there could be bent and unduly pressed in wrestling and could even
slip a little towards the inside--but let this be regarded rather as
a conjecture than as an actual fact. The hip, placed as an axis
for the members above and below it, should be supple, easy to
turn and to rotate. This is effected by its length and, by Zeus, by
its extraordinary fleshiness. The part below the hip should not be
without sufficient flesh nor yet with too much; the one is a sign of
weakness, the other of lack of exercise--but let it project marked-
ly, in a way suited to the prospective wrestler. Sides that are

flexible and that give mobility to the chest make men able to wrestle on the offensive or the defensive; for when they lie beneath their opponents, men such as these are hard to overpower and, on the other hand, they are no easy burden for the one who lies beneath them. Narrow buttocks are a sign of no strength, too wide ones of indolence, but those well-formed are suited to everything. A well-built thigh turned outwards combines strength with beauty and gives good support, and even better if the leg which supports it does not bow outward, and the thigh rests on a straight knee. Ankles which are not straight, but slanting inward, trip a person up, just as bases which are not straight spoil the balance of firmly fixed columns.

Such is the wrestler and such a man will be able to compete in the ground pancratium, though he will do less well in the handholds. Perfect contestants for the pancratium are those who are more adapted to wrestling than boxers, and more adapted to boxing than wrestlers.

(36) Notable athletes, too, are the "big little men." As such we may consider those who in size fall short of the men built foursquare in symmetry and yet have a body magnificently well-knit beyond what you would expect from their size; and all the more so if, instead of appearing emaciated, they show a tendency to corpulence. Wrestling, preferably, shows them off to advantage, for they are lithe, supple, impetuous, nimble, quick, and equable in tension. Many of the dangers and difficulties of wrestling they surmount by bracing themselves with their head as well as with their feet. But they are not good candidates for the pancratium and boxing as they are shorter than the one striking them and, in a ridiculous fashion, have to raise themselves from the ground, whenever they want to hit back. An example of the "great in little" type is found in the statues of Maro the wrestler whom Cilicia once produced. Persons from this group with a long trunk should be rejected, for, though they too can dodge in wrestling, they are of no account in getting the opponent down, because of the weight of their legs.

(37) The lion type, eagle type, splinter type, and what they call the bear type are the following kinds of athletes. Those resembling lions are strong in their chest and arms but rather lacking at the back. The eagle variety is similar in shape to these but thin in the groins just as the eagle is, when in an upright position. Both of these types appear daring, vehement, impetuous, but rather apt to lose heart at any failure, which should not occasion surprise, if we call to mind the characteristics of lions and eagles.

(38) The splinter type and the strap type are both slender with long
legs and very long arms but they differ from each other in important and unimportant particulars. For the former appear stiff,
sharply outlined, and well-articulated, whence I suppose their nick-
name was derived; but the latter are loosely put together and more
relaxed and limber and for these reasons are likened to leather
thongs. The former are bolder in the holds, while the strap-shaped
ones are more restrained and more dissembling.

(39) Of athletes with endurance, the types are hard, muscular, well-
defined waistline, animated expression--but more dependable
among these are the phlegmatic kind, for the choleric ones on account of the liveliness of their nature may even change to insanity.

(40) Those likened to bears are rotund, flexible, fleshy, not so
well articulated, and stooped over rather than straight, hard to
wrestle with, squirming out of holds and strong on dissembling.
And these breathe noisily just as bears do when they run.

(41) The equal-handed, or in other words, the ambidextrous, a
freak of nature seldom met with, are of unbreakable strength, hard
to guard against, and untiring; of course this gift of ambidexterity
gives them a better development of both sides of their body than
that of normal persons. Whence comes this last piece of information, I will now state. The Egyptian Mys, so I heard from my
elders, was not a very big fellow but he used to wrestle far in advance of scientific rules. He fell ill and his left side increased.
When he had given up the idea of competing again a dream came to
him to encourage him in his illness telling him that he would be
stronger in his impaired side than in the side that was sound and
unhurt. And the vision proved true, for he devised for his injured
side wrestling holds that were hard to resist. He became dangerous to his opponents and had the advantage from his illness, that
the side which troubled him became strong. This is a marvelous
story and should not be told as a usual occurrence, but as a single
instance, and should be regarded as a case where a god was working a miracle for mankind.

(42) Now on the topic of body proportions and whether this sort of
person or that sort is better, there are, of course, differences of
opinion about the fine points among those who have not examined
this topic thoughtfully, but as regards temperaments, however
many they are, it never has been denied and never would be, that
the best temperament is the warm, moist one. For, like costly
statues, it is made of pure and perfect material. Free from dregs,
impurities, and excessive secretions are those in whom the
stream of phlegm and gall is scanty. They hold out well in neces-

sary toil, are of good appetite, seldom ill, quickly recuperate from
any illnesses; they are easy to train and obedient to the rein in intricate gymnastic exercises because they are fortunate in their
temperament. Choleric athletes are warm but dry in temperament
and as unproductive of results to the coach as hot sands are to the
sower. They are strong, however, in presence of mind, for they
possess this in abundance. The phlegmatic type are slower in their
behaviour because of their frigidity. These should be trained with
much prodding, but the choleric slowly and with time out to breathe--
the former type is in need of a spur, the latter, a check rein. The
phlegmatic type need to be contracted by applying dust, the choleric
need to be moistened with oil.

(43) So much may be said concerning temperament according to
modern gymnastics. The old school did not even recognize such a
thing as temperament but trained only physical strength. By gymnastics the ancients meant physical exercise, of any kind whatso-
ever. Some took exercise by carrying heavy burdens, some by vying in speed with horses and hares, some by straightening or bending thick pieces of wrought iron, while some were yoked with
strong draught oxen, and others forced back the necks of bulls and
even of lions. These were the gymnastic exercises of men like
Polymestor, Glaucus, Alesias, and Pulydamas from Scotussa.
Tisander, the boxer from Naxos, used to swim around the promontories of the island, and his arms took him far out to sea; thereby
receiving exercise themselves and furnishing exercise for his
whole body. Rivers and springs provided baths for these men;
they trained themselves to sleep on the ground, some stretched out
on oxhides, while others mowed a bed for themselves from the
meadows. Barley cakes served as their food and unleavened bread
of unsifted wheat, and their meats were of the ox, the bull, the
goat, and the roe, and they anointed themselves richly with oil
from the wild olive and the oleaster. In this way they were free
from illnesses when training and grew old slowly. Some of them
used to compete for eight Olympiads (32 years), and others for
nine; they were excellent in hoplite service, and used to fight in
defence of the ramparts, not falling there either but meriting
prizes and trophies. They regarded war as training for gymnastics, gymnastics as training for war.

(44) But when the change set in, men were without military service instead of being soldiers; they became inactive instead of
active and soft instead of hard; the Sicilian style of dainty living
gained force; the sinews of the athletic fields were cut and all the
more so since the vogue of coddling was introduced into gymnastics. Medical science introduced this practice of coddling by

adopting the system which is good as an auxiliary in medicine, but
too effeminate for athletes. Moreover, the doctors taught habits of
indolence, especially the habit of sitting down before the period of
exercising, gorged with food so as to be heavier than loads carried
by an Egyptian or Libyan. Medical science, too, brought in luxurious chefs and caterers by whom men were made into epicures and
gluttons, treated to indigestible bread sprinkled with poppy seed;
contrary to regulations they made use of fish as a food discoursing
on the nature of fish from their habitat in the sea: saying that those
from swampy places are fat; that soft ones come from near cliffs;
fleshy ones from the deep sea; that seaweed produced thin ones
and other kinds of sea moss produced a tasteless kind. Still further, the doctors brought on the flesh of swine with wondrous tales
about it, directing that herds of swine down by the sea should be
considered injurious on account of the sea-garlic which grows in
abundance along the shore and coast, and prohibiting the use of
those near rivers because they may have fed on crabs. The only
kind of pigs they recommended eating, while training, were those
fattened on cornel berries and acorns.

(45) Such a luxurious mode of life also was a keen incentive to love,
and started violations of the law among athletes in regard to money,
and the buying and selling of victories. For some sell their chances
of renown, I suppose, because they are in great need, while others
buy a victory requiring no exertion, as a result of their soft living.
Laws against temple-robbers vent their wrath on those who steal
or mutilate a silver or gold votive offering, but the wreath of
Apollo or Poseidon, for which even the gods themselves competed
in mighty contests, it is safe to sell, safe to buy, with the exception that in Elis the olive is still inviolate in accordance with its
age-old glory. As for the rest of the contests, let me give one
instance out of many--it will tell the whole story. A boy won the
Isthmian wrestling contest by agreeing to pay three thousand drachmas to one of his opponents for the victory. When they had come
to the gymnasium the next day, his opponent asked for his money
but the boy claimed that he did not owe it, for his opponent had
tried not to let him win. As no settlement was reached, they re-
sorted to an oath and went to the Isthmian temple. The one who
had given away the victory swore in public that he had sold the
god's contest, bargaining it away for three thousand drachmas.
And he confessed this in a clear tone, not in any shamefaced
manner. The truer the story shows itself to be from having been
told before witnesses, the more sacrilegious and infamous it
appears. For he took this oath at the Isthmus before the face and
eyes of Greece. What then might not be happening in Ionia, and

in Asia, to disgrace the contests! I do not exonerate the coaches
of blame for this corruption. For they come to do their training
all provided with money, and they lend the athletes money at higher
rates of interest than traders braving the sea have to pay; in no
way do they look out for the good repute of the athletes but give
them advice in the buying and selling of victories, bearing in mind
their own gain, either by usurious loans to those who are buying,
or by failing in their obligations to those who have sold. So much
may be said, then, regarding this trafficking, for thinking only of
their own interests, coaches certainly do traffic in the merits of
their athletes.

(46) But they err also in the following particular: they strip and
train a boy athlete as if he were a grown man, bidding him to over-
load his stomach beforehand, and to walk away in the midst of his
training, and belch in hollow fashion. In this way just like poor
teachers, they rob the boy of his youthful liveliness and train him
in habits of indolence, procrastination, sluggishness, and in the
habit of being less daring than his youth would warrant. Motion
should be used here just as in the wrestling school. By motion,
however, I mean the passive sort, applied to the legs in a soft
massage movement and to the arms with hard kneading. The boy
should also clap, since exercises like these are more enlivening.
The Phoenician Helix took this sort of training not only as a boy,
but when grown to manhood, and he was more wonderful than words
in comparison with all of those who I know are now cultivating
this fad of relaxation (see Dio Cass. LXXX 10, cited in the Introduction, above).

(47) The tetrad system, as practised by the coaches, should not be
considered at all, for it is because of this that the whole system of
gymnastics has gone to rack and ruin. By the term "tetrad system"
I would have you understand a cycle of four days, in which something different is done each day. The first day's work is to prepare the athlete; the second to exercise him intensely; the third,
to relax him, and the fourth to exercise him moderately. The one
to prepare him is an energetic, short, quick exercise designed to
arouse the athlete and to get him ready for the coming exertion;
the intensive is an unmerciful test of the latent power in his constitution; the relaxing one is a time for reviving his activity in a
reasonable way; while the fourth, the moderate exercise, consists
in dodging one's adversary and not letting go when the latter is
trying to escape. While in routine fashion they are going through
this system and are repeating these cycles of four days, they are
absolutely ignoring the personal element, the condition of the
athlete himself. For it is the food which is hurting him, the wine,

the furtive lunching, worry, exhaustion, and many another factor, voluntary and involuntary. How shall we cure this fellow by our system of tetrads and routine assignments?

[In Chapters 48-53, hints are given for detecting persons of faulty living habits; corrective exercises are suggested.]

(54) An argument against the "tetrad system" which I rejected, is the serious mistake in regard to Gerenus, the wrestler, whose gravestone stands in Athens on the right hand side of the road to Eleusis. This man was a native of Naucratis, and one of the champion wrestlers as is shown by the victories which he won in contests. He had had the good fortune of winning at Olympia; on the third day afterwards, because he was drinking to his victory, entertaining his friends, indulging in rich food contrary to his usual habit, he was thrown off from the usual path of sleep. Now, the next day he reported at the Gymnasium as usual, though he admitted to the coach that he was upset and had something the matter with him. But the coach was irritated, listened to him angrily, and was severe on the man for breaking training and interfering with the "four day" plan, until through sheer ignorance he caused the death of the athlete right in the midst of his exercise, by not prescribing the exercises which he should have seen were necessary, even if the man had kept still. With a tetrad system like this and a coach so untrained and untutored, extraordinary mishaps follow. Isn't it really a serious mishap to lose such an athlete as Gerenus from the stadium? Furthermore, what will those who are so enthusiastic over the tetrad system do with it when they come to Olympia? Down there is the dust which I have pictured, the prescribed gymnastic exercises, and the Olympic judges exercise athletes not according to previous instructions, but with everything improvised according to the occasion, even threatening the coach with a whipping, if he should do anything contrary to their orders. Their commands are unalterable, and it is possible to exclude from the Olympic games any who refuse obedience. So much then for my opinion of the tetrad system; and if my advice is followed we shall prove that gymnastics is a science, we shall strengthen the athletes, and athletic fields will become rejuvenated under a system of training which is beneficial.

(55) The jumping weight is an invention of the pentathletes, and was invented for use in jumping, from which it derives its name. For the rules regard jumping as one of the more difficult exercises, and allow the jumper to be spurred on by the flute and they give him wings by means of this jumping weight; it is a sure guide for the hands and brings the feet firmly to the ground in good form.

The rules show of what value this latter point is, for they do not
permit the jump to be measured unless the footprints are just
right. The long jumping weights afford exercise for the shoulders
and hands, the round ones for the fingers as well. These should be
used by light athletes as well as heavy, in all exercises, except
during those for relaxing.

(56) Now of the kinds of dust, that from clay is adapted to cleaning
and to restoring normal condition to those with an excess of secretions; brick dust serves to open the closed pores and to bring out
perspiration, while that from asphalt warms the chilled frame.
Black and yellow dust are both from the earth and are useful in
massaging and building up the system, but yellow dust also adds
lustre and is prettier to look at, that is, on a noble, well-developed
body. The dust should be scattered over the body with the wrist
supple and with the fingers sprinkling it spread apart, rather than
throwing it against the person, so that the powder-like dust may
settle down upon the athlete.

(57) A punching bag should, it is true, be hung up for the boxers,
but far more important is it that there should be one for those who
practice the pancratium. The one for boxers should be light, since
the boxers' hands are to be trained only in opportune striking; the
one for the use of the pancratiasts should be heavier and larger,
so that they may be trained to keep their footing at the sudden onset of the bag, and again that their shoulders and fingers may be
exercised by striking against something that offers resistance.
The athlete should dash his head against the bag, and should practice all the positions of the upright variety of the pancratium.

(58) Some people take sun baths without discretion, all doing so
indiscriminately, in every kind of sunshine, but those who are
sensible and experienced do not take them at all times, but only
whenever they are beneficial. During a north wind or a calm the
sun's rays are pure and beneficial because they are transmitted
through clear air; during a south wind or in a partly cloudy day,
they are damp and too scorching, so that they weaken rather than
warm those in training. The days with the beneficial sunshine I
have, then, described. The phlegmatic type should bask in the
sun more than the others, so as to sweat out the excess of secretions, but the choleric type should refrain from this so that fire
may not be poured over fire. Those who are advanced in years
should lie quietly in the sun, exposed to the sun's rays in the same
way as though they were being roasted, but those who are young
and vigorous should take sun baths, actively, with all the exercises prescribed by the men of Elis. As for the vapor bath and

the pure oil bath, since these belong to a cruder system of gymnastics, we will leave them to the Lacedaemonians whose exercises
bear no resemblance to the pancratium or to boxing either. The
Lacedaemonians themselves declare that they practise thus not for
the sake of a prize contest, but merely to harden themselves, and
their system of flogging bears out this assertion, for their law
prescribes cruel whipping at the altar.*

BIBLIOGRAPHY

A. Abbreviations for Periodicals and Collections

[Abbreviated names of classical authors and abbreviated titles of their works are generally only slightly shortened. For abbreviated titles of modern works, always preceded in the text or notes by the author's name, see part B, below.]

AJA	American Journal of Archaeology
BCH	Bulletin de Correspondance Hellénique
BSA	Annual of the British School at Athens
CAH	Cambridge Ancient History
CIA	Corpus Inscriptionum Atticarum
CIL	Corpus Inscriptionum Latinarum
CP	Classical Philology
C P Herm	Corpus Papyrorum Hermopolitanorum, Part I, ed. C. Wessely (Studien zur Palaeographie und Papyruskunde, V)
CR	The Classical Review
FGH (Jacoby)	Fragmente der griechischen Historiker
FHG (Müller)	Fragmenta Historicorum Graecorum
IG	Inscriptiones Graecae
IGA	Inscriptiones Graecae Antiquissimae (Roehl)
IGB	Inschriften Griechischer Bildhauer (Loewy)
Jahrb.	Jahrbuch des kaiserlich deutschen archäologischen Instituts
Jahresh.	Jahreshefte des österreichischen archäologischen Institutes
JHS	Journal of Hellenic Studies
Ol. Ins.	Die Inschriften von Olympia, ed. Dittenberger-Purgold (Curtius-Adler, Olympia, V)
P Lond	Greek Papyri in the British Museum, Vol. III, ed. Kenyon-Bell

P Oxy	Oxyrhynchus Papyri
PW	Realencyclopädie der classischen Altertumswissenschaft, ed. Pauly-Wissowa-Kroll
Rev. Phil.	Revue de Philologie
Riv. Fil.	Rivista di Filologia
Röm. Mitt.	Mitteilungen des deutschen archäologischen Instituts, Römische Abteilung
SIG	Sylloge Inscriptionum Graecarum, ed. Dittenberger
TAPA	Transactions of the American Philological Association
Wiener Denkschr.	Denkschriften der Akademie der Wissenschaften in Wien

B. Select Modern Works

[Full data on other books, cited only once, will be found in the notes at the place of citation.]

Brauchitsch, G., Die Panathenäischen Preisamphoren, Leipzig 1910.

Chrimes, K.T., Ancient Sparta, Manchester 1949.

Daremberg-Saglio, Dictionnaire des antiquités grecques et romaines, Paris 1877-1919 [Daremb.-Saglio]

Dörpfeld, W., Alt-Olympia, Berlin 1935. 2 vols.

Dyer, L., "The Olympic Council House and Council," Harvard Studies in Classical Philology, XIX (1908) 1-60.

Farnell, L.R., Pindar, London 1932. 3 vols.

Ferguson, W.S., Hellenistic Athens, London 1911.

Forbes, C.A., Greek Physical Education, New York 1929 [GPE]

Förster, Hugo, Die Sieger in den olympischen Spielen, Ostern (progr.) 1891-2.

Frazer, J.G., Pausanias, London 1916. 6 vols.

Friedländer-Wissowa, Darstellungen aus der Sittengeschichte
    Roms, 9th ed. Leipzig 1920. 4 vols. [Friedl.]; English tr.
    of 7th ed. by Freese and Magnus, New York 1908-13. 4 vols.

Frost, K.T., "Greek Boxing," JHS 26 (1905) 213-25.

Gardiner, E.N., Greek Athletic Sports and Festivals, London
    1910 [GASF].

-----, Athletics of the Ancient World, Oxford 1930 [AAW].

-----, Olympia, Its History and Remains, Oxford 1925 [Olymp.].

-----, "Pankration and Wrestling," JHS 26 (1906) 4-22 [P and W].

Gow, A.S.F., Theocritus, Cambridge 1950. 2 vols.

Hyde, W.W., Olympic Victor Monuments and Greek Athletic Art,
    Washington 1921.

Jüthner, J., Über antike Turngeräthe, Wien 1896 [Jüth. AT].

-----, Philostratos über Gymnastik, Leipzig 1909 [Jüth. Philostr.].

-----, Körperkultur im Altertum, Jena 1928 [Jüth. KA].

Knab, R.. Die Periodoniken, Giessen 1934.

Krause, J.H., Olympia oder Darstellung der grossen Olympischen
    Spiele, Wien 1838.

Magie, D., Roman Rule in Asia Minor, Princeton 1950. 2 vols.

Méautis, G., Hermoupolis-la-Grande, Lausanne (diss.) 1918.

Mezö, F., Geschichte der Olympischen Spiele, München 1930.

Mitteis-Wilcken, Grundzüge und Chrestomathie der Papyrusur-
    kunde, Berlin 1912. 2 vols., 4 parts.

Mommsen, A., Feste der Stadt Athen im Altertum, Leipzig 1898.

Myres, J.L., Who Were the Greeks?, Berkeley 1930.

Richter-Young, Kouroi, Oxford 1942.

Schröder, B., Der Sport im Altertum, Berlin 1927.

NOTES

2. See below, Chap. VII A and note, for further mention of Vergil's games (Aeneid V 114-604); Chap. VII H, for note about Statius' funeral games (Thebaid VI 389 ff); and Chap. IX final note, for details about the games described by Quintus Smyrnaeus (The Fall of Troy IV 180-595).

3. Passages quoted from the Iliad are from the transl. by Lang, Leaf and Myers (London 1883). See also Richmond Lattimore's vivid, swift-moving version, couched in modern English (Univ. of Chicago Press 1951).

3 (chariot-racers). For a discussion of chariot races and for illustrations see Gardiner, GASF 14-17 and 451-66; also Hyde 257-282.

4. For Sophocles' description of just such an accident see below, Chap. IV D with note.

5. See below, Chap. IX D, for remarks by Philostratus (On Gymn. 43) about the informal training received by athletic competitors in the early days.

14. For the history of boxing among the ancient Greeks see esp. Frost 215-225; Gardiner, GASF 17-19 and 402-34; AAW 197-211; Mezö 90-99; Schröder 144-52. Ancient accounts of other formal and informal boxing matches are cited below: from Homer, Section C of this chapter; from Theocritus, Chap. VI B; from Polybius, Chap. VI E; from Dio Chrysostomus, Chap. VII H.

15. For an authoritative history of the various styles of hand covering used in boxing, with illustrations, see Jüthner, AT 65-95; for ancient testimony, see Pausan. VIII 40, 3 and Philostr. On Gymn. 10 (cited Chap. IX D).

16. For a discussion of Greek wrestling matches and for illustrations, see Gardiner, GASF 19 and 372-401; AAW 181-97; Hyde 228-234; Mezö 78-90; Schröder 121-9. See also the wrestling match described by Heliodorus, cited below Chap. IX C, and the additional evidence for ancient wrestling cited there in a note. See also Chap. III G 2, note on Milo.

17. For a discussion of foot racing among the ancient Greeks see Gardiner, GASF 20 and 270-94, AAW 128-43; Hyde 190-209; Mezö 68-78; Schröder 101-110. Also see below, Chap. VI A note.

19. For the importance of this contest throughout Greek history, and for a citation of the literary evidence, see Daremb.-Saglio s.v. "Hoplomachia."

20. For contests in throwing the discus and other weights see Gardiner, GASF 22 f. and 313-337; AAW 26 and 154-68; Hyde 218-22; Jüthner, AT 18-36; Mezö 118-27; Schröder 118-121. For other ancient evidence on weight throwing, see below, Chap. III and note.

21. See Gardiner, GASF 22; AAW 27; Daremb.-Saglio s.v. "Arcus"; Butler, Sport in Classic Times (London 1930), 195 ff.

22. Gardiner, GASF 22; AAW 25; and his article "Throwing the Javelin" JHS 27 (1907) 249-73; Hyde 8; Jüthner, AT 37-65.

22 (Cretans). For characteristics of early Cretan athletic sports, with illustrations, see Gardiner, GASF 9-11; AAW 9-14; Hyde 1-7; and esp. W. R. Ridington, The Minoan-Mycenaean Background of Greek Athletics (Diss. Philadelphia 1935).

23. Selections quoted from the Odyssey are from the transl. by Butcher and Lang (New York 1893, 3rd ed.).

24. The Greek word here translated "a man of thy hands" is athlêtêr, literally "a winner of prizes." This is the earliest occurrence of the word (later athlêtês) from which the English word athlete is derived. See Chapter VIII D, below, for an amusing etymology proposed by Galen (Exhorta. 11), and Chap. II E for another fanciful one proposed by the fourth-century Eusebius.

27. For other ancient games of ball see passages cited below, Chap. VIII C and notes.

30 (thirty-three heroes). See Ludolf Malten, "Leichenspiel und Totenkult" Röm. Mitt. 38-39 (1923-4) 300-340, esp. 307 f.

30 (Cypselus chest). For a comprehensive study of this chest see H. Stuart Jones, JHS 14 (1894) 30-84 and Plate I; also Hyde pp. 12 ff.

30 (Pausanias). Translation by W. H. S. Jones, the Loeb
Classical Library; reprinted by courtesy of the Harvard University
Press.

33. On the dating of events and persons in prehistoric Greece,
see Section C, below (Phlegon 1, note), and Section E, Eusebius.
See also Clinton, Fasti Hellenici (Oxford 1834), I 77 ff. and 128 ff.,
who gives a detailed list.

34 (Olympian Ode). Translation by Sandys, Loeb Classical
Library; courtesy of Harvard University Press.

34 (Heracles). I. e. the younger Heracles. Herodotus, a younger contemporary of Pindar, discusses at length the subject of an
older Heracles, god from Crete, and a younger Heracles from
Argos. His conclusions are (II 44): "The facts obtained by personal investigation show clearly that Heracles is a very old god. And
I think those Greeks are most nearly correct who have installed
two Heracles, giving to one sacrifices as though to a god whose
last name is Olympian but to the other bringing offerings as though
to a late hero." Compare also a similar account given by Diodorus
(V 76).

34 (Pelops). See Dörpfeld I 118-24 for an analysis of his 1929
excavations on the site of Pelop's tomb.

34 (iron blows). See Pausanias V 1, 9-10 (cited D below) for
the details of this "menial service."

35 (victors). See also Olymp. Ode III, for an account of Heracles' other activities in behalf of Olympia, in which Pindar assigns
him credit for having introduced the olive trees there.

35 (in very deed). See Pausanias V 8, 4 (cited in D, below) for
a different list of victors for these same games, sounding less
like "solid citizens" than Pindar's precisely named men. The
events listed by Pindar correspond in general to those mentioned
by Homer (Il. XXIII 625 ff.) for this neighborhood and period (i. e.
at Bouprasion in Nestor's boyhood). But a four horse chariot race
for those times is probably an anachronism in which Pindar is
following the style of his contemporary fellow artists and sculptors
(cf. those famous sculptured scenes of the chariot race with four
horses each of Pelops and Oenomaus set in place in the pediment
of the Zeus temple perhaps in Pindar's day and still to be seen in
restored fragments in the museum at Olympia).

36 (Strabo). Transl. by H. L. Jones, the Loeb Classical Library; courtesy of Harvard University Press.

36 (Pisatis). Whether there was a city by the name of Pisa or whether there was merely a federation of towns forming a district known as Pisatis or Pisa was a question discussed even by ancient scholars. Strabo writes in detail on the matter (VIII 3, 31). Dörpfeld, I 55 ff., feels certain that excavations have revealed a Pisa going back to the fifteenth century B.C. See also Dyer 11 ff.

37. See Introduction to Pausanias selection (cited D below) and note, for a discussion of this information taken from Homer's Iliad.

38 (the Olympian). It is difficult to see how the absence of a wreath as prize would prove whether or not the brilliant athletic meets attributed by tradition to a Pelops or a Heracles before the Trojan War actually occurred. Strabo, in fact, seems here to have done little research and excerpting on the matter of the awards, or, indeed, on the origin of the four great national athletic festivals of Greece.

In Homer's account of the funeral games for Patroclus and on that old chest of Cypselus the victors were pictured as having led off or carried off as awards whatever gifts the generous host felt minded to give at his personally sponsored festival gathering. That the wreath as prize at Olympia was not introduced until the seventh Olympiad (752 B.C.) Strabo seems not to have read in his sources (but cf. Phlegon 11, cited C below) or that awards of cash value in the early days were the common practice, e.g. the grain awarded to victors in that old athletic festival at Eleusis which Aristotle is said to have listed as the oldest in Greece (Foucart, BCH (1884) 199 ff.; Schol. Aristid. FHG (Müller) II 282; IG II 834 b).

Herodotus (I 144) mentions an age-old practice of dedicating bronze tripods won in ancient games of Triopian Apollo.

The miniature two horse chariots and tripods, votive offerings found on the site of Olympia, have been eloquently explained by Dörpfeld (I 51 ff.) as prizes dedicated by Olympic victors in the pre-Troy era, but recent scholars have pointed out cogent reasons why these objects cannot reasonably be used as evidence for such early centuries (Searle-Dinsmoor AJA 49 [1945] 62-80).

38 (prizes). Il. XI 699. Strabo's interpretation, it would seem, is hardly justified when one studies the contents of the whole anec-

dote and examines the general background of affairs in those districts as hinted by other writers. A fuller discussion is promised
in an article, "Homer and the Olympic Games."

38 (Ephorus). See G. L. Barber, The Historian Ephorus (Cambridge 1935) 189 ff., for an analysis of the fragments remaining
from this author's new style World History and esp. 26 f. for a
discussion of Strabo's use of Ephorus.

39 (Iphitus). But between Oxylus (dated by Thucydides [I 12] as
80 yrs. after Troy) and Iphitus there was a gap of centuries!

39 (Aristotle). See Jüthner, Philostr. 60-70, for a discussion
of the ancient victor lists.

39 (source). Perhaps from records kept by the Iamidae-Clytidae
family of seers, always in residence at Olympia, whose origin and
connection with Delphi's Apollo are gloriously described by Pindar
(Olymp. Ode VI 19 ff.) and whose members are mentioned many
times by Pausanias.

40 (Phlegon). Translated from FGH (Jacoby) 2 B 257, 1160 F.

40 (Peisos). Dörpfeld (I 39 and 50 f.) seeks to identify Peisos
with a Clymenus of Crete mentioned by Pausanias V 8, 1, cited D
below.

40 (Heracles). For an idea of the approximate century when
these personages are reputed to have lived, see the useful discussion of dates of the prehistoric period by Wace, CAH I 178. Professor Wace would place Pelops at about 1283 B.C.; but also see
Myres 304 f., who would place Pelops a little later (1260 B.C.)
and Heracles about 1230 B.C. See also the note above referring
to page 33 of this chapter.

40 (Heracles and Deaneira). Phlegon here cites the generations
according to a list of Eurypontid Spartan Kings, the same list
apparently as was used by a Simonides of the 5th Century B.C.
(Plutarch, Lycurg. 1, 3) and by Pausanias (III 7). But Herodotus
(VIII 131) gives a Eurypontid list whose names and their sequence
are in some cases different. For Spartan King Lists -- their
variations, their reliability, their use by ancient writers in dating
events from the century before the Trojan War down to 776 B.C. --
see Prakken, Studies in Greek Genealogical Chronology (Columbia
Diss. 1943).

40. Iphitus, the reorganizer of the games, and his immediate kinfolk were figures evidently shrouded in haze to the ancient view, though he was so important in Olympia tradition that the statuary group representing him as being wreathed by Lady Truce was, in 460 B.C., placed in full view as one entered the front door of the Zeus temple at Olympia (Pausan. V 10, 10; 26, 2). Phlegon here hesitates about Iphitus' lineage (cf. Pausanias V 4, 6, cited below, D with note).

41 (discus). Plutarch (Lycurg. 1) mentions that Aristotle (4th century B.C.) had seen the discus at Olympia with the name Lycurgus still legible upon it. An ancient-looking discus kept in the temple of Hera next to a bit of Pelops' wife's furniture, it seems, was still being shown to visitors at Olympia in A.D. 174. Pausanias saw and described it as follows (V 20, 1): "The discus of Iphitus has inscribed upon it the truce which the men of Elis announce at the time of the Olympic Games, not inscribed in a straight line but the letters on the discus run around to form a circle."

41 (Peloponnesian). Judging from the way the story turns out, blurred as its outlines are, the word "Peloponnesians" includes all the folk except the Eleans. The Eleans had apparently without due authority assumed the directorship of the festival and thereby, perhaps, caused the general feeling of dissatisfaction.

41 (oracle). A book notice of Phlegon's work written by Photius (ix cent. A.D.) appraises Phlegon's style in words which still awaken a sympathetic response in a reader lately come from the tedious oracles (FGH [Jacoby] 2 B 257): "In language it is not so very lowly in style; still it does not preserve the Attic exactly. Besides that, in the section concerning the Olympiads, the recital of names of the contestants and their deeds, the inappropriate overfondness and overattention to oracles, bringing his audience to exhaustion and not allowing them to get a peek at hardly anything else in the story -- all this points to an unentertaining narrative and gives evidence that it had no style. He used all sorts of oracles in excess."

42 (superintending). Phlegon's account implies that it was due to pressure from Delphi and that it was with considerable reluctance on the part of the Pisatans and the others that Elis obtained the management of the Olympic Games at the time of this Renewal. Though Pisa's ancient claim to priority at the Olympic Games was well recognized (Xen. Hellen. III 2, 31) she had of course lost a

great deal of her power there with the coming of Oxylus (see Strabo VIII 3, 30, cited B above), so that it could be expected that Delphi would favor the more progressive federation. Dyer (41 ff.) cites considerable ancient evidence to show that two Hellanodicae, one an Elean and one a Pisatan, presided over these early games. If this was the fact, we must conclude both that Phlegon's version is a bit slanted and that Pausanias is in error (V 9, 4).

42 (wreath). Earlier awards were no doubt of cash value (see Strabo VIII 3, 30, above, and the notes to page 38).

42 (Iphitus). This is a younger Iphitus, as I understand it, and not to be confused with the Iphitus whom Phlegon mentioned above (2). The latter is clearly described as being the contemporary of Lycurgus of the early ninth century B.C. Scholars who assume that only one Iphitus figures in Phlegon's narrative and on that assumption put Iphitus, Lycurgus, and the Reorganization all just before 776 B.C., overlook the fact that Phlegon's narrative, like that of Strabo, is not a continuous history. (See Jüthner's inadequate statement Philostr. 63 ; Weniger, "Das Hochfest des Zeus in Olympia" Klio V (1905) 187 f.; Gardiner's non-committal statement, Olymp. 84; and Chrimes' seemingly illogical assertions about the date of Iphitus, 322.) There is at (9) in Phlegon's account a time lapse of uncertain length indicated by the general expression "after this." According to Pausanias' chronology for the Helos incident (III 2, 7), this probably amounted to three generations. The rest of Phlegon's story is not a continuous history but merely a recital of two more Delphic oracles which shaped later Olympia history. Even such an important event as Coroebus and his first officially recorded victory (776 B.C.) is omitted.

Scholars who insist on one Iphitus must picture him as old enough to have reorganized the games with Lycurgus and young enough to be able to travel to Delphi twenty years after 776 B.C. To accomplish this they ignore Phlegon's statement (2) about Lycurgus' place in the genealogical table of Spartan Kings and emend the clause (1) about the length of time the games lapsed or omit it completely (as one scholar suggests!).

43. Pausanias' intricate report is cited in full as its incidental stories will serve to explain allusions scattered throughout the authors. For a brief discussion of the legends of early Olympia see Gardiner, Olymp. 58 ff.; and as an example of the uncritical account too frequently met, see Hyde 14-18, in his otherwise useful work.

44 (Pausanias). These games just mentioned, it would seem, were held under a general supervision and with the sanction of Pisa, to whose territory the shrine seems continuously to have belonged during the century and a half from the time of Pelops to that of Oxylus. Pausanias' report (V 3, 1) that Delphi's Apollo ordered Heracles to spare Pisa (though no objection had come from that shrine at the fate of Elis and Pylos) points to Pisa's importance at Olympia at the time of Heracles. Strabo's mention (VIII 3, 30) that some believed that Pisa took no part in the Trojan War, being considered sacred to Zeus, and again (VIII 3, 33) that it was from "Achaeans" (i.e. Pisatans) that Oxylus wrested control of Olympia (?1104 B.C.) also indicate Pisa's importance at Olympia.

44 (Bronze Age). Lorimer, Homer and the Monuments (London, 1950) 46; but cf. Carpenter, Folk Tale, Fiction and Saga in the Homeric Epics (Berkeley 1946) 178 f.

44 (Zeus). The Pylos-Elis ships could have been manned by a total of 10,000 active combatants if Thucydides' estimate (I 10) of the number on a full ship in Homer's day is accepted. Cf. the estimate of numbers of heroes on the Argo, Jason's ship (cited Chap. VI C note).

46 (merged). This whole question of the dating of Iphitus and whether there was a Senior and a Junior by that name is an important one for the students of Greek History. The undisputed statement that a Lycurgus and an Iphitus were contemporaries has been the main peg upon which scholars ancient (cf. Plut. Lycurg. 1) and modern (cf. Chrimes 319 ff.) have fastened their thesis as to whether the great Lycurgus belonged to the eight hundreds or the seven hundreds B.C. and whether or not the Reorganization of the Festival and Coroebus' first recorded victory occurred at one and the same time (See below Pausan. V 4, 5 note and above C, Phlegon 10, note).

46 (Pausanias). Transl. by W. H. S. Jones, The Loeb Classical Library; courtesy of Harvard University Press.

46 (Curetes). But cf. Strabo's opinion of such tales (above, B).

47. "Deucalion's flood," a rainfall in the Copais Lake district of central Greece so heavy that memory of it persisted from one generation to the next, is one of the more definite points upon which early Greek chronology was made to depend. It is commonly dated as 1430 B.C. (Myres, 248).

47 (Heracles). For possible dates of Pelops and Heracles see Phlegon (1) and note, above.

48 (pancratium). But cf. Pindar's list of victors, A above and note.

48 (Iphitus). More than three centuries of events at Olympia are thus summarily dismissed. But some scholars have failed to note seriously the information available in other chapters of Pausanias about this period. These are therefore quoted in this section.

48 (Asia). That this story of Pelops was no invention of the later Roman writers, as is sometimes asserted, is shown by the fact that, six centuries before Pausanias, Thucydides (I 9) had expressed the opinion that this tradition about Pelops rested on credible authority: "It is said, furthermore, by those of the Peloponnesians who have received the clearest traditional accounts from men of former times [Is this a reference to the Priests of Elis?] that it was by means of a great wealth which he brought with him from Asia into the midst of a poor people that Pelops first acquired power, etc." (Transl. by Smith, The Loeb Classical Library; courtesy of Harvard University Press.

50. See the discussion of this passage above, page 44 and note.

51. That is for about six generations -- in round numbers 1070-884 B.C., reckoning three generations to a century according to the norm laid down by Herodotus (II 142). The date used here for Lycurgus (and his contemporary Iphitus) was also set by Herodotus (I 65; VII 304) and closely followed by Thucydides (I 18). See Chrimes Chap. IX, for a resumé of modern scholarship on the date of Lycurgus.

52 (himself). But cf. Phlegon's account (cited C above) which came, probably, from a Pisatan source.

52 (name). Apparently the Greek people did not take too seriously official pronouncements of Elis, if two statements in writing could not shake the popular belief. The inscription alluded to, I suppose, refers to the one on the statue of Iphitus (mentioned in V 10, 10): "As you enter the bronze doors (i.e. of the temple of Zeus) you see on the right, before the pillar, Iphitus being crowned by a woman, Echecheiria(Truce), as the elegiac couplet on the statue says."

53 (Eusebius).   Transl. from Schoene's ed., I (1875).

53 (Greeks).   See Gardiner, GASF 50 f., for a clear discussion
of this Register; and Jüthner, Philostr. 60-70, for a more detailed
treatment.

54 (Peloponnesians).   See Phlegon (C above) for a longer form
of these same oracles.

54 (added).   Most scholars regard this statement (and also Pausanias' similar report [V 8, 5-11] as well as Philostr. On Gymn.
12) as an absurdity, in view of the evidence furnished by funeral
games; see Gardiner GASF 51 f.

54 (Aristodemus).   Cf. also the ninth-century statement of
Photius (FGH [Jacoby] 2 B 257): "Phlegon of Tralles (see page 39),
freedman of the emperor Hadrian, published a collection entitled
"Olympic Victors and Annals." ...   The collection begins with the
first Olympiad (i. e. 776 B.C.) because earlier events (and practi-
cally all other writers agree with this statement) did not meet with
any accurate and trustworthy listing, since different persons were
listing different events, with no agreement, according to each
writer's individual preference.   But Phlegon began his list, as we
said, with the first Olympiad.   It goes down to the time of Hadrian
(A.D. 117-138), as he himself states; I read it as far as the 177th
Olympiad 72-68 B.C.)."

55.   Substantially the same story, with Callimachus cited as
his authority, is recounted by a late scholiast on Lucian (ad Rhet.
praec. 9, see below Chap. IX intro.)   Some scholars explain this
smaller number of Olympiads as indicating an original festival
held every ninth year instead of every fifth.   See Gardiner, Olymp.
68 ff.

56.   Translated by H. G. Evelyn-White, The Loeb Classical
Library; courtesy of Harvard University Press.

58 (Register).   For a list of these victors, arranged chronologi-
cally and accompanied by ancient evidence, see Förster.

58 (August).   An Orsippos of Megara is listed as the winner of
the foot race in 720 B.C. and is also credited with having introduced an innovation in athletic costume (see below D, Anacharsis
36, note).   He was destined to become a great statesman who
changed the boundaries of his city.   Onomastus of Smyrna is

credited not only with the physical strength and skill to win in boxing at Olympia in 688 B.C. but also with the brains to compile the
first set of regulations which was to become the standard book of
rules on boxing (Pausan. V 8, 7; Philostr. On Gymn. 12). Chionis
of Sparta, assistant founder of Cyrene, for ten years in his youth
was acclaimed as a champion in the foot race, having won seven
victories in the long and short race beginning with his Olympic
victory in 668 B.C. (Pausan. III 14, 3). Cylon of Athens in 640
B.C. was the winner in the double foot race, on the strength of
which he was to win as wife the daughter of the wealthy Theagenes,
Tyrant of Megara. Later, still counting on his fame as a recent
Olympic victor, he is said to have tried without success to seize
control of all Athens (Thucyd. I 126; Herodot.V 71). Phrynon,
later to be the famous general sent by Athens to win Sigeum, was
victor in the pancratium match of 636 B.C. (Strabo XIII 38).

There must have been many more such prominent men who were
victors at other games, though chance has not preserved their
names.

58. On Pheidon of Argos see P. N. Ure, The Origin of Tyranny
(Cambridge 1922) 159 f.

58 (a talent). This is a sum which compares favorably with the
amount awarded a victor at the Olympic Games by Solon in this
same generation (see below, B and note). If, as seems plausible,
Solon's five hundred drachmas were in part a reimbursement for
the month or more consumed by the journey to Olympia and the
required residence there -- then twelve times that amount (i. e. a
talent) for a year's absence would represent generosity on the
same scale. See also below, Chap. VII E, for mention of sums
paid athletes for maintenance during their residence for training.

59 (local ones). For some notion of their numbers and programs
see Ringwood, Agonistic Features of Local Greek Festivals, etc.
(Columbia Univ. Diss. 1927), and A. Mommsen.

59 (Herodotus). This quotation and VI, 130 above and II 160
quoted below are transl. by A. D. Godley, The Loeb Classical
Library; courtesy of Harvard University Press.

59 (legislation). For accounts of the work and life of Solon see
Kathleen Freeman, Work and Life of Solon (London 1926); Ivan
Linforth, Solon the Athenian (Berkeley 1919).

59 (Inscriptions). See Jevons, "Work and Wages in Athens"
JHS (1895) 239-47. Diogenes Laertius, of probably the 3rd cent.
A. D., mentions these awards by Solon (I 55). He follows the statement with his personal analysis of Solon's motives. His indictment
of excesses of professional athletics in Solon's time shows a complete lack of information on the background of athletic and economic
life in the days of Solon. Diogenes' remarks are in reality a denunciation of athletic excesses of his own day and contain the several
commonplace utterances which became the stock-in-trade of such
rhetorical efforts.

This later writer, visualizing the purchasing power of money
with which he had personal experience, asserts that Solon's idea
was to curtail athletics by granting small sums of money! In that
case how disappointed Solon must have been at the upsurge in athletic enthusiasm and at the increase in valuable prizes awarded
in his city's Panathenaic Games under the warm patronage of his
successor, Pisistratus, who had gold mines as well as silver
mines at his disposal.

It is unfortunate that some modern scholars are still quoting
Diogenes Laertius' opinion as their chief witness for athletics in
Solon's day without proper appraisal of all the other evidence for
that period.

60. Transl. by Bernadotte Perrin, The Loeb Classical Library;
courtesy of Harvard University Press.

61. From Pausanias it is clear that relations between the Olympia management and that of the Isthmian Festival were far from
smooth, though his stories as to the real cause of the feud are a
bit confusing (V 2, 5; VI 3, 9 and 16, 2.)

62 (Lyceum). Two late lexicographers, Harpocration and
Suidas, quote the statement of Theopompus (fourth century B.C.)
to the effect that the Lyceum gymnasium was built by Pisistratus
(560-527 B.C.); see Grenfell-Hunt, Hellenica Oxyrhynchia (Oxford
1909), fragm. 132 of Theopompus. Since Solon was alive during
part of the Age of Pisistratus, Lucian's setting for this dialogue
follows the historical tradition.

62 (writers). See Herodot. IV 76; and an interesting note on the
passage in How and Wells, A Commentary on Herodotus (Oxford
1912).

62 (Lucian). Transl. by A. M. Harmon, The Loeb Classical Library; courtesy of Harvard University Press.

66. Of course the "amphitheatre" of Solon's day was merely a grassy slope. See Emil Kunze and Hans Schlief, "Bericht über die Ausgrabungen in Olympia," Jahrb. 53 (1937-8) 5-27 "Das Stadion"; also Mrs. E. P. Blegen, "News Items from Athens" AJA 43 (1939) 338 f. For Nemea, an excavation conducted by the Univ. of Cincinnati has brought precise information: "At Nemea where everything always remained simplicity itself there was no stone construction whatever except for a water channel. The spectators stood or sat on the ground itself which descends in a regular, and certainly artificially made, slope to the floor of the stadium" (Carl P. Blegen, AJA 31 (1927) 421-440.

68. Anacharsis paid dearly for such lessons in the Greek way of life for, according to Herodotus (IV 76), on his return home to what is now Russia, King Saulis put him to death with an arrow shot because "he left his country for Hellas and followed the customs of strangers."

71. This remark is more appropriate for the fifth century B.C. when the graceful "Pentathlon" ideal produced an all-round harmonious development so evident in the work of the famous artists of that period. See below Chap. IV, Intro. and notes.

76. Lucian is here following the testimony of most vase paintings, which show that nudity was the rule in Greek sport for that period. Pausanias (I 44, 1) ascribes the introduction of that custom to Orsippus of Megara in 720 B.C., at least for the foot races.

Thucydides, usually a reliable witness, has baffled scholars by his statement (I 6) which clearly does not agree with most archaeological evidence: The Lacedaemonians, too, were the first who in their athletic exercises stripped naked and rubbed themselves over with oil. But this was not the ancient custom; athletes formerly, even when they were contending at Olympia, wore girdles about their loins, a practice which lasted until quite lately (i.e. the close of the fifth century B.C.)(Smith's transl., Loeb Classical Library, courtesy of Harvard Univ. Press). Strangely enough, a few black-figured vases from the end of the sixth century B.C. do show the loin cloth in use. See Gardiner, AAW Figs. 163 and 182 with notes.

78. For a discussion of the physical education system at Sparta see Forbes,GPE Chap. II, with bibliography.

79 (scholars). Hyde 326 f.; Richter-Young 125 f.

79 (Imagines). Transl. from Benndorf-Schenkl ed. (Leipzig 1893).

79 (Philostratus). Whether this is the same Philostratus who was the author of the Handbook on Gymnastics (Chap. IX D below) or that man's uncle has not yet been satisfactorily proved in spite of the extensive literature on the subject. See Christ-Schmid-Stählin, Griech. Literaturgesch. (Müller's Handbuch, etc. 1924 VII 2) 772-785.

80 (backward). That is, using the MS reading hyptiasmòn approved by Westermann (Paris 1849) and not hypòpiasmòn (sufferings) preferred by Benndorf-Schenkl.

80 (gouging). For a discussion of the positions of each opponent at the various stages of this contest see Jüthner "Gymnastisches in Philostrats Eikones," Eranos Vindobonensis (Vienna 1893) 327-30.

For further description of the pancratium see Gardiner,GASF 435 ff., and esp. his illustrated article "The Pankration and Wrestling" JHS 26 (1906) 5 ff.

81 (Pausanias). Transl. by W. H. S. Jones, the Loeb Classical Library; courtesy of Harvard University Press.

81 (time). But on the stone statue found at Phigalia there is an inscription across the chest, which fact has provided an additional argument for those not willing for stylistic reasons to identify it as a likeness of Arrhichion; see Richter-Young 125 f.

82. The list includes a Pagondas of Thebes--the first victory on the records with four horses (680 B.C.); an Archidamus from Dyspontion, Elis (672 B.C.); Myron of Sicyon (648 B.C.) who, as a votive offering, dedicated two solid bronze building models of nineteen tons weight; the immensely wealthy Alcmaeon of Athens (between 612-592 B.C.), Periander of Corinth (beginning of 6th century B.C.); Cleisthenes of Sicyon (576 or 572 B.C.), see A above; Callias of Athens (564 B.C.), first of a long line all renowned for their wealth; and of course the Miltiades-Cimon-Pisistratus victories for Athens (559-524 B.C.) mentioned in this selection.

82 (coins). See C. T. Seltman, Athens, Its History and Coinage (Cambridge 1924) 137 f.

83 (Herodotus). Transl. by A. D. Godley, The Loeb Classical Library; courtesy of Harvard University Press.

83 (writers). See Förster for a resumé of the ancient evidence for athletes mentioned in this chapter.

84 (Nemea). One such victor is known from a sixth century "boustrophedon" type inscription found on a re-used poros block in the area of the old gymnasium on the site of Nemea; "Aristis, son of Pheidon of Kleonai, four times victor in the Nemean games." See C. Blegen, "Excavations at Nemea, 1926" AJA 42 (1927) 421-40.

84 (Pausanias). Transl. by W. H. S. Jones, The Loeb Classical Library; courtesy of Harvard University Press.

85 (wrestler). See below, Chap. IX D (Philostr. 11 and note) for remarks on ancient wrestling; also above, Chap. I A "Wrestling Match" and note. For an appraisal of this contest, with explanation of technical terms and holds and illustrations, see Gardiner, P and W 4-22.

85 (eater). Aristotle (Nic. Eth. II 6, 7 [1106 b]) leaves a significant story as to what his idea of a "huge eater" was: "Suppose that ten pounds of food is a large ration for anybody and two pounds a small one; it does not follow that a trainer will prescribe six pounds, for perhaps even this will be a large ration, or a small one, for the particular athlete who is to receive it; it is a small ration for Milo, but a large one for a man just beginning to go in for athletics." But compare this with the amounts of food quoted below for Milo by later writers.

86 (Strabo). Transl. by H. L. Jones, The Loeb Classical Library; courtesy of Harvard University Press.

87 (beasts). This anecdote occurs in several other writers, e.g. Pausan. VI 14, 8; Aulus Gellius XV 16; Galen, Protrept. 13.

87 (Pausanias). Transl. by W. H. S. Jones, The Loeb Classical Library; courtesy of Harvard University Press.

87 (statue). Portions of a circular, discus-like base found at Olympia have been identified by some as the remains of Milo's statue. There is a depression in it where a statue may have stood and the letters which remain are of sixth cent. B.C. style and look like a part of the name "Dameas" (IGA [Roehl] 589; see also Hitzig-Blumner, Pausanias [Leipzig 1901] II, 602).

87 (pomegranate). Aelian (third century after Christ) gives an irreverent version of this feat (Var. Hist. II 24): "Some have exploded the story of Milo's great strength, telling the following: 'No opponent could snatch from him the pomegranate which he grasped. But his sweetheart used to take it away with no trouble as often as she grappled with him.' From which it is clear that Milo was strong in body but weak in mind." There were several reports by authors that Milo's success was due to a lucky charm which he carried, e.g. Plin. Nat. Hist. XXXVII 54: "Alectoria ... a stone found in the crop of poultry ... crystal in appearance-- large as a bean--Milo of Croton was thought to be in the habit of carrying this stone, a thing that rendered him invincible in athletic contests."

87 (Philostratus). Transl. by F. C. Conybeare, The Loeb Classical Library; courtesy of Harvard University Press.

88 (Titormus). If his brother was actually at Cleisthenes' party in 570 B.C. (Herodot. VI 126, see A above), Titormus would have been quite advanced in years at the time of this contest. Milo's career did not begin until 536 B.C.

88 (Athenaeus). Transl. by C. B. Gulick, The Loeb Classical Library; courtesy of Harvard University Press.

89 (halter). For a discussion of the jumping contest, an event in the pentathlon, see Gardiner, "Phayllus and his Record Jump" JHS 24 (1904) 70-80 and 170-94. See also the description of an early stone halter found at the site of the Isthmian Games in the recent Univ. of Chicago excavations. O. Broneer, Hesperia XXII, 3 (1953) 194 Plate 60.

89 (Jüthner). Jahresh. 29 (1935) 32-43.

89 (stone discus). See Gardiner's important article "Throwing the Diskos" JHS (1907) 1-36 with illustra.; and Chap. I A for further information on discus contests.

90 (bronze). Previously translated: Exoidas dedicated me, the bronze discus etc.

90 (Phocion). Using the reading of these two baffling words as suggested by S. Accame, "L'epigraphe di Bybone," Riv. Fil. 16 (1938) 167-9.

91 (diatribes). For an elaborated discussion of this simple protest see Bowra, "Xenophanes and the Olympian Games" in Problems in Greek Poetry (Oxford 1953) 15-37.

91 (Xenophanes). Ed. Diehl, trans. by W. A. Oldfather.

92. Pindar mentions many such fifth century B.C. athletes with a family tradition of athletics. Among them were: Hippocleas of Thessaly, 490 B.C. (Pyth. Ode X); Megacles of Athens, 486 B.C. (Pyth. Ode VII); Timodemus of Acharnae, 485 B.C. (Nem. Ode II); Pythias of Aegina, 485 B.C. (Nem. Ode V); Melissus of Thebes, 478 B.C. (Isthm. Ode IV); the Lampon family of Aegina, 476 B.C. (Isthm. Ode V and VI); the Timasarchus clan of Aegina, 473 B.C. (Nem. Ode IV).

93 (praise). Isocrates, born about the time Pindar died, remarked (Antidosis 166), to an Athenian audience who would have been in a position to check his veracity, that Athens paid Pindar 10,000 drachmas for that one complimentary sentence (that is, twenty times Solon's award for an Olympic victor). This gives an idea of what sums of money lyric poets may have received from wealthy patrons for athletic odes. Later writers give the story a different slant, stating that Thebes fined Pindar 1000 dr. for complimenting Athens, and that the fine was paid by Athens for Pindar (Eustath. Vita Pindari 28).

93 (Olympia). See Gardiner, Olymp. 106 f.; and the important papyrus fragment P. Oxy. II 222, which gives a list of the victors from 480-468 B.C.

93 (vases). Walters, History of Ancient Pottery (London 1905) esp. I, p. 417 f.; Christine Alexander, Greek Athletics (New York 1925) 31 pp. of illustra. only. Gisela Richter, Attic Red-Figured Vases (Yale Univ. 1946) with useful bibliog.

93 (sculptors). See Hester H. Stow, Greek Athletic Festivals in the Fifth Century (Boston 1939) 40 plates with explanatory comments; Hyde, for many illustra. of statues of athletes; and A.

Furtwängler, Die Bedeutung der Gymnastik in der Griechischen
Kunst (Leipzig 1905) 15 pp.

94 (pay). Schol. to Aristoph. Peace 695; Suidas s.v. "Simonides";
hinted at by Pindar Isthm. Ode II, 10.

94 (Lyr. Gr.). These selections from Simonides are translated
from Edmonds' edition (1924).

94 (embrace). A convenient line to memorize for the events of
the pentathlon.

95 (Dandes). A runner votive statuette was discovered at Olympia in 1937 with an Argive inscription which perhaps mentions
Dandes; see Hampe-Jantzen, Jahrb. 52 (1937) 77-82, Taf. 23, 24.

95 (Pindar). See also the selection quoted from Pindar, Chap.
II A above.

95 (Pythian). These selections transl. by Sandys, The Loeb
Classical Library; courtesy of the Harvard University Press.

97 (steps). Cf. the clearer translation of this troublesome line
by Lattimore (Univ. of Chicago Press 1947).

97 (refrain). A scholiast's note to this passage preserves two
lines of this famous song for victors composed in the seventh century B.C.: "O fair victor--hail Heracles! him and Iolaus--both
champions--tenella Victor!--tenella Victor!--tenella Victor!"
This "Song of Archilochus" was used as a substitute for a lyric
ode and in an impromptu hailing of the victor immediately after
his victory. The words "tenella, tenella, tenella," as screamed
with a twang by the crowd, were supposed to represent the sound
of the missing lyre. See Chap. VII G for Nero's use of this same
song.

98 (remedy). The cloaks given as prizes at Pellana are often
mentioned by the writers (see esp. Cohn, Paroemiog. 79, cited
by Edmonds in Lyr. Gr. II p. 306.

98 (Diagoras). For a more complete account of Diagoras and
his famous family, see Pausanias as quoted below in this chapter,
B 2.

98 (bronze). For a discussion of this festival and the following
ones see Farnell II 56 f.; also see Irene R. Arnold "The Shield of
Argos" AJA 41 (1937) 435-40.

99. Pindar's prayer was evidently answered, since the Scholiast
records that this ode was dedicated in letters of gold in the temple
of Athena at Lindus, Rhodes. It is by no means certain whether
letters of gold cut into a marble surface are to be understood or,
as seems more probable, that a parchment or leather roll on which
the ode was transcribed in letters of gold was dedicated. See
Graux's discussion, Rev. Phil. V (1881) 117-121.

100 (sea). Before competing for this victory at Olympia (464
B. C.), Xenophon had vowed, if successful, to dedicate an offering
of a hundred girls to the temple of Aphrodite in Corinth. A fragment of Pindar's song written to accompany the victory dance of
those girls is preserved (frg. 122, Sandys ed.); in it Pindar admits
that he was dubious about the reaction toward him of the city fathers
at Corinth for having used his talent for such a composition.

100 (Praxidamas). See Chapter III G.

100 (drawn). In Lucian (Hermotimus 40) are to be found the details of lot drawing and rules governing the "bye" in pancratium
and wrestling matches. Also see Farnell's discussion of it, II
286 f.

101. This Melesias, whose pupils had just won the thirtieth
victory for him, was probably the greatest teacher of wrestling in
Greece during the early fifth century. Wade-Gery plausibly reasons that Melesias was the father of the Athenian statesman
Thucydides and sets forth the evidence that wrestling was the diversion of this aristocratic family for three generations (JHS 52 [1932]
208-11).

102. The selections from Bacchylides are translated from
Jebb's ed. (Cambridge 1905). Thanks are due Prof. Forbes for a
critical reading (1930) of this translation in its original version.

103. There have been found at Delphi the inscribed bases for
these tripods, set conspicuously before the temple of Apollo, thus
confirming the poet's words. See Jebb, Bacchyl. Appendix 452 ff.

104 (wrestling). The prize was evidently awarded to a person
winning only three victories in the five events of the pentathlon.
See also Aristeides III 339 (ed. Dindorf).

104 (four laps). This was evidently the double double-race (four laps instead of two), known as the Hippios (horse-race) and especially popular at the Nemean and Isthmian Games.

105. The selections from Pausanias in this chapter are transl. by W. H. S. Jones, The Loeb Classical Library; courtesy of Harvard University Press.

105 (Aegina). A flippant third-century B.C. epigram about Theagenes' statue is reported by Athenaeus (X 412 e): "And on a bet I once ate an ox from Maeonia (Asia Minor). The food in my native land, Thasos (an island), would not have sufficed Theagenes. However much I ate I always asked for more. Therefore I stand here in bronze--holding out my hand!"

106. See Philostr. On Gymn. 17, cited below, Chap. IX C; and Pausanias' more detailed account (V 6, 7).

107. Photius (413, 20) quotes a sentence written by Simonides about this same Astylus of Croton: "What man of our times tied on to himself so many victories in local contests with their myrtle leaves and rose wreaths?"

109 (games). In 380 B.C. an ambitious woman, Cynisca of Sparta, entered her horses in the chariot race at Olympia and won. But of course she did not appear there in person for this first woman's victory (Pausan. III 8, 1; VI 1, 6). Bases of the statues which were set up for her at Olympia still exist (IGB 99 and 100).

109 (women). See Gardiner, Olymp. 75.

109 (statues). See the inscriptions cited below, Chap. VII F, for three girl victors at the sites of other major festivals.

110. Some forty miles from the new city of Elis, founded in 471 B.C. and devoted almost exclusively to the care and training of contestants. See Pausanias' description of its athletics plant (VI 23); also Gardiner, GASF 115 ff., Olymp. 105 f.

111 (Thucydides). Transl. by Smith, The Loeb Classical Library; courtesy of Harvard University Press.

111 (pancratium). Thucydides here dates the year by the winner of the pancratium match. It was not until Hippias had compiled the Olympic Register in the next century and the historian

Timaeus had used it for reckoning dates by Olympiads that the custom arose of dating the Olympiad by the winner of the foot race, the
first event.

111 (minas). Some idea of what a very large fine this was can be
gained from a remark in Thucydides of about the same time. The
daily pay for a rower in the fleet sent against Sicily was one drachma (VI 31). Two minas (120 dr.) would therefore equal 4 mos. pay,
though of course hoplites were probably better paid than rowers.

112. Jüthner, Jahresh. 29 (1934-35) 38-40.

113 (audience). If the Antaeus, a tragedy by Phrynichus (beginning of 5th cent. B.C.), were extant, athletic history would be
still further enriched, as in it was described a wrestling match
between Heracles and his earth-born foe. The manner in which
Aristophanes (Scholiast Frogs 686) refers to this play shows that
this description of the wrestling bout was still famous after a century.

113 (poet). Sophocles is said (Athen. I 20, cited below, Chap.
VII C) to have delighted an audience by his exhibition of ball-playing
when an actor in his own play "Nausicaa." Tradition also reported
that as a boy he won prizes in athletic contests (Vita Soph. 3).

113 (Sophocles). Transl. by F. Storr, The Loeb Classical
Library; courtesy of Harvard University Press.

115 (sight). Pindar (Pythian Ode V 40 f.) gives a good idea of
how frequently such accidents did happen at Delphi. Out of forty
chariots only one came through unbroken in the twelve lap race
(462 B.C.).

115 (victories). See Isocrates' account of these victories, cited
in Chap. V A and notes.

115 (Thucydides). Transl. by Smith, The Loeb Classical
Library; courtesy of Harvard University Press.

116 (over). For example, it was a favorite custom to take
along an Olympic Victor as Official Founder of a new colony; see
V. Ehrenberg, Aspects of the Ancient World (New York 1946) 117.

116 (Autolycus). Transl. by W. A. Oldfather from Nauck's
Trag. Graec. Frag., Euripidis fr. 282.

118 (Lysippus). C. Morgan, "The Style of Lysippos," Hesperia
8 (1949) 228-234.

118 (Vases). Gardiner, GASF 407 fig. 135; and Brauchitsch,
throughout.

119 (athletes). But as P. Shorey writes: It is not historically
speaking quite correct to regard professional athleticism as a de-
generation from an earlier ₁ormulated ideal. Yet we are tempted
to think of it in this way because those earlier centuries appear to
us transfigured in the odes of Pindar. In those odes the background of professionalism discernible by the student disappears in
the dazzling radiance of absolute poetry ("The Spirit of Greek
Athletics," Chautauquan 57 [1909-10] 255-273).

119 (contestants). One must not imagine, however, that among
the Greeks all impromptu, informal athletic competitions had gone
out of fashion. Xenophon leaves evidence that in 400 B.C. the fun
of athletics still remained much as in Homer's day. For after
132 days of dangerous marches Xenophon's volunteer soldiers
from all over the Greek world celebrated their safe arrival at
Trapezus in a typical Greek way with sacrifices to the gods followed by athletic games (Anabasis IV 8, 25-28):

> They held an athletic meet on the mountain where they were
> encamping. They selected Dracontius a Spartan ... to choose
> the course and to preside over the contest. After the sacrifice
> they handed the hides (for prizes) to Dracontius and bade him
> decide where the course should be laid out. Pointing to where
> they happened to be standing, he said: "This ridge is an excel-
> lent spot for a race wherever one wishes." "But how will they
> be able to wrestle" they said, "in a spot so rough and over-
> grown?" "The one who falls will be all the more hurt" was his
> reply. Young men entered the stade race, most of them cap-
> tives; for the long distance race more than sixty Cretans ran
> and for wrestling and boxing ... (gap in text). It was a wonder-
> ful spectacle. Many entered the competition and because their
> comrades were watching there was a great deal of rivalry.
> Horses raced, too, and their riders had to guide them down the
> slope, turn around in the sea, and guide them back to the altar.
> On the way down many rolled over; going up the terribly steep
> slope the horses proceeded slowly with great effort; thereupon
> the spectators shouted loudly, laughed and cheered them on.

119 (period). IG II^2 2311; IG II^2 1356. See A. Mommsen's
discussion of these, 70 and 76 f.

119 (vases). See G. Brauchitsch throughout, and the thirty-
seven illustra. in his book.

120 (Isocrates). Transl. by L. VanHook, The Loeb Classical
Library; courtesy of Harvard University Press.

120 (surpassing him). For other accounts of this same victory,
see Thucyd. VI 16 (cited above, Chap. IV D 2); Plutarch, Alcibiades
11; and Euripides' Ode, Lyr. Gr. II p. 241 (Edmonds).

121. Transl. from Bekker's ed. (1853). Thanks are due Prof.
Donald Bradeen (Univ. of Cincinnati) for his collaboration in the
preparation of this selection.

122 (Pausanias). Transl. by W. H. S. Jones, The Loeb Classical Library; courtesy of Harvard University Press.

122 (Olympiad). This festival must have marked an all time
low in the proceedings at Olympia as compared with her usual high
standards: Dionysius' farce, a woman disguised as trainer (see
Chap. IV C 3) and this scandal! The fact seems to have been that
the prestige of Olympia and of her officials had been badly damaged
in the war between Sparta and Elis in 399-97 B.C. and that there
had not been time enough for a full recovery. The ban imposed on
Sparta (Chap. IV C 6) had proved a costly one for the Olympia
shrine (Pausan. VIII 8, 3). Her wealth in the form of cattle and
slaves had been ruthlessly pillaged by the Spartan King Agis; her
beautiful gymnasium in the new City of Elis had been damaged.
True, Elis was grudgingly left with the presidency of the shrine
but only because there was no one else in the neighborhood of
the calibre to assume it. Xenophon, who was a resident of nearby
Scillus, gives a vivid account of this Sparta-Elis trouble (Hellenica
III 2, 27-30).

123. These selections from Xenophon transl. by J. S. Watson
(Bohn 1848).

125. Transl. by B. Jowett (Oxford 1888, 3rd ed.). Plato
leaves a full discussion of military gymnastics also in his Laws
VII and VIII.

135. These selections from Aristotle transl. by J. E. C. Well-
don (London 1883).

136. See J. Chryssafis, "Aristotle on Physical Education," Journal of Health and Physical Education (Ann Arbor 1930) 3-19.

138. These selections from Dio are a revision of a privately published translation (Urbana 1923, from the Budé ed. Leipzig 1916) presented to the University of Illinois by its author, the late Professor C. M. Moss. Though Dio lived so many centuries later than Diogenes, he seems to have found reliable sources for his account of the Isthmian games in the fourth century B.C.

140. Ferguson 296 f.

141 (Rhodes). See L. Casson, "The Grain Trade of the Hellenistic World," TAPA 85 (1954) 168-88; esp. 171 for estimate of commercial importance of Rhodes.

141 (Leonidas). Many more athlete heroes of the third and second centuries B.C. who resembled in their achievements the popular victors of previous centuries could be mentioned: for example, Democrates of Tenedos, a wrestler, noted like Milo for his feats of strength. It is said that no one could dislodge him when he had taken a position behind a line (Pausan. VI 17, 1; Ol. Ins. 39; Aelian Var. Hist. IV 15). Evanidoras (252 B.C.), victor in junior wrestling, later became one of the Olympic umpires (Hellanodicae) and compiled an official Register of Victors (Pausan. VI 8, 1). See also Förster, II nos. 423-511.

141 (surroundings). Gardiner, GASF 148 ff; Jüthner, KA 48 f; Forbes, "Expanded Uses of the Greek Gymnasium" CP XI (1945) 32-42.

141 (honor). See Knab 4.

142 (long race). For details about all the foot races see Gardiner, "Notes on the Greek Foot Race" JHS 23 (1903) 261-91.

142 (fight). Gardiner, GASF 428-9, where a blow by blow analysis of this fight is entertainingly set forth.

143 (poems). These may be read conveniently in the recent edition by Gow.

143 (Argonautica). See the translation of this epic by R. Seaton, The Loeb Classical Library (Harvard Univ. Press). The tradition so often repeated by writers that Apollonius and Callimachus had

a serious literary quarrel about length of poems and that Apollonius
wrote his four-book epic deliberately to flout Callimachus, the exponent of short poems, has in recent years been shown to rest on
no reliable testimony. Discussion on the merits of long and short
poems, it seems, dates back at least to Aristotle. See Walter
Allen, "The Epyllion: A Chapter in the History of Literary Criticism," TAPA 71 (1940) 1-26. Therefore the theory (often stated)
must be discarded that Theocritus wrote his compact, polished account to rebuke Apollonius and to range himself on the side of Callimachus, using a short poem for the legend rather than a full-blown
epic treatment. A simple explanation would be that Theocritus
found the boxing theme personally to his liking, knew that his public would be similarly diverted by it, even though it had been treated
recently by a fellow poet, and chose to develop it along the lines of
his other idylls.

143 (ladder). An engraved picture of this very scene, ladder
and all, is on a bronze vanity box (Ficoroni cista) found in Prae-
neste and now to be seen in the Villa Giulia Museum in Rome. It
is usually dated as of the time of Theocritus or a little earlier.
See Gow II Plates XIV and XV; and the useful article by Phyllis
Williams "Note on the Interpretation of the Ficoroni Cista"
AJA 49 (1945) 348-52. The "crowd" probably should be pictured
as numbering fifty to sixty persons. Theocritus (Idyll XIII 74)
mentions for the Argo thirty rowing benches and Apollonius sup-
plies the detail of two to a bench (I 395) and besides gives a long
list of their names (I 23 ff.). Pindar (Pyth. Ode IV 301 ff.) lists
twelve of the heroes in his famous account of the Argo. See also
P. Williams "Amykos and Dioskouroi" AJA 49 (1945) 330-347,
for a description of statues which may represent the Polydeuces
and others of Apollonius' account.

144. For hand coverings in boxing see above, Chapter I A note;
and Pausanias VIII 40, 3.

146. For a description of the Panathenaic festival and of the
important part in it which contestants from abroad assumed in
this era, see Ferguson 291 f.

147 (Callimachus). Transl. from Pfeiffer's ed. (Oxford 1949).
I am indebted to Prof. Alister Cameron for helpful suggestions in
the preparation of this translation.

147 (Cromnites). This place is usually referred to by other
writers as "Cenchreae".

147. Whether this is a Sosibius belonging to the end of the fourth century and the beginning of the third or one who lived two generations later is a problem still under discussion (Pfeiffer, Philologus 87 [1932] 220 ff.). The only ancient testimony on this, aside from this poem, is that from Athenaeus (IV 144 e) who mentions that the Sosibius praised by Callimachus had written an "Essay on Kingship" for Cassander. Since Cassander died in 297 B.C., the youthful athletic victories of Sosibius, which of course preceded his literary essay, or were contemporary with it, would have had to occur in the fourth century, if Athenaeus' statement is correct. His chariot victories therefore, won when he had become a prominent, wealthy man, could not reasonably be put later than 275 B.C. This dating would also agree with Callimachus' statement about a boyhood victory under Ptolemy son of Lagus. Callimachus himself would then have been comparatively young when he wrote this poem about a recent victory. Still ahead of him was his work on "Berenice's Lock of Hair" and his 120 volume "Pinakes"-- a descriptive catalog of the books in the Alexandria libraries.

147 (boy). This is a clear example of the enigmatic style of writing which became the vogue in this "Golden Age" of Alexandrian poetry. Callimachus is merely stating, so obscurely that even his fellow members of the Museum must have had to use a mythological dictionary, that Sosibius had won a victory both at the Isthmian Games founded in honor of Melicertes-Palaemon and at the Nemean founded in honor of Opheltes.

Another characteristic of Alexandrian poetry, fondness for reciting the details in beautiful out-of-doors scenery, is clearly seen in the selection from Theocritus quoted above.

147 (dry knees). Quite possibly true, since Sosibius would have been returning home from these triumphs in May or June when the Nile was usually at its lowest point!

148 (Archilochus). See Chapter IV, note on Pindar Olymp. Ode IX, for the words of this ancient victory chant.

148 (Ptolemy). This seems to be a reference to Ptolemy Soter and some unspecified games, not, as some argue, to Ptolemy II and the Ptolemaia Games instituted in 279/8. It is easy to picture Ptolemy I (Pausan. I 6) as a sponsor of athletic games, Greek style, in Egypt, for he was proud of the Greek descent of which he boasted in an inscription at Olympia. He himself in 310 B.C. had won a victory at Delphi in the chariot race with colts, an event which had been recently introduced there (Pausan. X 7, 3).

148 (Heraeum). Clearly a reference to gifts of clothing to statues of the Graces (daughters of Euronyme) who are mentioned by
Pausanias (II 17, 3) as standing near the entrance of the Temple of
Hera in Argos. Pausanias (IX 35, 2) says that the Graces were portrayed as fully-clad figures in the earlier centuries and mentions
the fully-clothed figures of them executed by the great Socrates
(last half of fifth century) and placed at the entrance of the Acropo-
lis. He further states that he does not know which artist started
the style, current in his day, of portraying them nude nor the date
of the innovation. But this reference by Callimachus may be a
clue to the date, as it is difficult to explain it other than as a reference to a new fad in sculpture; for the Graces in front of the old
Heraeum were ancient images and surely belonged to the older,
fully clothed type. Callimachus cannot be serious in his remark
that clothes were needed by them. There is of course the possibility that the sentence is not to be taken literally but that it re-
echoes some proverb well known to his audience.

148. For an account of Attalus, see Magie I 3 ff.

149 (Fränkel). Also in E. Hoffman, Sylloge Epigrammatum
Graecorum (Halle 1893) no. 334. Transl. by Professor C. A.
Forbes, Ohio State University.

149 (barrier). See Chapter IV C 4, above, for Pausanias' fuller
description of this starting device, and Gardiner, JHS 23 (1903)
263, for ancient passages discussing this rope barrier.

149 (Pergamum). A poem cited by Diog. Laert. (IV 6, 30) and
attributed to the philosopher Arcesilaus (315-241 B.C.), a contemporary of Attalus, seems to refer to this same victory.

149 (Pausanias). See also Anthol. Palatin. IX 588, for an epigram by Alcaeus of Messenia purporting to be written for the
statue of Cleitomachus. It commemorates his extraordinary feat
at the Isthmus.

149 (Polybius). Transl. by W. R. Paton, Loeb Classical Library; courtesy of Harvard University Press.

150. Ptolemy IV, king of Egypt (221-205 B.C.).

151 (Plutarch). Dryden's transl. revised by A. H. Clough
(Boston 1881).

152. For other information on the history of the Greek gymnasium see Daremb. -Saglio, s.v. Gymnasium 1684-1705; Gardiner, GASF Chap. XXII and his Olymp. Chap. XVI.; Forbes, GPE 82 f. and esp. Chap. VII; and his article "Expanded Uses of the Greek Gymnasium" cited above (Intro., note); Dinsmoor, The Architecture of Ancient Greece (London 1950, 3rd ed.) 320-2.

153(Vitruvius). Transl. from Granger's ed. (London 1931). See also the description of the gymnasium in Elis City given by Pausanias VI 23, 1-7.

155. See Eugénie Strong, Art in Ancient Rome (1928) I, 33: The coarse and simple mosaic known as opus signinum ... of considerable antiquity ... is merely a pavement of pounded tiles and chalk into which rude geometrical designs formed by pebbles were inserted.

156 (Greeks). In 204 B.C., detractors at Rome of Scipio Africanus sought to discredit him in the eyes of his fellow citizens by alleging that he had adopted the habit,"un-Roman" and "unmilitary," of frequenting the Greek palaestra at Syracuse, Sicily (Livy XXIX 19); cf. also the remarks of Varro (De Re Rustica II 2).

156 (offerings). According to Pausanias (V 10, 5) these included twenty-one golden shields which were fastened above the columns on the outside of Zeus' temple, and a bronze Zeus (V 24, 8); there were also, it seems, equestrian statues, perhaps with a likeness of Mummius as the rider. The bases of these with his name inscribed on them are still to be seen (Ol. Ins. 278-81).

156 (foot races). This was of course because the Romans had themselves long excelled in foot races.

157 (ruins). See Frazer, I Intro. XIV, for further evidence on this point and a list of shrunken cities cited by Pausanias.

157 (determined). J. A. O. Larsen, Roman Greece (IV in An Economic Survey of Ancient Rome, Baltimore 1938), presents a synthesis of the ancient evidence for the general condition of Greece in this period (259-435). See esp. his conclusions (421-2) that Greece in these centuries may not have been as badly off as certain ancient writers lead one to infer.

157 (service). See Forbes' useful collection of evidence on this topic, GPE 184 ff.

NOTES

157 (neighbors). See Mommsen, History of Rome, I 3 and 10
(in Dickson's Eng. tr. [Everyman's ed.] 32 and esp. Chap. X
"The Hellenes in Italy").

However, it must be admitted in all candor that the final word
has as yet not been written on the subject of the Early Romans and
Greek Athletics. Dionysius of Halicarnassus (VII 70 ff.) emphasizes, among other Greek customs, a type of Homeric athletics
practised by Romans at a festival in the fifth century B.C. He
cites Fabius Pictor as his source and apparently does not agree
with his contemporary, Livy (cited just below), on the matter of
the date of the first Greek athletic events at Rome. The long,
curious passage would merit further study in the light of all of
the other evidence on athletics, esp. the pictorial evidence which
comes from Etruria. A. Piganiol has already made a worthwhile
contribution to the problem in his Recherches sur les Jeux Romains
(Strasbourg 1923).

158 (soldiers). The Greek Plutarch in his biographical sketch
of Cato the Elder (XX, 4) sketched the type of informal physical
training given in Rome at the beginning of the 2nd century B.C.:
"He (Cato) was his son's coach, teaching him not merely to hurl
the javelin and fight in armor and ride a horse, but also to box,
to withstand heat and cold, and to swim the seething currents of
the Tiber." For an account of Roman Sports see Gardiner, AAW
Chap. VIII 117-127; and Mezö 205 ff.

158 (combats). For a complete and well-documented account
of the several kinds of such spectacles enjoyed by the Romans
from the days of Augustus through the Antonines, see Friedländer
II, Section VIII: "Die Schauspiele" 1-112; English transl. by
Freese.

158 (young folk). Cicero in 44 B.C. wrote to Atticus (Epist.
XVI 5) a report of the Greek games: "The attendance was small
and I am not surprised. ... You know what I think of Greek
games."

158 (Augustus). From Dio Cassius in the third century after
Christ comes a statement about rewards of athletes in the time of
the Emperor Augustus which is often cited as evidence for this
period. The remarks are so applicable to conditions in Dio's own
day (Chap. IX below) that one hesitates to take them at face value
for times as early as the author indicates. Could it be that Dio
slanted his sources a bit with the hope of causing the current

administration to reflect on some needed athletic reforms? He reports (LII 30) that an adviser recommended to Augustus that he curtail grants to victorious athletes,saying: "as for the competitors in the games, the prizes which are offered in each event are enough, unless a man wins in the Olympian or Pythian games or in some contest here in Rome. For these are the only victors who ought to receive their maintenance, and then cities will not be wearing themselves out to no purpose nor will any athlete go into training except those who have a chance of winning; the rest will be able to follow some occupation that will be more profitable both to themselves and to the commonwealth" (transl. by E. Cary, The Loeb Classical Library; courtesy of Harvard University Press).

159. For an analysis of Vergil's funeral games see the informative article by H. W. Willis, "Athletic Contests in the Epic," TAPA 72 (1941) 392-417. This selection from Vergil is omitted in this source book since it is readily available to readers in many English translations and is besides of interest, chiefly, for the subject of Roman athletics.

160 (Photius). Transl. from FGH (Jacoby) 2 B 1163.

161 (Antony). Brandis ("Ein Schreiben des Triumvirn Marcus Antonius," Hermes 32 [1897] 509-22) is however of the opinion that this document may be dated 33 B.C., opposing Kenyon's verdict in favor of 41 B.C.

161 (Letter). Transl. from the text given in Kenyon's "A Rescript of Marcus Antonius," CR 7 (1893) 476-8. My thanks are due Professors Trahman and Bradeen of the University of Cincinnati for helpful suggestions.

161 (Asia). For the Commonalty or Federation of Asia see Magie I 74.

161 (Stephanitae). See J. Keil, "Die Synode der ökumenischen Hieroniken und Stephaniten," Jahresh. 14 (1911) Beibl. 123-34.

162 (Naples games). For a discussion of the probable two festivals merged into this one and an interesting study of the whole inscription see R. Geer, "The Greek Games at Naples," TAPA 66 (1935) 208-221.

162 (entrants). Compare with this Solon's plan of subsidizing athletes (Chap. III B).

163 (law). This provision of course takes care of both the Greek
style of nomenclature and that of the Romans. Inscriptions (Ol.
Ins. 220, 369 and 424) illustrate the two styles where one man is
referred to in both ways: "Apollonius, son of Apollonius also
called Tiberius Claudius Apollonius."

163 (supervisors). See Pausan. V 21, 13, cited below in this
chapter, for a story about one such late arrival at Olympia which
helps to confirm the view that the rules at Naples and at Olympia
were identical.

163 (Claudius). See Pomtow, Klio XV (1918) 71-78, for a discussion of this inscription and a proposed reconstruction of the
monument picturing the three sisters in a graceful pose.

163 (suspected). Ancient art and literature offer a few clues.
Both the Arcadian and Boeotian Atalantas, mythical prototypes of
the woman athlete, were famous in popular Greek legends as
winners in wrestling and footracing respectively. On the black-
figured storage jars in common use in the sixth century B.C. the
Greeks felt no repugnance, evidently, at scenes picturing a woman
clad in trunks, applying a technically perfect hold in wrestling
against her male partner, also a schooled wrestler (See Gardiner,
GASF Fig. 119, and Schröder 162-6 with illustra.) Sparta, from
the time of Lycurgus, emphasized athletics for women (Philostr.
On Gymn. 27, cited below, IX D), and Plato's warm approval of
the plan has been cited in Chap. V C 2. Though married women
were barred as spectators at Olympia, they could enter horses in
the hippic events. At the games of Hera held at Olympia, girls
had their own special foot races (see Chap. IV C 3). At the Panathenaic Games in Athens an Argive Polycrates and his three
daughters figured prominently from 190-178 B.C. as victors in
races (Ferguson 293). Domitian, forty years after the feminine
victories here listed, introduced foot races by girls to the Romans
in the Greek athletic games held in the new stadium in A.D. 86
(Sueton. Domitian 4). Athenaeus (XIII 566 e), writing in the early
3rd century after Christ, represents an ancient Greek dinner guest
as remarking on the pleasant sight of girls and boys wrestling together in the gymnasium at Chios (but when, is not stated).

163 (SIG). Transl. by Prof. Clarence A. Forbes (Ohio State
University).

166 (errors). Plutarch asserts unflatteringly (De Tuenda Sanitate, Praecepta 133 D) that gymnastic trainers had wrenched their

athletes away from their books and, by their training, had rendered them as glistening and stony as the pillars in the gymnasium.

166 (Dio). Transl. from Budé ed. (1919). Thanks are due Prof. Forbes for a critical reading (1928) of this transl. in its original version.

169 (leaving). From this same period there comes a description of boxing by Valerius Flaccus (died A.D. 90). In his "Argonautica" (IV 133-366) he includes an account of the Pollux vs. Amycus match. In the three and a half centuries since Theocritus and Apollonius this mythical bout, under the influence of Roman gladiatorial spectacles, seems to have gained only in matters such as duration of contest, adroit motivation, brutality of the giant, deadliness of the gloves, and severity of the final blow dealt by a Pollux who had increased in agility during the centuries (see transl. by Mozley, Loeb Classical Library).

Statius, also a contemporary of Dio Chrysostomus, leaves an important contribution to athletic games as conducted by the Italians. In his epic "Thebaid" (Bk. VI), following the Vergilian tradition, he includes funeral games supposed to have been held at Nemea in prehistoric times. They are for the most part a vivid account of contemporary games written by no "arm-chair" athletics fan. The games described are probably those which Statius must have witnessed many a time in his home town of Naples at the Sebasta festival. The reactions of the audience, the chariot race, and the incidents in the foot race seem distinctly Italian. But since the preliminary motions in the discus throw and the "heave throw" of the wrestling match are nowhere else as well described, no student of Greek athletics should omit reading them (transl. by Mozley, Loeb Classical Library).

169-170. These selections from Pausanias are transl. by W. H. S. Jones, The Loeb Classical Library; courtesy of Harvard University Press.

170. See the rule cited above in the Naples-Isolympia Games.

171 (Incomparable). In this age honorary titles for such stellar athletes were many and varied. To the older "Circuit Champion" (periodonikês) there were added such designations as "Unthrown" (aptôtos);"Undefeated" (aleiptos); "Incomparable" (paradoxonikês); "First of Mankind" (prôtos anthrôpôn); "Without dust" (akoniti) that is, victor without a contest; "Ungashed" (atraumatistos).

However, the title of "Successor of Heracles" for some reason was
abolished after A. D. 37 by the officials of the Olympic Games.
But, strangely, they kept secret their compact to do so. Before
that time seven individuals had won the designation for a victory
like the traditional one of Heracles, that is, in the pancratium and
wrestling on the same day (Pausan. V 21, 10). The Olympic officials had to do some very quick thinking to avoid awarding this
title on several later occasions. See below, Chap. IX Intro.; and
Mezö 105-6.

171 (day). See C. A. Forbes, "Ancient Athletic Guilds," CP 50
(1955) 238-52, for a valuable study of this difficult subject. It has
appeared too recently for inclusion here other than by title.

172. For the "Shield of Argos" festival see above, Chap. IV,
note to Pindar, Olymp. Ode VII.

173. Vitruvius, writing at the end of the 1st cent. B. C., gives
details of these honors (IX 1): For the honorable athletes who had
won at the Olympian, Pythian, Isthmian, Nemean games, the ancestors of the Greeks voted such great rewards that not only did
they receive applause as they stood in the assembly with their
palm and wreath but also on their return home with the victory
they were conveyed in triumph in a four-horse chariot inside the
city gates and to their father's home and they enjoyed for life a
fixed grant from the public treasury.

174. See P. Graindor, Hérode Atticus et sa Famille (Cairo
1930) esp. Chap. X; and, for a very readable account of the previous water system at Olympia together with a description of this
improvement of Herodes' which is, strangely enough, not mentioned
by Pausanias, see Frazer IV 72.

176. (papyri). C P Herm (Wesseley ed.). A very interesting
analysis of their contents has been written by Méautis.

176 (gymnasium). For example, Ploution, Asclepiades-Neilos,
Herminus-Morus who are mentioned in C P Herm 77, 78, 125, 119
verso 3 and P Lond III 935. It is tempting to think that the reaction of the common folk to the airs assumed by such men of the
gymnasium set is reflected in a fable in the Aesop collection (no.
37 Halm ed. Leipzig 1863): A Fox and a Crocodile were arguing
about their fine ancestry. The Crocodile had gone on at length
about the brilliance of his ancestors and had closed his remarks
with: "and I am from a family who were Directors of the Gymna-

sium!" The Fox interrupted: "But even if you didn't say so, your skin would make it plain that you have many years of gymnasium training behind you."

176 (returns). We know from abundant evidence in inscriptions that the Greek elementary and grammar schools of that day, especially in Asia Minor, continued the practice of stressing gymnastics quite as much as grammar. All the students in Galen's audience, then, would have had a good preparatory training, sufficient to make them eligible either for advanced courses in athletics or in the liberal arts. In Galen's birthplace, Pergamum, there were in his day no fewer than five gymnasia--a fact which shows the enthusiasm for physical education in his great city. Athens, which has been credited with the most gymnasia, had only two more (see Forbes, GPE Chap. VII 222).

177 (services). See C P Herm 54, 55, 56, 72, 73, 77, 78, esp. 119 and discussion by Méautis, Appendice B "Les athlétes d' Hermoupolis."

177 (Galen). Trans. from Koch ed. (1922). My thanks are due Professor Forbes for his critical reading (1928) of this transla. in its original version.

180. Galen explains this more clearly in Chapter 11, 42-44: "The gymnastics trainer (paidotribês) is a servant to the coach (gymnastês) just as a cook is to a doctor. The cook prepares beets, or lentil soup, or barley gruel in different ways at different times, but without understanding the virtues in the dish prepared nor which of the recipes is best. The doctor cannot prepare any of these dishes like the cook but he understands the virtues in each one after it is prepared."

181. This seems to be the same kicking exercise which was popular in Sparta in the fifth century B.C. (Aristoph. Lysistr. 82). According to Galen's contemporary, Pollux (Onomast. IV 102), it was recorded on the tombstone of one Spartan woman that she could jump and kick her buttocks one thousand times in succession.

182 (sculptor). In Athens three marble blocks were quite unexpectedly unearthed on which there were six life-like sculptured reliefs of athletic scenes. These are thought to be the work of sixth century B.C. sculptors. Two of the scenes illustrate ballplaying. In one picture two teams of three young men each are seen in an expectant position ready to catch a ball to be thrown by

one of the group. The pitcher is bent backward just as Pollux described in "Sky Ball," but the arrangement of the players also suggests the "Episkyros" game. The second picture shows two men in the foreground grasping hockey sticks in their right hands and bending over in an attempt to get control of a small ball, while others similarly equipped stand on either side. No record in literature to explain any similar game has as yet been found earlier than the 12th Christian century when a polo game is fully described in which players on horseback use a tennis racket type of club and a small ball: G. Cinnamus, Historia de rebus gestis a Joanne et Manuele Comnenis VI 5 [ed. Du Cange (1670) p. 154].

It is tempting, however, to see a reference to some kind of ball-game played with a club in Cicero's essay on "Old Age" (XVI 58): "Then leave the young folks their military weapons, their horses, their spears, their club and ball, their wild beast hunt and foot races." But commentators have been in the habit of interpreting Cicero's "clavam et pilam" as meaning two distinct games "Fencing foil" and "ball" and they cite Vegetius (De Re Militari I 4) to explain "fencing foil". However they fail to mention why "fencing foil" and ball should be so closely associated.

To cite only a few of the many illustr. articles on this find: S. Casson, "The New Athenian Statue Bases," JHS 45 (1925) 164-79; L. Van Hook, AJA 30 (1926) 283-7; S. Schipper, Archaeology I 5 (1952).

182. Harper's Class. Dict. under Pila conveniently summarizes the evidence and modern lit. on this subject; see also the important pamphlet by J. M. Marquardt, De Sphaeromachiis veterum (Gustrow 1879).

183. Inscriptions dating from the 1st century A.D. mention that Spartan boys regularly were divided into teams and played some game of ball similar to this. See M. N. Tod, BSA 10 (1903-4) 63 ff.; and Forbes, GPE 21.

184 (Athenaeus). Transl. by C. P Gulick. The Loeb Classical Library; courtesy of Harvard University Press.

185 (Galen). Transl. from Marquardt ed. (1884). Thanks are due Professor Forbes for a critical reading (1928) of this transl. in its first version. As in the other selections from Galen, some of the sentences involving his characteristic habit of repetition have been omitted.

185 (times). Galen is probably thinking of his celebrated pre-
decessor, Hippocrates, fifth century B.C. physician whose statement we still have (Anc. Medicine IV, Loeb Class. Lib.): Even at
the present day those who study gymnastics and athletic exercises
are constantly making some fresh discovery by investigating ...
what food and what drink are best assimilated and make a man
stronger.

186 (small one). Hippocrates, six hundred years earlier, in a
chance comment, had indicated the size and material of such a
ball (On Joints III, Loeb Class. Lib.): In the hollow of the armpit
one should put something round fitted to it (i.e. in case of a dislocated shoulder) ... the very small, hard balls such as are commonly stitched out of leather.

Aristotle in the next century after Hippocrates mentions the in-
expensiveness of a ball (Nic. Eth. IV 2, 18): for the finest oil-
flask or ball does not cost much--though it makes a magnificent
present for a child.

191 (Hygienist). For a discussion of this whole subject, see
Jüthner, Philostr. Intro. 1-69.

191 (Galen). Transl. from "Protreptikos," Marquardt ed.
(1884). Thanks are due Prof. Forbes for his critical reading of
this transl. in its original version (1928).

194. Here again, as was the case when expatiating on the
brainlessness of athletes, Galen seems to be talking with his
tongue in his cheek. He was surely enough of a student to know
the correct derivation of athlêtês: a man competing for an "Athlon"
(prize); cf. Homer's ref. to athlêtêr, Chap. I B above.

195. A superfluous remark--Galen knew, of course, of athletes
of his day who had become famous because of their military deeds.
For example, Mnasibulus, a renowned victor in foot races at
Olympia, had collected a group of fellow-citizens to defend Elatea
(in Phocis), had himself slaughtered a vast number of the invading
Costobocs (sometime between A.D. 166-180) and had fallen in the
fight (Pausan. X 34, 5); and there was the unnamed boxer who
played such a prominent role in defending Byzantium during the
three years' siege by the Romans (A.D. 191-4) that he was one of
the first captives to be put to death (Dio Cass. LXXV 14, 1).

196 (Hercules). See above, page 171 and note.

196 (Brayer). This is clearly a facetious reference to the fulsome victor inscriptions popular in that day. The whole address
must have evoked peals of laughter from his young audience.

197. Evidently a proverbial saying which originated when
Aristippus of Cyrene, disciple of Socrates, after being shipwrecked
off Rhodes, had earned money on that island by teaching; he had
then lectured his fellow passengers on the advantage of carrying
with them on a journey "goods which could swim ashore" (i.e. mental resources). Vitruvius tells the story (VI Intro.).

198. Transl. by Prof. Clarence A. Forbes (Ohio State University).

199 (Euryclea). An inscription at Sparta records this victory
won by Asclepiades (CIG I 1427).

199 (time) The retirement appears to have lasted for about
twelve years, and so Asclepiades was some thirty-seven years
old at the time of his last special appearance.

199 (Olympics). An even more famous athlete--Demostratus
of Sardis--a few years older than Asclepiades, has left in two inscriptions the full record of his sixty-eight victories and honors
granted by emperors from Marcus Aurelius through Caracalla
(IG XIV 1105; see Keil-Premerstein "Bericht über eine Reise in
Lydien" Wiener Denkschrift. 53 [1910] no. 37).

199-200. Letters (1) and (2) transl. by Prof. C. A. Forbes.

199. "Xystic" of course refers to the Xystos or enclosure
where athletes exercised. Pausanias derives the word from
"scrape" (VI 23, 1): The whole of this enclosure (i.e. gymnasium
at Elis City) is called Xystus, because an exercise of Heracles,
the son of Amphitryo, was to scrape up (anaxyein) each day all the
thistles that grew there.

202. His age actually was twenty-seven, a detail which may be
supplied from data in other papyri (P Lond III 935).

203. Gibbon, Decline and Fall of the Roman Empire (Bury ed.
1896) II 260 f.; Ammianus Marcellinus (XVI 10) gives a vivid first-
hand account of the Emperor Constantius' first visit to Rome in
357. He entered the city with the pomp of an oriental despot and

then, like any wide-eyed tourist, made the rounds of the ancient monuments which filled him with amazement.

204 (parent one). See Krause, Abschnitt II 202-35, for a learned discussion of the many games in the ancient world which were called "Olympia"; and also Daremb.-Saglio, s.v. "Olympia."

204 (portraits). Now in the Lateran Museum at Rome. No agreement has been reached among scholars as to whether these mosaics belong to the original building of the early third century or were added as a new feature in a fourth-century restoration of the Baths. Secchi, who first published them (Il Musaico Antoniniana [Rome 1845]), suggests the earlier date. But to some scholars the orthography of the three names on the mosaic--Iovinus, Iobianus, Benator--seems to suit the time of Valentinian rather than that of Caracalla. See esp. Huelsen-Jordan, Topographie der Stadt Rom im Altertum, I³ (Berlin 1907) 195.

204 (East). My remarks are based on an examination of the large scale photographs of them published by Nogara in his volume, I Mosaici Antichi del Vaticano e del Laterano (Milan 1910) "Atleti" 1-3; Plates I-IV. The various athletic implements, wreaths, and accessories of a palaestra are also included in this mosaic picture.

204 (Tusculum). For a discussion of this mosaic found in a priest's garden in 1862, see Hans Lucas "Athletentypen" Jahrb. XIX (1904) 127-36, 8 illustr.; and Gardiner AAW illustra. no. 70; see also Marion E. Blake, "Roman Mosaics of the II Century in Italy," Mem. Am. Acad. Rome XIII (1936) 67-214, 46 plates, esp. pp. 162-6.

205 (Heracles). See above, 171 and note.

205 (appreciation). See Mezö 211; and esp. Sawhill, The Use of Athletic Metaphors in the Biblical Homilies of St. John Chrysostom (Diss. Princeton 1928) 110 f.: "After reading the Biblical Homilies of St. Chrysostom for the purpose of noting all allusions to athletics, one cannot fail to be impressed with the spell the Greek Olympic games must still have exercised--when he addressed his congregations both in Antioch and in Constantinople ... Many technical points of interest regarding the games and the regulations prescribed for their conduct and that of the athletes themselves have been unconsciously revealed to us by St. Chrysostom."

205 (Daphne). These games were founded in the days of Augustus
by reason of a legacy left by a senator, Sosibius, for that purpose.
After magistrates had misused the money the games were reorganized in the time of Claudius and for a sum of money the officials
at Elis, according to the late historian, Malalas, gave permission
to use both the name "Olympia" and other distinctive features of
those games. These continued to be the most important games of
the East until 508. For a full citation of the literature, see
Downey "The Olympic Games of Antioch in the Fourth Century
A.D." TAPA 70 (1939) 428-38).

206 (Antioch). See also Pack, Studies in Libanius and Antiochene
Society under Theodosius (Diss. Michigan 1935) 61 f.

206 (Theodosian Code). Compiled in 438. See transl. by Pharr
and others (Princeton 1952).

207 (Moses of Chorene). History of Armenia III 40 (French
transl. by P. E. Le Vaillant de Florival, Venice 1841).

207 (Cedrenus). Compendium Historiarum, Xylander's version
I, 326, 122 D (Paris 1647).

208. Transl. from Tissot, Les Douze Livres du Code de
l'Empereur Justinian de la seconde ed. IV (Paris 1810).

209 (C P Herm 54). Transl. from Wesseley ed. (Leipzig 1905);
Wilcken no. 157.

209 (splendor). These epithets were regularly added to documents by boosters of Hermopolis after Hadrian had lavishly
founded a rival city, Antinoopolis, just across the river.

209 (months). For a sketch of the general conditions prevailing
in Egypt, see Hunt and Edgar, Select Papyri, II Intro; esp. xxxi f.
for an explanation of Egyptian months.

210. For other ancient evidence on wrestling see a fragment
of a drill-book used in a wrestling-school. This was found on a
2nd-century papyrus (P Oxy III 466; transl. in Freeman's Schools
of Hellas [London 1932] 131). See Gardiner's interpretation of
this papyrus: "Wrestling" JHS 25 (1905) 14-31; 263-93; 26 (1906)
4-22; also see above, Chap. I A "Wrestling Match" and note.

210 (Aethiopica). Transl. from Colonna's ed. (Rome 1938). Thanks are due Prof. Forbes for a critical reading (1930) of the first version of this transl.

212 (Philostratus). Transl. from Jüth. <u>Philostr</u>. Thanks are due Professor Forbes for a critical reading (1929) of the first version of this translation; to the student who would study this ancient essay more thoroughly, the edition by Jüthner with Greek text, German transl., full notes, and detailed introduction is indispensable.

215. See above, Chap. I A "Boxing Match," note.

216. A similar account is given by Pausanias (V 8, 6) and may be read in the English transl. of W. H. S. Jones, The Loeb Class. Lib.).

232. A fourth century version of Homeric funeral games written by Quintus Smyrnaeus in his epic "The Fall of Troy" (IV 180-595) is here omitted because of limitations of space. It is readily accessible in an English transl. by A. S. Way (The Loeb Classical Library). Quintus' version of the athletic games supposed to have been held in honor of Achilles reflects the author's own world in the time of the Emperor Julian. Its general tone is far different from that of Homer's account. There is an abundance of sentimentality and medical detail: heroes kiss one another and patiently stand about while ointments and bandages are sympathetically applied. Boxing and wrestling are described with considerable enthusiasm, but the chariot race, so important to Homer, and the other events show little variation in the men participating or in the final outcome. Quintus includes such a glaring anachronism as Aias standing forth the undisputed champion in the pancratium-- a contest not known in the Homeric Age. The introduction of contests in jumping and in horse racing is also a departure from the Homeric program of events.

INDEX OF ORIGINAL SOURCES

[Numerals following parentheses refer to pages of the text and notes, above. Passages merely discussed or mentioned are marked with an obelisk (†). Asterisks indicate translations by the author. The translators of other passages are acknowledged in the notes.]

GENERAL INDEX

accidents in chariot-racing 6, 48, 114, 121, 256; in foot-race 18; with the discus 51; ball-playing least dangerous of sports 190.

Aetolus exiled because of chariot-race accident 48; gave name to Aetolians 48.

Alexandrian poetry, characteristics of 261.

Amphitheatres, Lucian's anachronism 66; only an embankment of earth 109; type at Olympia 248; at Nemea 248.

Alcibiades, chariot racing 115, 119.

Anacharsis discusses athletics with Solon 62 ff.; comes to Greece to learn Greek ways 68; his visit interested Greek writers 247; the penalty he paid for interest in foreigners 248.

Antioch-Olympic games 205; referred to by Libanius 206; the enlargement of the plethron 206; literature on 274.

Apollonius of Rhodes, Pollux vs. Amycus 143; literary quarrel with Callimachus 260.

Aratus, his athletic career 151.

Archery contest in Homer's Iliad 21; literature on 237.

Archibius, professional athlete of 1st cent. A.D. 171-2.

Archilochus, old victory chant 97, 253, 261.

Argo, Jason's ship 143, 213, 260.

Aristotle, date of 135 (see also Index of Sources); revised Olympic Register 39; bodily condition of athlete not good for fatherhood 136; in children gymnastics should precede mental training 136; brutality toward children in Sparta 136; light type of exercises for children 137; calls festival of Eleusis the oldest 239; saw discus of Iphitus 241.

armor, contest in Homer's Iliad 19; literature on 237.

Arrhichion (Arrhachion), famous pancratiast 79 ff.; his statue at Phigalia 81, 249.

Asclepiades, famous athlete, career as citizen 176; career as athlete 198-9; athletic career of his father, Demetrius 198, 201; his victory inscription at Sparta 272; his age at retirement 272.

Astylus of Croton altered citizenship for fee 107; statue of 107; epigram on, by Simonides 255.

Athenaeus, date of, etc. 183 (see also Index of Sources).

athletes, derivation of word according to Homer 24, 237; to Eusebius 53; to Galen 194, 271;

interest shown by King Ptolemy in 150; psychology of spectators 149-50.

Callimachus (see Index of Sources), date of, etc. 146, 261; literary quarrel with Apollonius 259-60.

chariot race in Homer's funeral games 3-16; Peisistratus' exchange with Cimon for victory in 82 f.; starting device for 109, 262; description of by Sophocles 112; victories in, won by Alcibiades 115, 119; new types of races introduced 148; Attalus' victory in 149, 262; four horses for Heracles' time, an anachronism 238; list of wealthy victors in, during 6th cent. B.C. 249.

Christians and athletics 205, 273.

Cimon, victor twice at chariot races 83.

Cleisthenes of Pisa 33, 40.

Cleisthenes of Sicyon, victor in chariot race 58; holds athletic competitions for suitors 58; gives one talent to each athlete suitor 58, 246.

Cleitomachus, boxing match of 149; epigram on 262.

Clymenus of Crete, held games at Olympia 47; identified with Peisos 240.

codes, see Justinian, Theodosius.

Coroebus, winner of foot-race in 1st Olympiad of Olympic Register 37, 40.

Crete, style of athletics practised in 237.

Croton, city in Southern Italy, its fame in athletics 86.

Cypselus chest, funeral games depicted on 30; literature on 237.

dates, from Troy to 776 B.C. reported by Eusebius 53; of events and personages in prehistoric Greece 238, 240; reckoned from Spartan King lists 240; reckoned from Olympic register of victors 53, 255; dating of year from pancratium victor, by Thucydides 255.

Delphi, advises on Olympic affairs 41; assists in enforcing Olympia's fines, 122.

Demetrius of Hermopolis, see Asclepiades.

Demostratus of Sardis, famous athlete, high officer in Heracles Guild 201; career of 272.

Deucalion's flood 47; date of 243.

Diagoras of Rhodes, famous athlete, career according to Pindar 98; his athletic family, according to Pausanias 106; see also Pherenice.

Dio Chrysostomus, date of 137 (see also Index of Sources).

Diodorus of Sicily on Ephorus 36 (see also Index of Sources).

Diogenes the Cynic, date of 137; his antics at the Isthmian festival 138.

Diogenes Laertius, see Index of Sources.

discus used in simile by Homer 7; described by Lucian 71; of Exoidas of 6th cent. B.C. 89-90; of Iphitus 241.

discus contest (see also weight throwing), in Homer's Iliad 20; in Odyssey 25; literature on 237.

Dörpfeld, excavations of Pelops' tomb 238; of Pisa 239; on the votive offerings at Olympia 239 f.

dust, use of by athletes 63; benefits of 72; varieties of 231.

1981
more...New Books

Arangio-Ruiz, V., & Olivieri, A., INSCRIPTIONES GRAECAE SICILIAE ET INFIMAE ITALIAE AD IUS PERTINENTES. [321-9] $25.00

Bell, H.I., EGYPT: FROM ALEXANDER TO THE ARAB CONQUEST. [354-5] $12.50

Bevan, E., STOICS AND SCRPTICS. [364-2] $12.50

Brodrick, M., & Morton, A.A., A CONCISE DICTIONARY OF EGYPTIAN ARCHAEOLOGY. [303-0] $7.50

Budge, E.A. Wallis, THE ROSETTA STONE. [331-6] $3.00

Clairmont, R., A COMMENTARY N SENECA'S APOCOLOCYNTOSIS DIVI CLAVDII. [342-1] $15.00

Davis, W.H., GREEK PAPYRI OF THE FIRST CENTURY. [332-4] $6.00

Dawkins, R.M., THE NATURE OF THE CYPRIOT CHRONICLE OF LEONTIOS MAKHAIRAS. [334-0] $4.00

Day, J.W., THE GLORY OF ATHENS: THE POPULAR TRADITION IN AELIUS ARISTIDES. [346-4] $15.00

Demitsas, M.G., (ed.) SYLLOGE INSCRIPTIONVM GRAECARVM ET LATINARVM MACEDONIAE. [324-3] 2 vols. $125.00

Dodds, E.R., SELECT PASSAGES ILLUSTRATING NEOPLATONISM. [302-2] $12.50

Dudley, D.R., A HISTORY OF CYNICISM. [365-0] $15.00

Herter, H., DE DIS ATTICIS PRIAPI SIMILIBUS. [360-X] $12.50

Hyde, G., DE OLYMPIONICARUM STATUIS, A PAUSANIAE DESCRIPTIS. [341-3] $15.00

Kapsomenakis, S.G., VORUNTERSUCHUNGEN ZU EINER GRAMMATIK DER NACHCHRISTLICHEN ZEIT. [294-8] $12.50

Kenyon, F.G., BOOKS AND READERS IN ANCIENT GREECE AND ROME. [340-5] $12.50

Klee, T., ZUR GESCHICHTE DER GYMNISCHEN AGONE AN GRIECHISCHEN FESTEN. [336-7] $12.50

Klotsche, E., THE SUPERNATURAL IN THE TRAGEDIES OF EURIPIDES. [343-X] $10.00

Knab, R., DIE PERIODONIKEN. [330-8] $15.00

Kretschmer, P., GRIECHISCHEN VASENINSCHRIFTEN. [347-2] $25.00

Loewe, B., ANCIENT GREEK THEOPHORIC TOPONYMS. [333-2] $10.00

Marmor Parium, CHRONICUM PARIUM (ed.) F. Jacoby. [362-6] $15.00

Mead, G.R.S., APOLLONIUS OF TYANA. [350-2] $12.50

Milligan, G., SELECTIONS FROM GREEK PAPYRI. [335-9] $15.00

Muthmann, GRIECHISCHE STEINSCCHRIFTEN ALS AUSDRUCK LEBENDI-GEN GEISTES. [372-3] $15.00

Naumann, GRIECHISCHE WEIHINSCHRIFTEN. [371-5] $12.50

Negris, P., ANCIENT UNDERWATER RUINS. [338-3] $4.00

Parker, H.M.D., ROMAN LEGIONS. [356-1] $15.00

ON ANCIENT ATHLETICS

7020 N. WESTERN AVENUE, CHICAGO, ILLINOIS 60645

COMPLETE YOUR LIBRARY

Just Mail your order form to: **ARES PUBLISHERS, INC.,**